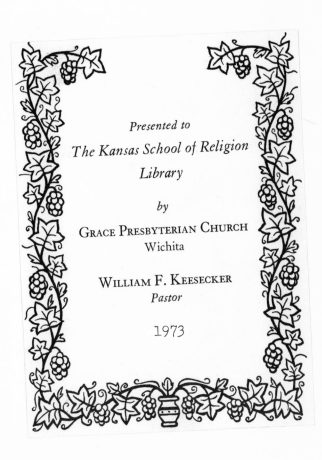

Presented to

The Kansas School of Religion
Library

by

GRACE PRESBYTERIAN CHURCH
Wichita

WILLIAM F. KEESECKER
Pastor

1973

THE CHURCH OF ENGLAND, THE METHODISTS AND SOCIETY 1700–1850

The Church of England, the Methodists and Society 1700–1850

ANTHONY ARMSTRONG M.A.

Rowman and Littlefield

Totowa, New Jersey 07512

The first verse of Thomas Hardy's
Afternoon Service at Mellstock (*circa* 1850),
first published in *Moments of Vision* (1917),
appears on p. 34 by kind permission of the
Trustees of the Hardy Estate and of the
publishers: Macmillan, New York

First published in the United States 1973
by Rowman and Littlefield, Totowa, New Jersey

Library of Congress Cataloging in Publication Data

Armstrong, Anthony.
  The Church of England, the Methodists and
Society, 1700–1850

  (London history studies [9])
  Includes bibliographical references.
1. Great Britain–Church history–18th century.
2. Great Britain–Church history–19th century.
1. Title
BR758. A66 1973   274.2   72-11862
ISBN 0-87471-160-6
ISBN 0-87471-164-9 (pbk)

Printed and bound in Great Britain

CONTENTS

INTRODUCTION

One of the most persistent, appealing, and useful hypotheses used to interpret English history in the eighteenth and nineteenth centuries is a simplification of the religious developments of the time. On 24 May 1738 Wesley was converted. From that moment, so it is argued, a corrupt and lifeless Established Church was faced with the shock of the Methodist Revival. The Methodists, persecuted by mobs and forbidden to preach in many Anglican churches, were at length driven from the Church of England. Their impact, however, continued through their spiritual descendants, the Evangelicals. These Evangelicals (to continue the hypothesis) did not effect a takeover of the Church of England, but rather a takeover of the whole nation, imbuing it with their values and creating Victorianism. The Methodists' main appeal was to the working classes. Besides accomplishing the civilization of a section of those classes, the Methodists imposed a degree of conservatism upon them which was providential, since the French Revolution and the Industrial Revolution together created uniquely powerful tensions which otherwise might have brought about the disintegration of society.

A great amount of work in ecclestiastical and social history has collected on these themes since they were first enunciated. Some parts of the hypothesis seem secure now, others shaky. The whole question of what constitutes Victorianism (if it existed) is too vast to handle here; but this book may serve as an introduction to some of the recent work on the religious aspects of English history between 1700 and 1850 — aspects which are often excised in schools.

My debt to the authors of the books given in the reading lists and elsewhere in the text will be obvious. It will perhaps be even more obvious that the late Norman Sykes taught me at Cambridge, though many of the interests shown here would not have been his. His *Church and State in England in the Eighteenth Century* (Cambridge University Press, 1934) has been as indispensable to me as to all other students of this period. I am

grateful to those who secured copies of the more obscure books
for me. The general editor, my sixth formers, my typist, and
(especially) my wife have been very tolerant towards me during
my long absorption in church matters.

PART I
The Church of England and Dissent in the Eighteenth Century

Most Victorians thought nothing of the eighteenth-century Church; since the 1930s, however, attitudes have changed. In part this is due to detailed investigation, which has revealed the bishops to be rather more than indolent time-servers. In part it is due to a more sympathetic view towards the eighteenth century in general, so that its plain little preaching-boxes have become churches in good taste. There is, too, some wonder now at the degree to which the Church was effectively involved with society at so many levels. Even its favourite doctrines seem now to be a response to prevailing scientific developments, rather than mere cold morality.

[1] THE ESTABLISHED CHURCH

The presence of the Established Church was to be seen throughout politics, law, and society. The position of the bishop indicated in the most obvious form the connection between Church and State. The twenty-six bishops in the House of Lords had a vital block of votes. The Lords comprised 213 members in 1714, and

by 1780 had increased only to 224. Even in important divisions
the number present rarely exceeded 120 to 145; the bishops'
votes therefore mattered, and on some occasions saved the
Government from defeat. The bishops did not often speak in the
Lords, though they took part in the full range of business there,
even down to sitting on committees considering enclosure bills.
From November until May the bishops were accordingly expected
to reside in London unless their health forbade it. The Duke of
Newcastle showed his customary concern for the details of
parliamentary management when some of the bishops did not
appear for the trial of the rebel lords after the Jacobite rebellion
in 1746. Potter, the Archbishop of Canterbury, produced for him
a detailed catalogue of reasons:

1. The Bishop of Peterborough hath lately been very ill, and was
scarce able to write. 2. Chester hath sent a certificate from his physician
and apothecary that he is under a course of medicines for the stone,
and not able to take a journey to London without hazard of his life.
3. Carlisle is four score and last winter contracted such an illness as
hath ever since adhered to him. 4. Ely is very infirm at Ely. 5. St
David's is in his remote diocese, where he is wanted, and cannot
return thither, the season being so far advanced.

The hold over the bishops by the Government was considerable. The salaries of the various bishops varied greatly –
the 1762 list given in *The Correspondence of George III* has the
bishopric of Bristol at the bottom with £450 a year and Canterbury at the top with £7,000; and translation of favoured divines
could be very rapid. Brownlow North had good reason to con-
gratulate himself that his half-brother, Lord North, was in office
for so long. He became Bishop of Lichfield at 30, Bishop of
Worcester at 33, and Bishop of Winchester at 40. This preferment he held for thirty-nine years, and he used his influence to
bestow further clerical posts on his family.

The church-state connection was displayed in many other
ways besides. The dominance of the Anglican Church was
expressed in legislative form by the Test and Corporation Acts,
which had confined the reality of political power to members of

the Church of England. The Prayer Book, enforced by the Act of Uniformity of 1662, of course expressed in its forms the identity of Church and State. It contained until 1859 forms of thanksgiving for the deliverance of King and Parliament from the Gunpowder Plot, for the 'unspeakable mercy' of having put an end to the Great Rebellion, and for the 'happy arrival' of William III.

Practically, the intertwining of Church and State and Church and Society was demonstrated by the extent of the control exercised by the laity over appointments to the Church. To the Crown belonged the appointment of bishops and deans and the nomination to 1,048 livings, while the patrons of over half the livings in England were laymen. An advowson (i.e. the right to present to a living) was a piece of property. The elaborate machinery of the law courts was in part operated by the Church. The ecclesiastical courts – a bishop's court, in which the bishop's chancellor normally presided, and in most dioceses, archdeacons' courts – continued to control matters relating to wills, as well as to regulate more obviously church matters. Although the supremacy of statutes and of lay courts had long been established over the church courts, such courts continued in effective operation.

It was, of course, at the parish level that the Church formed the closest connection with society. The parish, so far from being merely a unit of local and church government, was until the nineteenth century a most intricate complex of legal obligations and property interests, and the gentry were the predominant interest in it. Addison's description of Sir Roger de Coverly, who was responsible for beautifying the church, who increased the stipends of the vicar and the clerk, who provided the vicar with the best sermons in English to be read Sunday by Sunday, and who presided over the Sunday congregations with such rigorous eccentricity, must always stand as the most effective description of this, heavily idealized as it is.

The incumbent of a parish secured his income from several sources. There was the land directly attached to his living – the glebe – which the clergyman might let out or farm himself.

There was his income from tithe – the great tithe, one tenth of
the corn of each grower in the parish, payable in kind, and the
small tithe, including contributions in hay and other produce.
Then there were the fees for the clergyman's services. The whole
of this income, from all sources, went either to the incumbent,
who would then be styled *rector*, or more usually elsewhere. It
could be *appropriated* to the bishop or the dean and chapter of a
cathedral, or *impropriated* to a local gentleman, commonly the
lord of the manor, or to a body of local gentry. Part of the
proceeds was then made over to the vicar. Every one of these
sources of income was a variable, and consequently 'good
management' by the incumbent was often a prerequisite to a
comfortable existence, sometimes indeed to an existence at all.
The description of Parson Trulliber in Fielding's *Joseph Andrews*,
whom Parson Adams found

stript into his waistcoat, with an apron on, and a pail in his hand,
just come from serving his hogs; for Mr Trulliber was a parson on
Sundays, but all the other six might properly be called a farmer,

was an awful warning as to what might happen to a country
parson. 'Good management' might take other forms than actual
farming: it might mean astuteness in all legal matters affecting
income, such as the process of enclosure. Such involvement was,
of course, 'worldly' and made parsons subjects of caricature.

Another basic concern of the parish was the maintenance of
the parish church. Addison's picture of Sir Roger suggests,
perhaps, that the squire kept up the church fabric. So he might,
if his instincts were as sound as Sir Roger's; but more usually the
maintenance of the parish church required such a degree of
co-operation that repairs were delayed for years. The obligation
of repairing the chancel fell upon the impropriators, and it was
exceptionally difficult to use any kind of compulsion to make
them act. As for the nave of the church, its upkeep was the
obligation of the parishioners.

This mass of legal complexities is simplified if one considers
what the interior of an eighteenth-century parish church looked
like. The royal arms, carefully picked out in gilt, were emblematic

of the church-state relationship; and the way in which the high box-pews were disposed according to a fixed plan made the church at service time a kind of map of village society. The impropriators were entitled to seats in the chancel – seats provided with canopies, cushions, coats of arms, and even fires. They often impeded a congregation's view of the altar, and since certain pews were an obvious badge of rank, they were the cause of endless dispute. Vaults, monuments, and hatchments made clearer still the position of the squire in the parish.

Of course, the complete identity of Church and State was no longer maintained. The Civil War and the Commonwealth had demonstrated the power of the Presbyterians, the Independents, and the Anabaptists, but rigorous legislation against them after 1660 attempted to exclude them from both local and national political activity, and put severe checks on their religious activity. Attempts to 'comprehend' the Presbyterians (i.e. to incorporate them within the Church of England) between 1660 and 1689 all failed. At any rate the Dissenters enjoyed the protection of the Toleration Act of 1689, and the two attempts made by the Tories in Anne's reign to reduce their status were short-lived (see p. 37).

The alliance between Church and State has often been represented as a disaster which clogged the workings of the Church and impaired its effectiveness. As a melancholy example it is usual to give the suspension of Convocation, the official representative body of the Church, in 1717 – a suspension which lasted for more than a century. According to some good judges – Overton and Relton, writing in 1878, and Professor Gordon Rupp, writing in 1965 – Convocation, had it existed, might have tackled the problems to which the coming of Methodism gave rise. The history of Convocation since the Restoration, however, scarcely gives grounds for thinking that its continued existence would have effected anything to the credit of the Church. In 1664 the power of the Church to tax itself through Convocation was surrendered by the Archbishop of Canterbury – in return, the clergy were given the vote in parliamentary elections – and no sittings of Convocation took place between 1664 and 1689.

After the Revolution there was a total failure to agree on new canons (laws) for the Church. An acrimonious struggle between the Upper and Lower Houses marred most of the reign of Anne, until the appointment of Francis Atterbury, the prolocutor of the Lower House, to the bishopric of Rochester in 1713. In the few months before Anne's death Convocation managed to undertake some minor (though useful) administrative reforms in the Church. However, delay occasioned by the succession of George I, and controversy arising from Bishop Hoadly's views on the nature of the Church, disturbed this brief period of work, and Convocation was suspended in 1717.

So much for the relation between Church and State in practice. Practice was justified and rationalized in a variety of theories. William Warburton's *Alliance between Church and State* (1736) saw the relationship as a compact between two independent powers for their mutual support. The Church gained by it the endowment of its clergy, the presence of the bishops in the House of Lords, and the coercive power of the church courts – but lost its power of independent action. The State gained the beneficent influence of religion in all its workings, and the support of an institution which, if it were independent, might prove a dangerous enemy. William Paley, writing more than a generation later, was even more explicit than Warburton in setting out and justifying the situation as it was in England:

A religious establishment is no part of Christianity; it is only a means of inculcating it. The authority of a church establishment is founded upon its utility, and whenever, upon this principle, we deliberate concerning the form, propriety or comparative excellency of different establishments, the single view, under which we ought to consider any one of them is that of a scheme of instruction; the single end we ought to propose by them is, the preservation and communication of religious knowledge.

In a number of works he elaborated this simple theme with elegant and commonsense observations. He apologized (for instance) for giving large revenues to some because of the necessity of encouraging study, and the desirability of having independence of view. When the French Revolution came, and authority in Church and State was threatened, Burke asserted that Church and State formed a unity quite indissoluble; the church Establishment had 'solemnly and for ever consecrated the commonwealth and all that officiated in it'.

At the same time as the fusion of Church and State was thus justified, the Church's organization was increasingly justified on grounds of social utility. The parochial system, so eminently geared to a rural society, and so doubtful a means of ministering to industrial England, was idealized at the end of the eighteenth century and the beginning of the nineteenth century as the means to social harmony, due subordination, and the civilizing of the lower orders. The essential ingredients of such a parish were a resident squire, a resident parson, and (it was increasingly felt) a school.

[2] DOCTRINE

The ideals of the eighteenth-century Church of England, cool and reasonable though they were, sprang from the intellectual crisis of the preceding century. By 1700 the principal concern of the theologian was to defend Christianity from attack – an attack which came from the philosophers, the scientists, and the explorers. But the sorry experience since the Reformation of theological wranglings, religious persecution, and war produced an inclination towards calm. In the opening decades of the seventeenth century, Bacon had sought to divorce religion from philosophy altogether; in the middle years of the century, Hobbes's attitude had been virtually atheistic, and more concerned with matters physical than matters spiritual. The scientific revolution of the seventeenth century, observable in the discovery of the barometer and the telescope, the exposition of the laws of Newton, and the vogue for experimental philosophy,

produced an intense elation and strengthened the conviction
that a Supreme Being or 'Divine Author' existed. However, such
a revolution was ultimately hostile to some of the fundamentals
of the faith – miracles, for example. The geographical discoveries of the time posed another set of problems. These peoples
who had never heard of Christianity – were their souls to be
saved?

Answers to some of these problems were suggested by the
Cambridge Platonists, a group of philosophers largely associated
with Emmanuel College, Cambridge. Their most influential
members were Benjamin Whichcote (1609–83) and Ralph
Cudworth (1617–88). They were pre-eminently concerned with
two things: re-establishing the intellectual respectability of
Christianity; and ending the Baconian divorce between philosophy and religion. Some of their inspiration they drew from
Holland – when Burnet visited Holland in 1663, he found that
'the moderate men had larger and nobler thoughts of God and
of the design of the Christian religion than the zealots had' –
and much of the appeal of the Platonists was that they were
moderate men appealing to moderate men. The violence of
religious controversy had to be toned down; doctrines which had
formed the subject of, or the fuel for, such disputes were no
longer to be stressed. Much of the traditional imagery of Christian
thought and expression was ignored; concepts, rather than
images, mattered. Thought and conduct were the essentials –
'The state of religion lies in a good mind and a good life', says
Whichcote; 'all else is about religion, and men must not put the
instrumental part of religion for the state of religion.' Elsewhere
he details the essentials of a good life: 'sobriety, modesty, gentle-
ness, humility, obedience to God and charity to men'. Such
virtues were natural to mankind.

The Platonists gave to reason an authority in religion second
only to that of the Bible.

To go against reason is to go against God [said Whichcote]; it is the
self-same thing, to do that which the reason of the case doth require
and that which God himself doth appoint; reason is the divine
governor of man's life; it is the very voice of God.

All this sounds very prosaic, but the Platonists redeemed their theories from ordinariness by their intense desire that the Christian should not merely be virtuous but should strive towards a knowledge of God.

Scientific developments from Copernicus to Newton, by demonstrating that the universe was subject to law, suggested a fresh line of defence for Christianity, which might be summed up in the title of a once-famous book by John Ray – *The Wisdom of God in Creation* (1697), often described by the title of another by William Derham – *Physico-Theology* (1713). The wonders of nature demonstrate the greatness of the 'Divine Author' and the 'Divine Oeconomy'. Psalm 19 was to hand for those who took this line of defence, and Addison's version –

> The spacious firmament on high
> And all the blue ethereal sky
> And spangled heav'ns, a shining frame
> Doth his Creator's power display

– is a familiar exposition of it. This defence is most engagingly set forth, however, by Gilbert White in his *Natural History of Selborne*. This Hampshire clergyman, whether engaged in weighing a harvest mouse's nest, or declaiming Latin verse to test the clarity of an echo, saw clearly the hand of God:

> Say what impels amidst surrounding snow
> Congeal'd the Crocus' flamy bud to grow;
> Say, what retards amidst the summer's blaze
> Th' autumnal bulb; till pale declining days?
> The God of Seasons! Whose pervading power
> Controls the Sun, or sheds the fleecy shower;
> He bids each flower his quick'ning word obey
> Or to each lingering bloom enjoins delay.

Europeans, whether as missionaries, explorers, or traders, were now penetrating most parts of the world. Their memoirs and published descriptions encouraged not merely idle curiosity, but theological speculation. The tone of their work towards the people they found or converted was normally more than friendly; it was often idealizing. It was unthinkable that these virtuous Indians and Chinamen should be denied salvation.

These observations encouraged two tendencies of thought already prevalent from the middle of the seventeenth century: 'natural religion' – that is, the belief that religion and morality were essential parts of man's nature, and 'deism' – that is, a vague belief in a First Cause or Supreme Being, but without any of the distinctive tenets of Christianity. The greatest exponents of natural morality were the philosopher–Earl of Shaftesbury and Bishop Butler. Shaftesbury (his *Characteristicks of Men, Manners, Opinions and Times* was published in 1711) opposed Hobbes's ideas of the low self-interest and competitiveness which distinguished human conduct, and emphasized the satisfying characteristics of virtue and cheerfulness. Butler, later, dissected human nature into appetites, passions, affections, and a 'principle of reflection' which 'plainly bears upon it marks of authority over all the rest, and claims the absolute direction of them all, to alter or forbid their gratification'. Virtuous conduct might produce pleasure, but that is not the reason why it is done; it is done because it springs from human nature. As for deism, it is most neatly expressed by the (Roman Catholic!) Alexander Pope in his *Universal Hymn*:

> Father of All! in ev'ry Age
> In ev'ry Clime ador'd
> By Saint, by Savage and by Sage
> Jehovah, Jove or Lord.

The existence of the Deity accorded well with the ordered view of the universe which Newton suggested; belief in Him seemed to be an instinct of all ages and races. But the complications of Christian doctrine had to be swept away. The appearance of Toland's *Christianity not Mysterious* in 1696 brought the whole subject into the arena of literary controversy, and Christianity defended itself successfully, though in the process its doctrines were reduced to a minimum. The essentials of Christianity had to be plain and obvious, such as a reasonable man might comprehend. Archbishop Tillotson's address on I John 3, 'And His

commandments are not grievous', in which he demonstrated how
easy the performance of the Christian religion is, and how con-
sonant with our interest it is, is a celebrated example of this line
of thought. It is also a demonstration of why George Whitefield
in the next generation should observe that Tillotson 'knew no
more about religion than Mahomet'. The use of Tillotson's
sermons as models in both form and content emphasized the
tendency to minimize the essentials of Christian doctrine. This
inclination was a cause of frequent comment in sermons and in
addresses to clergy. Chancellor John Waugh at Carlisle in 1747,
drawing heavily on a sermon of Edmund Gibson, Bishop of
London, spoke of the necessity of insisting

upon such points as are purely Christian, the true understanding and
the practical belief and profession of which are of great import and
necessity to salvation. We daily see infidelity, Deism and profaneness
gaining ground; the doctrine of the glorious and ever-blessed Trinity,
the grand mystery of our redemption by the Incarnation of the
eternal Son of God and the merits of His Life, Death, Resurrection
and Ascension; the gifts of the Holy Ghost, and His preventing and
assisting grace; the necessity of repentance, the sure and certain
hopes of a resurrection, a future judgement, and eternal life; either
despised and trampled on, or little regarded and attended to.

Years later, Secker, when Archbishop of Canterbury, was to
declare to his assembled clergy that: 'We have in fact lost many
of our people to sectaries by not preaching in a manner sufficiently evangelical.'

What place had revelation in all this? Christian teaching
insists that knowledge of God arises not only from man's reason,
but from revelation – that is, from actual disclosure of knowledge
to man from God. The climax of the controversy over revelation
came with the appearance of Bishop Butler's *Analogy of Religion*
in 1736, a work which ingeniously compared the workings of
revelation to those of nature. Just as nature works in uncertain
ways, so does revelation. Man is ignorant and unable to conceive
how events are related to each other; the workings of God are
likewise obscure to man. Butler was able to assume the existence

of a Divine Author, and felt that there was altogether sufficient evidence in our own nature to demonstrate that He governed the world righteously – the operation of our own conscience, for example.

This great revolution in thought was accompanied by a change of tone in sermons and in writing. Appeals to 'the reasonable man' must be expressed reasonably and in his own language: the style of pulpit oratory and printed controversy of the eighteenth century was adjusted accordingly. John Tillotson (1630–94), the Archbishop of Canterbury, who in the matter of his sermons was such a model to the eighteenth century, was also so in manner. He jettisoned energy and metaphor in favour of the plainer speech of a Restoration gentleman. Burnet, writing of Tillotson and others, says:

These were the greatest divines of their times; and it is to their example and good taste that the method of preaching in England, which before was overrun with pedantry and mixed quotations, with points of controversy and different expositions, in a style either flat or low, or swelled up to a false sublime, was so wonderfully reformed. For the style of their discourses was generally clear and plain; they gave a short paraphrase of their text, laying aside all unnecessary shows of learning, and applying themselves directly to the matter, in which they opened the nature and reason of things so fully, and with that simplicity, that their hearers felt another kind of instruction than what they were accustomed to; and many, by their means, were won off from their prejudices against the church.

By 1711, a letter to Mr Spectator is complaining good humouredly of clergymen that 'affect a rakish negligent air by folding their arms and lolling on their book' and of a set of readers 'who affect, forsooth, a certain gentleman-like familiarity of tone, and mend the language as they go on, crying instead of "pardoneth and absolveth" "pardons and absolves".'

To the eighteenth-century churchman, enthusiasm had two meanings: zeal was one, and the other was Johnson's dictionary definition – 'a vain belief of private revelation; a vain confidence of divine favour or communication.' Both were anathema. The case against 'imprudent fervours of religion' as Addison states it is formidable – 'Where it is once laudable and prudential, it is an hundred times criminal and erroneous.'

... I love to see a man zealous in a good matter, and especially when his zeal shows itself for advancing morality, and promoting the happiness of mankind. But when I find the instruments he works with are racks and gibbets, galleys and dungeons, when he imprisons men's persons, confiscates their estates, ruins their families, and burns the body to save the soul, I cannot stick to pronounce of such a one that (whatever he may think of his faith and his religion) his faith is vain, and his religion unprofitable.

The ideals of the Cambridge Platonists, then, were subject to a steady process of vulgarization. Once they reach Tillotson and Addison, indeed, they are in a fair way to being vulgarized, since Tillotson's sermons and the *Spectator* essays were immensely popular throughout the eighteenth century. Eventually these ideals percolate to a provincial and parochial level – as we may see from the sermons of Spencer Cowper, Dean of Durham; John Lloyd, Vicar of Epping; Anthony Hastwell in the North Riding; and James Woodforde at Weston Longeville, who in the course of a sermon on prayer exhorted his hearers to 'such a fervency as was a gentle, pleasing, heavenly flame, and not a headstrong and outrageous fire, which hurries men into enthusiasm'.

But at any rate the preaching of simple virtues did have some remarkable effects. Hannah More dubbed this epoch 'the Age of Benevolence', and every kind of philanthropic activity or 'practical Christianity' appeared to flourish – whether it was the direct giving of alms, the musical festival in aid of the county hospital, the bequeathing of stock to provide for poor widows of the parish for ever, or the setting up of charity schools in all parts of the kingdom. M. G. Jones, in her famous study of the Charity School Movement, has distinguished between the Puritan conception of 'charity promoting the glory of God by promoting the usefulness of man' and 'the craze for philanthropy which at intervals seized upon the fashionable world'. The eighteenth-century charity school was not an exercise in disinterested charity, but an attempt to keep the lower orders in their places; and doubtless names were added to hospital subscription lists for reasons of fashion. But the achievements of Georgian benevolence are so wide-ranging that it is clear that at least one of the themes of pulpit oratory was more than just a pulpit ideal.

[3] THE CLERGY

A bishop has always been expected to have a near-impossible collection of virtues: to be a scholar, to be an administrator, and to be physically strong. The modern view of his functions may (without much exaggeration) be said to date from Samuel Wilberforce, who became Bishop of Oxford in 1845 and died as Bishop of Winchester in 1873. He, however, lived during the railway age and during an era of intense reform in ecclesiastical boundaries and finances; the political functions of a bishop were in decline. The eighteenth-century bishop, on the other hand, had more affinities with his medieval predecessors than with his modern successors. His political services were much less distinguished than those of the great clerical civil servants of the Middle Ages, but they were hardly less time-consuming. His social standing, at least in his own county, remained high. His position was still inordinately expensive to maintain. He was still hindered by bad communications. In consequence of all these things, he took very much the same formal view of his spiritual functions as many of the medieval bishops took. These functions included ordination of clergy, confirmation, and visitation, that is, a triennial investigation of the affairs of a diocese, conducted by touring the diocese and meeting clergy and officers at various centres.

The duty of attending and voting in the Lords (as we have seen) was virtually enforced, and those bishops who did not live near London were obliged to live in London from November until May. Episcopal participation in civil affairs did not end there. The bishop was a leader of his county set – attending the assizes, dining with the judges, visiting and being visited by the principal laity as well as the clergy – generally, in fact, sharing the activities of his own social class. Electioneering was not scorned; it was often expected. George Selwyn once referred memorably to the clergy as being 'as so many turnspits ready to be put into the wheel, and to turn it round as the Minister pleases'.

A bishop's life was an expensive one. There were several causes for extraordinary spending on his part – the expenses involved in elevation to a bishopric, the annual stay in London, and the standard and extent of the entertaining expected of him. When Samuel Bradford was offered the bishopric of St David's in 1710 without its being supplemented by another living, he rejected it

since the whole of his private fortunes at that time would have scarce enabled him to get into possession of this preferment, nor would the annual revenue of it alone have been sufficient for him to live upon with a decency and charity becoming such a situation.

Repairs to an episcopal palace sometimes were burdensome, and indeed sometimes there was no residence at all – the major reason Richard Watson, the Bishop of the poor see of Llandaff between 1782 and 1816, always gave for his remote control of his diocese from his house by Lake Windermere. The bishoprics (as we have seen) differed widely in their revenues, and they formed a series of stepping stones, beginning with Bristol and the Welsh dioceses. Permission was frequently given to hold additional preferments – livings *in commendam* – to make such posts endurable.

There were physical difficulties as well as pecuniary ones. The differences between the areas of the several dioceses in England and Wales were enormous. Bishops in the Middle Ages had the assistance of roving bishops (those consecrated to sees *in partibus infidelium*); the nineteenth century saw the reintroduction of bishops suffragan; but the eighteenth-century bishops had no assistants. The right of aged bishops to resign, necessary under such conditions, was denied, and there are many examples of the difficulties of very elderly bishops in large sees. Carlisle,

Rochester, or Hereford presented little difficulty to healthy men.
But the diocese of Lincoln contained 1,312 parishes and six
archdeaconries; it stretched over five counties. The population
of the archdeaconries of Lincoln and Stow alone was over
125,000. The diocese of St David's had 903 parishes and chapel-
ries. The physical difficulties involved in the performance of
visitation and confirmation were therefore immense. Before
setting out at Lincoln, William Wake had to plan his itinerary
beforehand with an eye on distance, on harvest weather, on
market days, and on the condition of the roads. Edmund Gibson
was compelled to split his visitation of that diocese in September
1720 and carry out the rest of it in 1721, though at that time he
was only in his early fifties.

Confirmation, which was ordinarily carried out with visitation
and at the same centres, was often a laborious, if not positively
dangerous, activity for a bishop, because of the number of
candidates involved. Zachary Pearce, the Bishop of Rochester,
had the task in 1773 of confirming seven hundred at Greenwich
when he was 82, and 'found himself next day unable to speak,
and never regained his former readiness of utterance'. He had
made repeated but unsuccessful efforts to resign ten years
before. When Dr White Kennett succeeded the aged and
incapable Cumberland as Bishop of Peterborough in 1718, it
took him several years to repair the neglects of his predecessor:

I have entered on my stages of confirmation [he wrote to Wake, the
Archbishop of Canterbury, in July 1722] and began at Uppingham in
Rutland, within which county they have had no confirmation these
forty years. The numbers as taken by one of my attendants were
1,700 and odd. I appoint it on Sundays after noon, because the good
folks have their best clothes and horses to spare; otherwise we should
have very few upon these dripping days when they must wait upon
their hay and corn. I intend constantly to preach myself in the
morning and have evening prayer over before 3, and to spend the
remainder of the day in that office. I had not done at Uppingham till
after ten at night.

In spite of all the difficulties surrounding the holding of visitations
and confirmations, Wake in 1718

believed the confirmations had never been so regular throughout the
kingdom as within the last thirty years, nor the episcopal visitations
and that by the bishops in person, so constant.

The administration of the Church had always been beset by
physical problems, but a series of shifts and devices made it
possible to overcome them. These solutions were always considered normal before the nineteenth century; since then, they
have been considered discreditable. Ordination and confirmation
could not be performed other than by a bishop, but almost every
other function could be delegated – and, to a great extent, to
study the administration of the eighteenth-century Church is to
study the working of delegation in all its forms. (The procedure
of using deputies was open to the obvious abuse of overworking
and underpaying the deputy, of course.)

To judge whether the Church of England of that period was
efficiently run or not, it is necessary to look at the activities of
clergymen several rungs below the level of a bishop. Dr John
Waugh, a minor dignitary already quoted, was the son of a
Bishop of Carlisle and in consequence found himself chancellor
of that diocese in 1727 while still in his twenties. He resided in
Carlisle until 1751, when the deanery of Worcester was added
to his existing preferments. During that time, under three
bishops, he effectively ran the diocese. As chancellor he presided
over the network of ecclesiastical courts and conducted visitations. He investigated virtually all the parishes of the diocese
personally, and his observations on them survive. During the
incursions of the Jacobites in 1745 he was the effective leader of
the clergy in Carlisle. When in 1751 he secured his due reward
for such services and left Carlisle for Worcester, the administration of the diocese still presented no problem – there was always
the archdeacon and, for the court business, a large number of
substitutes (or surrogates).

Archdeacon Paley, who cloaked most things in the Church of
his day with a respectable theoretical justification, defended the
division of the clergy into bishops, priests, and deacons on social
grounds:

It secures tranquillity and subordination amongst the clergy themselves [and] provides for the edification of each rank, by stationing
in each an order of clergy for their own class and quality.

The threefold division is too neat, but it is a helpful approxi-
mation. The formality surrounding a bishop was impressive, and
it was noticed as a sign of conduct 'beyond measure condescend-
ing and courteous' when Warburton, the Bishop of Gloucester,
'even graciously handed some biscuits and wine on a salver to
the curate who was to read the prayers'. Below the bishop were
the parochial clergy, of whom James Woodforde, the Rector of
Weston Longeville in Norfolk between 1774 and 1803, is now
the best-known example. With £300 a year, he was lucky,
though; the average of the hundred livings in the diocese of
Carlisle in 1747 was only £59. At the foot of the clerical ladder –
the profession was often referred to in this way, and even more
often as a lottery – was a miscellany of curates. The poorest of
their kind were the curates of the Lake District. At Martindale
at the opening of the century the endowments of the chapelry
were made up of

contributions from the inhabitants, £2.16.9½; from the Lord of the
Manor 10s; in hay 1/6; in land and houses £2.17.4; interest of £100
(£3.14.0).

The social and financial divisions among the clergy may be
studied from a variety of sources. Dr J. H. Plumb's half-sen-
tence (in his *England in the Eighteenth Century*, Pelican, 1950,
p. 44) dismissing most of them as 'not quite gentlemen' seems in
fact to be as near correct as a three-word generalization can be.
The definition is wide enough, and would include Parson Woodforde, accustomed to dining with the Custances at the local big
house but uneasy with those of a more aristocratic station, as
well as that Vicar of Irthington in Cumberland described by his
bishop as

the wretched and beggarly father of ten poor children, seven whereof
are with him. One girl he has at service; one a boy 'prentice to a glover
at Brampton, and another to a blacksmith.

The status, income, and conditions of the clergy were rising throughout the century. There were various reasons why this should be so. The operation of Queen Anne's Bounty was one cause of improvement. Bishop Burnet had suggested this scheme to Queen Mary in the 1690s; he later enlisted the support of William, and subsequently of Godolphin and of Anne's favourite prelate, Archbishop Sharp. The two taxes on ecclesiastical offices known as 'first fruits' and 'tenths' had been taken over by the Crown in 1534, and the proceeds were not used for church purposes. These taxes represented a severe burden on smaller livings, their collection was difficult, and payment was often in arrears. From 1704, the royal proceeds from first fruits and tenths – something like £17,000 a year – were devoted to the assistance of poor clergy, and arrears of tenths by the poorer clergy were remitted. From 1708, livings of £50 a year were discharged from payment of first fruits and tenths (see G. F. A. Best, *Temporal Pillars*, esp. pp. 21–8).

Under this arrangement also, livings of under £50 a year were augmented – though it was an uncertain operation, since livings to be improved were chosen by lot, unless they could attract a private donation. In the diocese of Carlisle, for example, out of 39 livings which had qualified under the scheme, 26 had benefited, some repeatedly, between 1707 and 1762. The major reason for the improvement in clerical incomes was, however, the increased value of land, arising from agricultural and industrial development. Tithe increased as the land brought into cultivation during the agricultural revolution increased; new agreements for changing tithe into a money payment instead of a payment in kind were frequently made at the time of enclosure; and by various means the clergy succeeded in revising old settlements so as to make their income approximate to contemporary values. Everywhere, as we have already seen, the virtues of 'good management' by the clergy were commended. 'Improvement' resulted not merely in increased stipends but in more expenditure in poor relief, church restoration, and the construction of parsonage houses.

What, among all this, were the standards of clerical duty in the parishes ? One tentative observation may be made: whenever generalization is attempted, the eighteenth-century clergyman gets the worst of it; and whenever detailed study of individual clergy is made, they emerge with credit. The publication of part of the diary of James Woodforde (in five volumes, 1924–31) illustrates this last point well enough. Woodforde's concentration on what he ate – especially his 'plumb puddings' – cannot obscure the more positive virtues among his activities at Weston. His Sunday duty was one service, either morning or afternoon; and Communion was celebrated quarterly. The particular virtue of his time – benevolence – he practised constantly; and his payment of doctors' bills for his parishioners; his gifts of money, food, and drink; and his attendance at the musical festivals in aid of the County Hospital at Norwich, are not unimpressive. The picture presented in this diary, of a parson aware of the personal needs of all his parish and in harmony with his parishioners, is almost enough on its own to revise the customary low view of the eighteenth-century clergyman. Other evidence confirms this impression. Ollard and Walker, introducing Archbishop Herring's Visitation Returns of 1743 for the diocese of York, thought that:

It seems from these records that the Chuch was, on the whole, doing her work far better and more thoroughly than is commonly supposed, yet she lacked the 'zeal' and 'fire' which the Revivals . . . supplied

and that the parish clergy were

a body of conscientious and dutiful men.

Holding more than one living – pluralism – and non-residence were widespread enough. All were agreed, of course, that the residence of a clergyman in his parish was desirable – partly because the working of a parish was a matter of great complexity, as has been seen; partly, too, because it was a guarantee of the health of society. Dr Johnson once wrote to a young clergyman:

The Dean of Carlisle, who was then a little rector in Northamptonshire, told me, that it might be discerned whether or no there was a clergyman resident in a parish, by the civil or savage manner of the people.

Dr William Nicolson became Bishop of Carlisle in 1702 and moved from the parish of Great Salkeld in Cumberland 'leaving the parishioners, as I thought, in a perfect unity and peace among themselves'. But his successor was non-resident:

Mr Archdeacon Fisher continuing at Burgh and rarely coming at them, they are now in great heats and divisions.

To the clerical administrator, the major difficulty was the neglect of the church and the parsonage house.

Certainly [says a popular legal handbook of the time, *The Parson's Counsellor*] there can be nothing more unbecoming the dignity of a clergyman than non-residence and dilapidations, which for the most part go hand in hand.

That pluralism was an abuse needs no elaboration; but it was permitted to a great variety of persons on a great variety of grounds, as Dr Sykes observes:

The unreformed Georgian Church did not question the inherited medieval tradition that ecclesiastical revenues existed for the support of ecclesiastical persons, irrespective of their residence in the locality from which their income was drawn.

All offices 'without cure of souls', such as deaneries and prebends, could be held with another benefice; chaplains, whether to the king or to lords spiritual or temporal, and those holding higher degrees, could hold more than one living. Canon 41 of 1604 hedged this privilege about with regulations, not always observed, that a pluralist should have a dispensation from an archbishop, as well as that the livings should not be more than thirty miles apart, and that a sufficient preacher should be employed where an incumbent did not reside. Such arrangements account for the familiar phenomenon of the underpaid curate of uncertain tenure, one of the most miserable figures of eighteenth-century society. To assume that a substitute always came under this description, however, would be mistaken; Gilbert White of Selborne, the most celebrated of all country parsons, was a curate for upwards of forty years.

All kinds of customs and difficulties reconciled administrators to the idea of pluralism. Two or three livings were often bestowed on a man for administrative or literary merit. They were necessary to support certain dignities – an archdeaconry, for example. Of course, too, the families of lay and ecclesiastical patrons had to be rewarded. The most common form of pluralism was, however, the holding of two or more adjacent livings in order to secure a living wage. Ollard and Walker, in their observations on the situation in the diocese of York as it was in 1743, observed that about half the clergy of the diocese held more than one living, many of them for the last reason. In the Carlisle diocese in 1747, something like twenty-eight clergymen held more than one living; but little fault might be found, for example, with Mr Christopher Walton who was curate of the adjacent parishes of Walton and Scaleby and who made a total of £33.10.0 a year for his exertions.

[4] CHURCHES AND PARISHES

The Georgian Church of England often stands accused of neglect of church building and of want of decency inside the buildings it had. More seriously, the lack of resilience in its parochial organization made it unfitted to face the challenge of an expanding and proletarian population.

It is difficult to make out the first charge. In 1702, Nicolson (already mentioned), an exceptionally high-minded and vigorous antiquary, was made Bishop of Carlisle. Since his diocese was small – about 100 parishes – he was able to make a personal parish-by-parish survey between May 1703 and March 1704. His account came into the hands of Chancellor Waugh, who made an equally detailed survey of the same parishes in the 1740s, in parallel with Nicolson's. Since the registers and court books for the diocese also exist for this period, there is an opportunity to examine the improvement in church maintenance and church provision at this time. (Nicolson's account has been in print since 1877, as *Miscellany Accounts of the Diocese of Carlisle*, ed. R. S. Ferguson. Ferguson also transcribed Waugh's observations. This transcription is in Tullie House, Carlisle.)

Various pressures were producing a demand for change: a revolution in architectural taste which rejected the Gothic as barbarous, or at least as nothing more than an antiquarian curiosity; a concern for decency and order; an intense desire for pews which indicated social status; the perennial difficulty of maintaining large medieval buildings; redistribution of population; and the need to produce a building which approximated to the needs of preaching and Prayer Book worship, rather than to the conventions of medieval worship. The ideal church interior envisaged by the Georgian churchman was one in which the royal arms and the commandments and creed, with a monument or two, would appear on plastered, whitewashed walls; a gallery would be erected at the west end; box-pews would be carefully assigned, and present no obstructions; an altar would stand north and south at the east end, and be carefully railed off; a three-decker pulpit, with a sounding-board over, would provide accommodation for the clerk, the parson's reading desk, and the point from which to preach. Such interiors might best be provided by complete rebuilding; otherwise the surviving Gothic building had to be adapted.

The account which Nicolson gives of the churches of his diocese in 1703 shows that they were very far from these standards. The region was poor economically. Since there was often no school-house, the school was sometimes conducted inside the church. At Westward the Bishop wrote:

I was glad, to find the curate, Mr Holme, surrounded by so good a number of scholars; though I could have wished to see them elsewhere than in the chancel, and spoiling Mr Barwis's monument with writing their copies on it.

The presence of numerous Dissenters in a parish sometimes obstructed improvements; so did quarrels between the impropriators. Nicolson wrote at Bridekirk:

The quire has rails, but everything else (in and about it) looks very scandalous . . . the walls and floor are most nasty and the leads very much decayed and full of drops. 'Tis crowded with the seats of the joint impropriators. *Hinc illae lachrymae*. They cannot or they will not adjust their proportions to the expense.

Sometimes a slovenly rector was at fault – at Stapleton

the quire . . . is most intolerably scandalous. No glass in the windows, no ascent to anything that looks like an altar.

At Torpenhow (where the Bishop himself had been vicar), however, much improvement had taken place through the co-operation of the vicar and the local squire, who had provided various additions in return for 'a seat answerable to his quality'. The desire to secure a suitable pew was indeed a valuable aid to church improvement. It was reported in the Bishop's register in 1709 that:

The master of the grammar school at Dovenby and the scholars want convenient seats in the church, so that the master's eye cannot behold their misdemeanours.

Mr John Muncaster was therefore

willing to erect a gallery at the low end of the said church and to make a pew therein for himself and his family and also seats for the said master and scholars, which will be no damage to the said church but rather an ornament thereto.

By the middle of the century the situation was much altered for the better. During the period from 1702 to 1768 the population remained more or less stationary in the diocese; there was no such increase as justified the rapid building of new churches in the nineteenth century. Nevertheless, seventeen churches and chapels were newly built or entirely rebuilt, either by the parish or, more rarely, with private backing. Every considerable point of population growth in the county of Cumberland – Carlisle, Wigton, Penrith, Maryport, Workington, and Whitehaven – was provided with a new church between 1700 and 1830; Workington and Whitehaven, indeed, with two each.

Forasmuch [reads the petition for the erection of Holy Trinity, Whitehaven, in 1715] as the inhabitants of the town of Whitehaven ... being greatly increased since the building of the present church or chapel there cannot now be all decently contained therein, whereby great numbers of the said inhabitants are put under a necessity either of staying at home, neglecting the public worship of Almighty God or of going to other churches in the country at a great distance and with much inconveniency, and several others may be induced for want of other accommodation to resort to the places of worship amongst those that dissent from the Church of England, and whereas the said town of Whitehaven being still in a growing condition some other place for public worship in the town is like to be daily more necessary and the want thereof attended with worse consequences.

Where churches were not rebuilt, the accommodation was often entirely renewed or galleries were added. Chancellor Waugh's account of the diocese, principally compiled in the forties, is full of other indications of improvement. His impressions he summed up himself when he made his notes at Torpenhow, which Nicolson had described in 1703 as 'the fairest inside of any parish church in the diocese'.. In 1747 'all about it was in laudable condition, though there are many better now in the diocese'.

So much for the situation in the North. All the evidence of recent architectural surveys and ecclesiological work points to similar conclusions all over the country. The notion that the eighteenth century had a deplorable record in church building and improvement is mistaken. The Oxford Movement and the romantic revival so affected ecclesiastical taste that determined attempts were made literally to erase or disguise the work of the previous age (see Basil F. L. Clarke, *The Building of the Eighteenth Century Church*, S.P.C.K., 1963, esp. Appendixes III, IV, and V).

As for the conduct of worship inside eighteenth-century churches, it has had the misfortune to suffer attacks from both John Wesley and the Tractarians. Knowledge of it survives best in Thomas Hardy, whose recollections are of a time before the Oxford Movement had affected many country churches:

> On afternoons of drowsy calm
> We stood in the panelled pew
> Singing one-voiced a Tate-and-Brady psalm
> To the tune of Cambridge New.

Tate and Brady's version of the psalms (1696) was commonly
bound up with the Prayer Book, and memorable and metrical
as the hymns might be, they were not distinguished verse:

> Lord, hear the voice of my complaint
> To my request give ear
> Preserve my soul from cruel foes
> And free my soul from fear

— and so on.

The parish clerk led the singing, sometimes after establishing the
tune or the note on a pitch pipe. A band often provided accompaniment. Indeed, as appears from a relatively large number of
survivals in East Anglia, the accompaniment could be provided
by a barrel organ: mechanical verses to mechanical tunes.

Though churches were provided, new parishes were not.
Before 1818, an Act of Parliament was required to set up a new
parish. The parish, far from being merely an area drawn on a
map, was (as has been seen) a complex of property interests; and
the clergy were as intent on protecting their fees for professional
services as were the impropriators on protecting their income
from land. The problem of attending to the spiritual needs of
new settlements brought about by industrial development was
therefore tackled by building chapels inside existing parishes.
There, morning or evening prayer was said by a curate, but
funerals and weddings, for which fees were payable, continued
to be held in the parish church. Proprietary chapels were also
erected in the cities – that is to say chapels were built as commercial speculations by or for capable preachers. Both solutions
were obviously unsatisfactory, though if new parishes had been
set up in exclusively working-class areas, the Church of England,
adjusted to a hierarchical society, would have found (and eventually did find) great difficulty in dealing with a one-class parish.

Here, as in so many ways, the identity between Church,

government, and society was so complete that adjustment to
change seemed hardly possible. The rise of Methodism, coincident
with industrial change, was to challenge many of the Church's
presuppositions all at once.

[5] DISSENT

There were small numbers of people outside the nicely ordered
society which assembled (at any rate in Sir Roger de Coverly's
parish) in the parish church – the Dissenters. Daniel Defoe, who
was one himself, sometimes gives a contrary impression; at
Southwold in Suffolk he wrote in the 1720s of being

> surprised to see an extraordinarily large church, capable of receiving
> five or six thousand people, and but twenty-seven in it besides the
> parson and the clerk; but at the same time the meeting house of the
> Dissenters was full to the very doors, having as I guessed six to eight
> hundred people in it.

The total number of Dissenters in 1715 in England and Wales is,
however, generally agreed to have been about a quarter of a
million out of a total population of five and a half million, and
though sizeable meetings might assemble in London and in the
older towns, the numbers in country parishes were often insignificant. The principal English Dissenting sects were the Presbyterians, who in the early part of the century were thought to
be two-thirds of the whole, the Independents, the Baptists, and
the Quakers; though the more extraordinary groups of the
Cromwellian period, such as the Muggletonians, continued their
existence for a long time.

This list of denominations suggests infinite variety, but in fact
what the Dissenters had in common at this time is more obvious
than the differences between them. Their heroic age had been
the Great Rebellion, and for the crime of rebellion they suffered
a common framework of restriction, and occasionally of persecution, for a century and a half. Their campaign against the

restrictions imposed on them at the Restoration gave them common opinions of protest. Moreover, in matters of belief they tended to become homogeneous as the details of Christian doctrine became blurred, and in matters of church government they all tended to slide into Independency as individual congregations assumed the management of their concerns. There was also a certain uniformity of class; if a Dissenter prospered exceedingly, he commonly went over to the Established Church. The Dissenters, too, created their own sub-culture. They brooded on their own history, like Calamy's account of the Ejected Ministers (1702) or Bogue and Bennett's *History of the Dissenters* (1814); they married members of their own denominations; excluded from Oxford and Cambridge, they formed and staffed their own places of education; and (a famous sidelight on the Industrial Revolution) they assisted each other in economic enterprises.

'Persecution' is a severe word for the treatment of the Dissenters in the period following 1689, but the legal apparatus of persecution remained on the statute book. The fate of the sects after the return of the monarchy in 1660 was not at first clear, and from time to time Anglican policy was to 'comprehend' or to include at any rate the Presbyterians within the Establishment. But the introduction of the Clarendon Code in the years 1661–5, and the Act of Uniformity in 1662, were decisive. The 1662 Act obliged ministers to swear unfeigned assent and consent to everything in the Book of Common Prayer, and thus the sectaries were ejected. The Corporation Act of 1661 excluded Dissenters from corporations; the Conventicle Act of 1664 made prayer meetings of more than four people who were not of the same household illegal, and specifically forbade field-preaching; the Five Mile Act of 1665 excluded dissenting ministers and schoolmasters from the towns. The Test Act of 1673 excluded the Dissenters from all public office under the Crown.

With the coming of William and Mary, the Dissenters (who were among their most obvious supporters) were rewarded with the Toleration Act of 1689. Under this, those who accepted thirty-six out of the Thirty-nine Articles were permitted to worship in premises licensed by the bishop or by the justices. The insistence that thirty-six Articles should be accepted excluded Unitarians from the provisions of the Act. Many of the Dissenters became Unitarians in the course of the eighteenth century, and the Articles requirement was waived from 1779. But the Clarendon Code and the Test Act remained on the statute book alongside the Toleration Act, and while they did, there was a considerable and often justified feeling of insecurity. The Dissenters identified themselves with the Whigs; the Tories, therefore, in the heyday of their power between 1710 and 1714, sought to restrict their power in two ways: by banning the Dissenters' practice of occasionally taking Communion in the Church of England to qualify themselves for public office (the Occasional Conformity Act, 1711), and by making Dissenting Academies illegal (The Schism Act, 1714). With the coming of George I, the Whigs undid these Acts (1718), and Dissent entered on a period of relative security. However, Hardwicke's Marriage Act obliged them after 1754 to marry in an Anglican church, and they could find themselves deprived of the right to burial in the churchyard if the incumbent questioned the baptism of the deceased. (There was often a general prejudice against them in the parishes because of their failure to pay church rates.)

The continued existence of the Test and Corporation Acts and the exclusion of the Dissenters from public life and from the universities produced a machinery for protest and a developing theory of liberalism among the Dissenters. It has often been observed that the burden imposed on them by the parliamentary Acts was not great. Steven Watson has investigated the years when an annual Indemnity Act was passed to lift the penalties incurred for breaches of the Test Act. The Indemnity Acts began in 1728, but they did not become a regular event until 1758. After that they were passed every year until the Test and Corporation Acts were themselves repealed in 1828 (see J. S. Watson, 'Dissent and Toleration' in *Silver Renaissance*, ed. Alex Natan).

Whether or not the burden was great, the effects of the Acts were. If the laws were to be lifted, some agitation was necessary; and agitation required direction and unity. The result was the formation of the Protestant Dissenting Deputies in 1732. Two deputies were chosen from every Presbyterian, Independent, and Baptist congregation in London and for ten miles round; from their number a committee of twenty-one was elected. The Deputies from that time forward became a permanent body to look after the Dissenters' civil concerns – not merely to lobby for the repeal of the obnoxious Acts, but also to take up cases of unreasonable discrimination on religious grounds. They retained operative links with their brethren in the provinces, through, for example, committees of correspondence, and were generally, though not always, in agreement with them (see B. L. Manning, *The Protestant Dissenting Deputies*, pp. 19–33).

The nature of the Dissenters' case against the restrictions imposed upon them was at first limited. Their calm statement of their case, printed for Members of Parliament in 1739, insisted that every man had a right to judge for himself in matters of religion, and insisted, like Locke, that matters of religion did not 'affect the public welfare and prosperity of the kingdom'. They maintained that to use the Holy Communion as a qualification for civic office was to debase that service, and that, as persons of property at least equal to that of their neighbours, and as friends of the existing Government, they ought to be admitted to civil office. But by George III's reign, when their case came to be stated by Dr Richard Price (1723–91) and Dr Joseph Priestley (1733–1804), the arch-representatives of 'Rational Dissent', the grounds of their protest widened. Somehow they had to unscramble the English Constitution – the alliance of Church and State as Warburton had defended it – and to secularize the State and their relationship to it. Priestley wrote in 1773:

As a Christian only, I acknowledge I ought to be content with the bare toleration of my religion and be thankful for it. But when the Christian is satisfied I cannot forget that I am likewise a man.

Their religious pleas became classic liberal demands for freedom of conscience and a career open to talents.

Their reaction to two other political issues of the period – the American and French Revolutions – confirmed the Dissenters' reputation for political radicalism (for their attitude to the French Revolution, see pp. 187–8). The leaders of Dissent maintained close contacts with Holland, with Scotland, and with the Thirteen Colonies – with their co-religionists, one might say – and also with the more original and reforming spirits in English politics, like Shelburne, Christopher Wyvil, and Fox. Price, a close friend of Franklin and a considerable theorist on the subject of national finance, was invited to take charge of the finances of the United States. Priestley eventually settled and died in America. During the American War Price produced an extremely influential pamphlet, the *Observations on Civil Liberty* of 1776, which sold 60,000 copies, and later some *Additional Observations* (1777). No one could have been a more enthusiastic supporter of the American cause.

Price was a moralist who brooded on the national sins he saw around him: misgovernment in India, excessive luxury and corrupt elections at home. The actions of the British Government towards America were a mere exertion of tyranny; to assert that unity must be preserved at the cost of enslaving the colonists was immoral. A solution might be an imperial parliament with equal representation. Magnanimity shown by withdrawing the British armies and protecting American rights of property would help. But the preacher was never far away: the real solution was for Britain to repent of her national sins. When the War was over, Price produced his *Importance of the American Revolution* (1784). He was inordinately enthusiastic:

Perhaps I do not go too far when I say that next to the introduction of Christianity among mankind, the American Revolution may prove the most important step in the progressive course of human improvement.

The advice he then gave the Americans was first to eliminate their public debt by setting up a Sinking Fund (a notion which Pitt the Younger derived from Price); to preserve peace; to establish full liberty of thought and discussion; to advance

education, though not by state action; to avoid hereditary
honours and do all they could to preserve their present happy
state of society, 'the middle state between the savage and the
refined'; to restrict foreign trade, which introduces luxury; and
to abolish the slave trade.

In belief, Latitudinarianism and a slide into general benevolence – characteristics, as we have seen, of the Church of England
– were also characteristics of the Dissenters. The theology of the
three major denominations had strong similarities. It was
officially Calvinist in asserting that a man was saved by his faith,
and that those to be saved had already been predestined to be
so; and of course it accepted the doctrine of the Trinity. The
crucial difference between the Baptists and the others was the
practice of adult baptism by immersion. The difference between
the Presbyterians and the Independents was one of church
government. The Independents gave decisive authority to the
individual congregation; in theory the Presbyterian system was
hierarchical. None of these divisions was critical in the eighteenth
century. The rigidities of Calvinism were often softened, though
they remained a talking point for congregations and an excuse
for expelling ministers if need be. There was a movement away
from belief in the Trinity into Arianism, Socinianism, or Unitarianism; that is to say, belief in the divinity of Christ was pro-
gressively diluted until it finally disappeared. In the case of the
Presbyterians, this movement towards Unitarianism became
something like a headlong rush.

The critical point in the history of the Three Denominations
came in 1719. The ministers of Devon and Cornwall, and after
them a committee of laymen, attempted to insist on public
affirmation by all ministers of belief in the Trinity. The problem
was referred to a meeting of Dissenters at Salters' Hall Meeting
House in London, and the advice there given was indecisive, and
a positive encouragement to splintering. By a majority of four
only, the meeting determined that it was undesirable that there
should be acceptance of creeds and confessions. Ministers could
be expelled if their congregations disliked their doctrine on the
Trinity: thus each congregation took control of its own affairs,

and Nonconformist history almost resolved itself for the rest of the century into a numberless series of squabbles in the meeting houses over doctrine and government. Authority from the centre did not exist. Just as political exclusion bred radicalism, so it has been argued that this atmosphere of argument in every meeting house encouraged individuality of view and attitudes singularly different from those produced by the authoritarianism and emotionalism of Methodism.

Proceedings inside the meeting houses underwent changes partly also to be observed inside the Church of England and among the Methodists. Isaac Watts (1674–1748) acted partly as a kind of Dissenters' Tillotson and partly as their Charles Wesley. Dr Johnson observed of Watts that:

He was one of the first authors that taught the Dissenters to court attention by the graces of language. Whatever they had among them before, whether of learning or acuteness, was commonly blunted by coarseness and inelegance of style. He shewed them, that zeal and purity might be expressed and enforced by polished diction.

In the art of hymn writing – in substituting elegant and emotional verse for pedestrian metrical psalms – he is of course celebrated: the author of 'O God our help in ages past' and 'Jesus shall reign where'er the Sun'.

Those who frequented the meeting houses formed in many ways 'a peculiar people'. They were educated apart in their own Dissenting Academies, though these did not exclude Anglicans. Such academies – crosses between boarding schools and universities – had originated in 1662, or, more properly perhaps, in the mind of Milton, whose treatise *Of Education* (1644) sets forth the ideals on which they were based. Many academics, ejected in 1662 as a result of the Act of Uniformity, kept body and soul together by acting as tutors to gentlemen's sons. They also set up academies, and between 1663 and 1690 twenty-three are known to have existed. Many flourished also during the eighteenth century: at Northampton, Gloucester, Daventry, Warrington, and Hackney, for example. None enjoyed a long existence – they were identified too closely with particular teachers; the maintenance of discipline often proved difficult; and in the case of the last of the famous foundations, Hackney (1786–96), hostility was incurred by the apparently revolutionary content of the curriculum. Priestley had indeed hoped in 1791 that the academies would 'educate such an illustrious character as those which are now conducting the glorious revolution in France'. The education provided at the academies was distinguished by its modernity of content and of method. Morton's famous institution at Stoke Newington, where both Daniel Defoe and Samuel Wesley were educated, had a laboratory with an air pump, a thermometer, and mathematical instruments. Priestley at Warrington, Doddridge at Northampton, and Jennings at Kibworth, taught history, partly the history of Nonconformity, and partly by way of political instruction. The political lectures delivered there – certainly the most famous of them, by Doddridge – were often formal and derived from Locke alone. The method of instruction was basically the lecture, in English; Watts and Doddridge also encouraged discussion (on this, see particularly A. Lincoln, *Some Political and Social Ideas of English Dissent*, Ch. III).

The academies no doubt provided a certain identity of view and helped to preserve the distinctness of Dissent. But who were the quarter of a million Dissenters? Two classes of Dissenters have been well enough analysed: the academics and authors already mentioned, and the innovators who contributed to industrial change. The Quakers, who usually married inside their own sect, and whose whole organization was held together by monthly, quarterly, and annual meetings, were particularly associated with the rise of industry. Dr M. W. Flynn writes that 'the tightly knit bands of Quaker industrial society promoted the welfare of both counting house and meeting house.' Together the Quakers dominated much of the iron industry. It has been argued that Puritanism is associated with something peculiarly conducive to success in business. The famous expression of this theory (by R. H. Tawney in *Religion and the Rise of Capitalism*) is that there existed for the Puritan a *calling*, both spiritual and temporal. A Christian has faith in God, by which he will be saved. This faith will be expressed in works – in working hard at his particular function in the world. The quarter of a million, however, were not made up altogether of divines, tutors, and business men. Dissenters in the villages were much more obscure, and met frequently for worship in barns and in front rooms licensed for the purpose. Professor Harold Perkin (in *The Origins of Modern English Societiey 1780–1880*, Routledge, 1969) has put forward a concept which would conveniently include all these groups. He sees the Dissenters as those who were free of dependence on society – who were not under obligation to landowners, to the Government for contracts, or to buyers of their goods and services – and who did not seek social advancement. This category comfortably includes manufacturers, yeomen farmers, and country craftsmen. Professor Perkin is able to define Dissent (at least in part) as an expression of 'social antagonism in the old society'.

In spite, therefore, of its small numbers, eighteenth-century Dissent has been given extraordinary significance as an expression of political and social, as well as religious, nonconformity. Its anomalous political position certainly encouraged political radicalism. The endless arguments over doctrine within local congregations doubtless encouraged questioning elsewhere and led to the rejection of authoritarianism. Their educational system intensified the same trends. E. P. Thompson, who views the impact of the Methodists on the labouring population with some regret, feels that if some section of Old Dissent had led the religious revival of the eighteenth century, then later Nonconformity would have become more 'intellectual and democratic'. The possibility did not exist, though. Not all Dissenters were Priestleys or Prices – or agreed with them; and from the anarchy and rationalism of Old Dissent no evangelical drive could be expected.

Further Reading

J. Beresford, ed. *The Diary of a Country Parson* (James Woodforde). Oxford University Press, 5 vols., 1924–31; also further abridged as a World's Classic, 1949.

G. F. A. Best, *Temporal Pillars*. Cambridge University Press, 1964. This is principally a study of Queen Anne's Bounty and the Ecclesiastical Commissioners, but has some distinguished contributions on the ecclesiastical machine in general, especially in Chapters II and IV.

J. Betjeman, ed., *Collins' Guide to English Churches*. Collins, 1958. The introduction contains a wonderful evocation of an English church in 1805.

B. F. L. Clarke, *The Building of the Eighteenth Century Church*. S.P.C.K., 1963. Architectural.

G. R. Cragg, *From Puritanism to the Age of Reason*. Cambridge University Press, 1950; paperback edition, 1966.
The Church and the Age of Reason. Pelican, 1960 (esp. pp. 117–40). 'The Churchman', in *Man v. Society in Eighteenth Century Britain*. Cambridge University Press, 1968.

J. M. Creed and J. S. Boys Smith, ed., *Religious Thought in the Eighteenth Century*. Cambridge University Press, 1935. Convenient extracts.

M. G. Jones, *The Charity School Movement*. Cambridge University Press, 1938.

D. Owen, *English Philanthropy 1660–1960*. Harvard University Press and Oxford University Press, 1964.

N. Sykes, *Church and State in England in the Eighteenth Century*. Cambridge University Press, 1934.
From Sheldon to Secker. Cambridge University Press, 1959.

B. Willey, *The Seventeenth Century Background*. Chatto and Windus, 1934; Peregrine, 1962.
The Eighteenth Century Background. Chatto and Windus, 1940; Peregrine, 1962.

E. N. Williams, *The Eighteenth Century Constitution*. Cambridge University Press, 1960 (Chapter V).

Dissent

E. D. Bebb, *Nonconformity and Social and Economic Life, 1660–1800*. Epworth Press, 1935.

N. Hunt, *Two Early Political Associations – the Quakers and the Dissenting Deputies in the Age of Sir Robert Walpole.* Oxford University Press, 1961.

R. Horton Davies, *The English Free Churches.* Second edition, Oxford University Press, 1963.

A. Lincoln, *Some Political and Social Ideas of English Dissent, 1763–1800.* Cambridge University Press, 1938.

B. Manning, *The Protestant Dissenting Deputies.* Cambridge University Press, 1952.

A. Natan, ed., *Silver Renaissance.* (The essays by Steven Watson and M. W. Flynn.) Macmillan, 1961.

C. Robbins, *The Eighteenth Century Commonwealthman.* Harvard University Press, 1959.

The Political Framework, 1660–1780

1660. Restoration of the Stuarts (Charles II, 1660–85; James II, 1685–8)

The possibility of something other than a simple restoration of the Anglican Church appeared to exist

1661. The Savoy Conference considered the fusion of the Presbyterians with the Church of England, but the Conference broke up, and Parliament instead imposed by degrees an apparatus of restriction on Nonconformity

Corporation Act restricted membership of corporations to members of the Church of England

1662. Act of Uniformity imposed a revised Book of Common Prayer on the Church of England, and required 'unfeigned assent and consent' by its ministers to its contents. Ministers of the Church had to have been ordained by a bishop. Thus under the Act about a thousand ministers were ejected from their livings

1664. Conventicle Act (revised 1670) forbade meetings for worship (other than in the Anglican form) in private houses or in the open

1665. Five Mile Act forbade Dissenting ministers to come within five miles of a corporate town, or to preach to any assembly without having sworn an oath against rebellion

1673. Test Act excluded Roman Catholics from all public offices

1687, 1688. James II's First and Second Declarations of Indulgence suspended the laws against the Papists and the Dissenters. But the circumstances under which toleration came from a Catholic King were suspect; he intended them as part of a programme to produce a Parliament sympathetic to him

1688. The Revolution (William III and Mary, 1689–1702)

November. William landed

December. James departed

The Revolution was critical in church history in two senses: the Church of England, absolutely identified with loyalty to the Stuarts, was subject to strain; and the Dissenters appeared to deserve some reward from the new Government for their loyalty to Protestantism

1689. A scheme for 'comprehending' the Dissenters within the Church of England was again propounded, but rejected

Toleration Act permitted all Nonconformists who believed in the Trinity freedom of worship. The Corporation, Conventicle, Five Mile, and Test Acts remained in force

A group of six bishops (including Sancroft, the Archbishop of Canterbury) and 400 clergy of the Church of England – the Nonjurors – refused to take the oath to William and Mary, and were deprived

1691–4. Tillotson Archbishop of Canterbury

1700. Effective sittings of Convocation resumed. Convocation consisted of an Upper House (of bishops) and a Lower House (of proctors or representatives of the lower clergy), and met at the same time as Parliament. The rights of Convocation, and in particular whether the decisions they took were binding on the laity, were the subject of controversy from the 1690s till the 1730s

1702–14. Queen Anne

The Tories' feeling against the Dissenters could take legislative form after Harley's ministry was formed in 1710

1711. Occasional Conformity Act sharply restricted the practice of some Dissenters of taking Anglican Communion merely to qualify themselves for public office

1714. Schism Act forbade both Papists and Dissenters from practising as tutors or schoolmasters

The Hanoverian Succession (George I, 1714–27; George II, 1727–60; George III, 1760–1820)

1717. Suspension of Convocation

1719. Occasional Conformity Act and Schism Act repealed

Salters' Hall Meeting. The three largest sects could not agree on the acceptance of any statement of belief, and gave decisive power to individual congregations, who could expel ministers whose doctrine was not acceptable

1727. Indemnity Act lifted the penalties to which office-holders were liable if they failed to take the oaths and Anglican Communion. The Act was an annual one, but only after 1758 was it passed as a matter of routine

1732. The Protestant Dissenting Deputies first appointed. This body became the accepted channel for putting the Dissenters' point of view to the Government

1753. Hardwicke's Marriage Act. No marriage was henceforth valid unless it was solemnized by a Church of England clergyman

after the calling of banns in the parish church on three succes-
sive Sundays. Jews and Quakers were exempted, but not other
Dissenters, or Roman Catholics. Thus in the 'Age of Toleration'
a new Dissenters' grievance was created, and not removed
until the Dissenters' Marriage Act of 1836

1772. Feathers Tavern Petition by some clergy of the Church of
England, asking that ordinands and ministers no longer be
required to subscribe to the Thirty-nine Articles. It was
rejected

1773. Unsuccessful move by the Dissenters to exempt their ministers
and teachers from subscription under the 1689 Toleration Act

1775–83. American War of Independence
Richard Price's pro-American pamphlets – *Observations on
Civil Liberty* (1776), *Additional Observations* (1777), and *The
Importance of the American Revolution* (1784)

1778. Catholic Relief Act removed restrictions on Catholic education
and on the right of Catholics to inherit land (on condition that
they took an oath of allegiance)

1779. Dissenters' Relief Act waived the requirement under the 1689
Act that Dissenting ministers and schoolmasters subscribe to
thirty-six of the Thirty-nine Articles and substituted a much
simpler declaration, to which Unitarians could subscribe

1780. The Gordon Riots. Popular anti-Papist rioting in London

PART II
The Methodist Revival

'Revival' is a word which implies deadness in the greater part of the Church of England and life in the new evangelical movements of the eighteenth century. Such an antithesis is often stated or implied. Deadness is an exaggeration, except in the technical sense: what was lacking was what Methodist converts called 'experimental' religion, and what is now properly called 'experiential' religion. The essentials of this were an initial sense of sin, followed by an experience of conversion. The convert believed that what alone was necessary for salvation was the conviction that Christ had died to secure the forgiveness of his own particular sins – the doctrine of justification by faith. The recognition of this conviction by the convert produced not only an assurance of salvation, but also an impetus to missionary activity such as may be seen at its most spectacular in the career of John Wesley, but at its most typical in the lives of lesser men than he, working inside smaller areas (see pp. 68–9). Such activity either required more dynamic and flexible forms of organization than the Church of England then provided, and produced in the end a separate connexion – the Methodists – or succeeded in staying inside the bounds of the Church of England or of existing Dissenting churches. Its consequences were not only religious but social.

A great number of conversion experiences – of which those of the Wesleys and of Whitefield are merely the most famous – were recorded in the period between 1730 and 1750. These marked the beginning of the Evangelical Revival, which emerged largely from the Church of England, though with some encouragement from contemporary events in the American Colonies and in Germany. What was generally accepted inside the Church of England – a cool Latitudinarianism in doctrine, a staid and gentlemanly form of preaching, and a close identification with the State and society – is clear enough. But inside the Church were unfashionable strands of thought and forms of organization which may be described as the beginnings of the Revival. The once-celebrated sections of the Church, the high churchmen and the Puritans, fell into total obscurity after 1714.

High Churchmanship

A high churchman in the previous age had believed that it was a sin to resist the will of the king, but the reign of the Catholic James II had modified that. Somehow, the high Anglican had been forced to adjust himself to the idea of Parliament's selecting monarchs in 1689 – if he had not, then he had become a nonjuror. During Anne's reign, he had felt easier in his mind: the Tories had introduced part of his political platform with the Occasional Conformity and Schism Acts. The Queen had shown a zealous interest in the Church, and Convocation had continued its proceedings noisily, if ultimately ineffectively.

After 1714, however, high churchmen were again disappointed – the Tory Acts were repealed, Convocation was suspended, and Hoadly, a bishop who did not believe in the necessity of a visible church organization at all, was rapidly promoted. Latitudinarians set little store by the high churchman's concern for tradition and continuity in the Church. His concern for the power of the Church as an institution, and for the respect and dignity which

he considered ought to be paid to the clergy, was ridiculed in the
1730s. This was seen more particularly in the controversy surrounding Dr Edmund Gibson, Bishop of London and church
adviser to Walpole, and his exposition of church law, the *Codex
Juris Ecclesiastici Anglicani*. Gibson was attacked, largely by
lawyers, for asserting that canon law applied to the laity as well
as the clergy; that church courts should be reformed to make
them effective; and that Convocation should have the power of
independent action. The book was first published in 1713, and,
as Dr G. F. A. Best puts it, 'did the Church nothing but harm in
the critical decades just after its publication'.

During the period since the return of Charles II, Anglican
clergymen and laymen had devised new modes of parochial and
philanthropic activity which survived effectively into the
eighteenth century. The most influential of these were the
'religious societies', groups designed to fortify and supplement
existing parochial organizations. The first of them appeared in
London in 1678, the result of the sermons of Anthony Horneck
in the Savoy Chapel. Horneck was a German, though educated
at Oxford. The societies formed under his direction, for those
confirmed Anglicans who had 'resolved upon a holy and serious
life', were to be directed by a minister of the Church of England.
The members met weekly for prayer and good discourse. *An
Account of the Rise and Progress of the Religious Societies in the
City of London,* by Dr Josiah Woodward, indicated how far they
had progressed by Anne's reign. The members were to 'frequent
the public exercises of the Church of England', though they were
to 'be careful withal to express due Christian charity, candour
and moderation towards all such Dissenters as are of good
conversation'. They were to contribute as they thought fit to 'a
public stock for pious and charitable uses, especially for putting
poor children to school'; and they were to avoid gaming and
'lewd Playhouses', and to take a stand against 'public profaneness'. Such societies were first advertised to the country at
large in *The Country Parson's Advice to his Parishioners,* which
appeared in 1680, and they were commended as 'an effectual
means for restoring our decaying Christianity to its primitive

life and vigour, and the support of our tottering and sinking Church'.

These societies enjoyed distinguished support in London – Archbishop Tenison and Bishop Beveridge, while still City clergymen, gave them their approval. Moreover, the societies were the basis of something bigger – the Society for Promoting Christian Knowledge (1699) and the Society for the Propagation of the Gospel (1701). The S.P.C.K. was formed for the support of schools, the circulation of books, and the encouragement of religion in the colonies; the S.P.G. was formed as an offshoot from it to take over the last aspect of its work. Both were largely supported by subscriptions from members of the religious societies.

Other activities, perhaps better known, were those initiated by Robert Nelson between 1699 and 1715. He was a high-church layman who supported the Society for the Reformation of Manners and was the presiding genius of the movement which eventually spread charity schools throughout the country.

Puritanism

By the 1730s Puritanism appeared even more decisively eclipsed than high Anglicanism. Still, traces may be discerned. Its literature survived. Bunyan's spiritual autobiography, *Grace Abounding to the Chief of Sinners* (1666), was the model for Whitefield's *Short Account of God's Dealings with the Reverend George Whitefield*. Pamphlets like Joseph Alleine's *Alarm to the Unconverted* remained in circulation. Alleine (1634–68) was a preacher who, like Bunyan, underwent persecution after the Restoration. Of his little book, Calamy, in 1702, wrote:

No book in the English tongue (the Bible only excepted) can equal it for the number that hath been dispersed; there have been twenty thousand sold under the title of the *Call* or *Alarm*, and fifty thousand of the same under the title of the *Sure Guide to Heaven*, thirty thousand of which were sold at one impression.

Whitefield also acknowledged that he was 'much benefited' by the book when he was at Oxford.

The Puritan preachers' open-air activities and their mode of speaking might also have served as models for the Evangelicals of the next century. Dr Robert South's attack on the Puritan preachers' 'crude incoherences, saucy familiarities with God, and nauseous tautologies' can certainly be paralleled many times with attacks on eighteenth-century Evangelicals!

Evangelism

Such techniques appear early in the eighteenth century. Griffith Jones, an ex-shepherd convinced in a dream that he was to be 'a peculiar instrument for rescuing many souls', became curate of Laugharne in 1710. His vision appeared to him as a command to evangelize in Wales, and he frequently preached in parishes other than his own. The attraction of large numbers to hear his sermons forced him to preach in the open air. Complaints of his intruding himself into other parishes led to his appearance before the Bishop of St David's in 1715, though the accusations against him were dropped. Jones became Rector of Llandowror in 1716, and from 1730 was a notable innovator in the movement to provide charity schools, or rather, travelling teachers, in Wales. Much later, he heard Wesley preach in Bath, and the two men met.

Daniel Rowland, a Church of England clergyman, and curate of Llangeitho in Cardiganshire, was converted by Jones in 1735. He became a famous itinerant whose sermons caused the kind of shriekings and tremblings more usually associated with Wesley's congregations. Howell Harris was a schoolmaster of Talgarth, Brecon, and wrote that he was 'convinced by the Holy Ghost that Christ died for me and that all my sins were laid on Him' in the course of Holy Communion at Talgarth on Whit Sunday, 1735. 'This', he continued, 'evidenced itself to be the true faith by the peace, joy, watchfulness, hatred to sin, and fear of offending God which followed it.' Harris was refused ordination, but in 1736 he became an itinerant preacher who, as George Whitefield observed, discoursed 'generally in a field, from a wall, a table, or anything else, but at other times in a house'. Harris also formed a number of religious societies which ensured the permanency of his work. Whitefield began the practice of open-air preaching in Bristol in 1739, a few weeks after he had made the acquaintance of Harris.

The phenomena of revival were also observable in Northampton, Massachusetts, in 1734–5. Jonathan Edwards, the Congregationalist pastor there, observed that in 1733 'there were more who manifested a religious concern than there used to be'. In 1734, he began to emphasize the doctrine of justification by faith, and this, he wrote later,

proved a word spoken in season here. . . . All would eagerly lay hold of opportunities for their souls, and were wont very often to meet together in private houses, for religious purposes: and such meetings when appointed were greatly thronged. . . . And the work of conversion was carried on in a most astonishing manner, and increased more and more: souls as it were did come by flocks to Jesus Christ. . . . This work of God . . . soon made a glorious alteration in the town.

Edwards's *Narrative* of these events was published in London in 1737.

Another Protestant element of great importance came from outside England – the Moravians, whose critical years of development were in the 1720s. The more determined supporters of the Bohemian reformer John Huss had formed a Brotherhood in 1457, and the Brotherhood, after many struggles, settled in Saxony in 1722 on a hill which they called Herrnhut, under the protection of the Lutheran Count Zinzendorf. Zinzendorf persuaded the Moravians to come to an understanding with the Lutheran Church. In August 1727 they attended Communion at Berthelsdorf church, and there took place an experience in which all the congregation shared. Each felt, Zinzendorf explained,

his lack of worth in the sight of God and each felt himself at this Communion to be in view of the noble countenance of the Saviour. . . . In this view of the man of sorrows and acquainted with grief, their hearts told them that He would be their patron and their priest who was at once changing their tears into oil of gladness and their misery into happiness. This firm confidence changed them in a single moment into a happy people which they are to this day. . . .

The Moravian Community – whose form of justification by faith was to be that which Wesley assumed – immediately set about missionary activity, and a group of them was sent to England the next year. They were intensely interested in the foundation and settlement of Georgia. General Oglethorpe had secured the foundation of this colony in 1732, with the intention of planting some of the inmates of debtors' prisons there. Others were encouraged to settle, and a group of Moravians led by August Spangenberg, a professor at the University of Jena, set out from England in February 1735. More missionaries from Herrnhut appeared later that year, and joined the ship which was also taking John and Charles Wesley to Georgia. George Whitefield was still in England, where, after undergoing 'innumerable buffetings of Satan', he had been converted some weeks after Easter.

John Wesley

In John Wesley all these differing and unfashionable strands of churchmanship converged. He was born in 1703 at Epworth, Lincolnshire, the son of Samuel Wesley, the Rector, and of Susanna, his wife. His ancestors over several generations had been clergymen. Both his grandfathers were Puritans ejected from their livings under the Act of Uniformity in 1662. His grandfather, John Wesley, had been a West-country incumbent; his other grandfather, Samuel Annesley, had been minister of St Giles's, Cripplegate, during the Interregnum, and after his ejection continued to be a leading figure among London Dissenters until his death in 1696. Both his parents, on the other hand, had ultimately taken up very high-church positions when they reached maturity. Samuel Wesley was educated successively at two London Dissenting Academies, but while he was engaged in 1683 in refuting a piece of controversial Anglican writing, he found himself agreeing with it. He went to Oxford, was ordained, and became a high churchman in every sense in which that term could be understood. Theologically, he emphasized the importance of the Early Church. Politically he was a

Tory, and he was at one time thought to have written the speech of Dr Henry Sacheverell when Sacheverell was impeached for impugning the Whig ministers and the Revolution Settlement in 1710. In matters of organization, too, he approved the Anglican practices of prison visiting and of forming religious societies.

Susanna's political position was even more extreme – she was a Jacobite. While her husband was acting as a proctor in Convocation between November 1710 and February 1712, she set up a religious society at her kitchen in the rectory. Originally for children and servants, at one time it had an attendance of two hundred. Both parents were also much concerned for missionary activity – Samuel even offered his services as a missionary to the East Indies in 1706. Notwithstanding this evidence of Susanna's high-churchmanship, however, her household is probably the best known of all examples of Puritan domestic management. As she considered that she was responsible under God for her children's souls, the first essential was to break their wills: 'Whenever a child is corrected, it must be conquered'. A celebrated letter, written to John in her old age, gives all the details of how she brought up her children – details which included teaching them to fear the rod at one year old. The effect on Wesley of this regimen has been much argued: his mother's dominance might have caused psychological damage, but it was obviously partly responsible for his fanatical concern for the effective management of his time.

Epworth, then a somewhat desolate village to which neither John nor his parents showed much attachment, also produced impressions of a different kind. In 1709 the rectory was burned down, allegedly by the villagers, and John Wesley saved himself from the flames by climbing on to a chest of drawers, from which he was taken on the shoulders of his rescuer. Ever afterwards he was fond of referring to himself as 'the brand plucked from the burning', and the incident became the subject of a steel engraving which still ornaments the band rooms of innumerable Methodist churches. The behaviour of the Lincolnshire peasantry may also have produced one of Wesley's deepest prejudices, visible throughout his career – a contempt for the agricultural labourer. Certainly Susanna deplored the effects of having to permit her children to consort with servants and village children after the fire:

That civil behaviour which made them admired when at home, by all which saw them, was in great measure lost; and a clownish accent, and many rude ways, were learned and not reformed without some difficulty.

From 1714 to 1720 Wesley was at Charterhouse, a period of his life of which little is known. Indeed, it may be that the events which most fascinated him at this time happened in Epworth. The calm of the new rectory was disturbed by a poltergeist during 1716 and 1717, and Wesley displayed the strongest interest in the disturbances, never doubting that they were supernatural. All his life he remained convinced of the existence of ghosts and witches, notwithstanding the fact that he lived in the 'Age of Reason'.

He went up to Christ Church, Oxford, in 1720, graduated in 1724, was ordained deacon in September 1725 by the Bishop of Oxford, and was elected Fellow of Lincoln College, Oxford, in 1726. Between 1727 and 1729 he acted as his father's curate at Wroot, near Epworth, but afterwards returned to Lincoln College until 1735. His contacts, his reading, and his spiritual development during his Oxford period have been charted in detail: they were all more extensive than was at one time imagined. His social life with friends both in the Cotswolds and at Wroot was agreeable – playing cards, dancing, and shooting peewits were included among more serious pursuits. His reading (listed by V. H. H. Green in *The Young Mr Wesley*), though certainly classical and theological for the most part, by no means indicates the religious-minded philistine. He read Milton and Spenser, Restoration plays, Clarendon, and works that were causing the literary furores of the 1720s, such as Burnet's *History of My own Time*, and *Gulliver's Travels*. Indeed, among the books which most powerfully affected his life was a medical one: Dr Cheyne's *Book of Health and Long Life*, which commended getting up early:

Valetudinary, studious and contemplative people ought to go bed by eight, nine or ten at latest, and rise by four, five or six

and riding:

the most manly, the most healthy, and the least laborious and expensive of spirits of any [exercise], shaking the whole machine.

What is most obviously to be seen in these years, however, is the making of a high churchman. It was then that he read Jeremy Taylor's *Holy Living* and *Holy Dying*, seventeenth-century classics which encouraged him in the direction of setting himself spiritual resolutions and of practising the utmost economy of time – a direction in which he was always inclined to go. (To Jeremy Taylor the world is obliged for inspiring Wesley to keep a journal, in which he charted his life and opinions in enormous detail.) Wesley's preparation for ordination in 1725 induced a degree of self-analysis and study. He wrote later:

I began to alter the whole form of my conversation, and to set in earnest upon a new life. I set apart an hour or two for religious retirement. I communicated every week. I watched against all sin, whether in word or deed. I began to aim at, and pray for, inward holiness.

The work of the nonjuror William Law, *A Serious Call to a Devout and Holy Life*, appeared in 1728 and greatly affected Wesley's thinking. It emphasized the necessity of devotion and morality as well as the externals of worship.

In November 1729, when Wesley returned from Wroot to Oxford, he found in existence the Holy Club, a group founded by his younger brother Charles, then an undergraduate at Christ Church. The Club seems to have been Charles's response to a circular of the Vice-Chancellor requesting college tutors to explain the Thirty-nine Articles and to encourage frequent and careful reading of the Bible. It seems also to have been a way by which Charles encouraged himself to study – three or four young men met in his rooms to study together as well as to pray together. They also attended Communion weekly. John took over the direction of this group down to 1735, and during that time it became an expression of all his dominant impulses. He fastened on it a whole series of religious exercises. The urge towards 'practical Christianity' showed itself when one of its members, William Morgan, began in 1730 the practice of prison visiting, and of preaching, confirming, and instructing in the prisons. Wesley's insistence on the necessity of early rising was characteristic. In the atmosphere of eighteenth-century Oxford, however, the Club was bound to incur criticism on account of its very strangeness; and when William Morgan fell into a pitiably mad condition and died in 1732, his fate was blamed on the strict régime of the Club. As for the effect of the Club on Wesley himself, Professor Martin Schmidt has observed that it

led him to a veritable 'martyr theology' which became ever more rigorous. It belongs to the true Christian life to be misunderstood, despised, persecuted, and this ought to be a matter of pride.

This attitude Wesley took with him to Georgia. When General Oglethorpe secured the planting of this colony, its white population came not only from London debtors' prisons, but also from various parts of Europe. John and Charles Wesley accepted invitations to join this little cosmopolitan community in 1735. (Before he set out, Charles was rapidly ordained deacon and priest by the Bishop of London.) John's first motive in going out to North America he gave as 'personal salvation'; the attraction of Georgia was that it provided him with a situation giving all the opportunities for missionary activity which the Primitive Church had once offered. He set out with a frenzy for self-denial, restricting his diet to biscuits and rice, and with a frenzy for exercising a mission to those crossing with him on the boat, to Red Indians, to negro slaves, and to the new settlers.

These intentions were frustrated by the realities of life in Georgia. Wesley himself was committed to being minister in Savannah, not to being a missionary, and the quarrels and difficulties of that tiny community took up most of his time. As

for the Indian tribes, there was continuous warfare between
them, and by October 1737 he was confessing in his Journal:

The reason for which I left [England] has now no force; there being
no possibility, as yet, of instructing the Indians; neither had I, as
yet, found or heard of any Indians on the continent of America who
had the least desire of being instructed.

There was, however, more to the Georgian experience than
disillusionment. In the course of the voyage across the Atlantic
and in the colony he came for the first time under the influence
of the Moravians; an influence decisive in determining his
development as a great missionary and as a great religious
organizer. On board the ship leaving for Georgia were twenty-six
Moravian brethren. Wesley was interested in their theology,
their mode of life, their hymns and their singing meetings, and
their organization. At the other side of the Atlatntic, as the ship
lay at the mouth of the Savannah River, Wesley had a conversation with their leader in America, August Gottlieb Spangenberg:

'Do you know Jesus Christ?' asked Spangenberg.
'I know that he is the Saviour of the World', replied Wesley.
'True; but do you know He has saved you?'
'I hope he has died to save me.'
'Do you know yourself?'
'I do.'
   'But', Wesley added in his Journal, 'I fear these were vain words.'

The doubt remained with him until 24 May 1738.
   On landing, Wesley stayed with the Herrnhuters of Savannah,
and he translated their hymns. In his work as minister there, he
continued the experiments in effective religious organization
that had begun, perhaps, with the Holy Club, but which at this
point seem based on the Moravian way of doing things. He wrote
in his Journal:

We agreed: 1. To advise the more serious among them to form themselves into a little society, to meet once or twice a week, in order to
reprove, instruct and exhort one another. 2. To select out of these a
smaller number for a more intimate union with each other, which

might be forwarded, partly by our conversing singly with each, and partly by inviting them all together to our house, and this, accordingly, we determined to do every Sunday in the afternoon.

Wesley continued at this time to display, in a way eccentric in such an outlandish community, all the prejudices of an Oxford high churchman. He condemned the Scots at Darien for praying extempore, and infuriated the people of Savannah by his insistence on following the Prayer Book to the letter. A dispute concerning Sophia Hopkey, the niece of the chief magistrate of Savannah, brought matters to a head. John hoped to marry her; she married somebody else. He excluded her from Communion, apparently on the ground of her irregular attendance at church services. Her husband took the exclusion as a slight on her character, and Wesley was prosecuted. While the case was undecided, Wesley departed for England.

In February 1738, when he landed from Georgia, he had therefore a profound sense of failure. It was while in this dejection that he had a long series of conversations in London, in Oxford, and between the two, with Peter Böhler, a native of Frankfurt and a Moravian who had been converted by Zinzendorf himself. Böhler insisted on the necessity of believing that salvation comes by faith alone, and on the need for conversion. He also urged the rejection of ethics and natural religion, the stock-in-trade of the eighteenth-century Church. Wesley resisted, though unwillingly. When he enquired of Böhler on 5 March whether, since he did not yet hold Böhler's beliefs, he ought to give up preaching, Böhler was positive:

Preach faith until you have it; and then, because you have it, you will preach faith.

The next day Wesley followed the advice in a sermon to a condemned prisoner, who was convinced of his salvation. Shortly afterwards he left for Manchester, 'resolved to lose no opportunity of awakening, instructing and exhorting any whom we might meet with on our journey'. Böhler left for America on 4 May, but Wesley continued to follow his instructions, and after sermons in several London churches, was banned from further preaching in them. Böhler had also introduced Wesley again to those Moravian forms of organization of which he had known something in Georgia. In Oxford, the German had set up 'bands' – very small groups (each presided over by a 'bandkeeper') designed so that the members might examine together their spiritual experiences.

On Monday, Tuesday, and Wednesday, 22–4 May 1738, Wesley wrote of his 'continual sorrow and heaviness of heart'. On the 24th, a day on which all the texts he came across – even the words of the anthem in St Paul's Cathedral – appeared to indicate approaching conversion, he was writing:

God is holy. I am unholy. God is a consuming fire: I am altogether a sinner, meet to be consumed. Yet I hear a voice (and is it not the voice of God?) saying 'Believe, and thou shalt be saved. He that believeth is passed from death into life'.

It was in the evening of that day that he went to the meeting in Aldersgate Street, 'felt his heart strangely warmed', and was 'saved from the law of sin and death'.

Wesley himself was not always convinced that this was the great event of his life. Though he insisted some days after that before the 24 May he was not a Christian, he had changed his mind by the end of the year. The psychological effect of the conversion was more important than the theological. It gave him confidence, not a new set of doctrines. He did not abandon his instinctive high churchmanship at that moment, if ever. Nor did he then acquire his passion for evangelism: this had always been one of his permanent characteristics, apparent in Oxford and in Georgia. Events, however, moved him fairly rapidly towards evangelistic activity on a larger scale. He paid a visit to Herrnhut. That October, too, while walking from London to Oxford, he read the 'truly surprising' account of Jonathan Edwards's activities in converting hundreds in Northampton, Massachusetts. On 2 April 1739, at Bristol, he accepted George Whitefield's invitation to preach 'from a little eminence in a ground adjoining to the City of Bristol'. His field-preaching career had begun.

(See in particular John Walsh, 'The Origins of the Evangelical Revival' in *Essays in Modern English Church History in Memory of Norman Sykes*, A. & C. Black, 1965, pp. 132–62; and A. Skevington Wood, *Inextinguishable Blaze*, Paternoster Press, Exeter, 1960, pp. 39–126.)

[7] JOHN WESLEY: ORGANIZER AND INNOVATOR

The career of Wesley as a travelling preacher, begun in this way in 1739, ended only with his death in 1791. It is not surprising that sheer wonder has sometimes overtaken Wesley's biographers as they have noted that he must have preached forty thousand sermons and travelled something like a quarter of a million miles in the course of these fifty-odd years. It is easy to picture the prim little man – 'in the year 1769 I weighed a hundred and twenty pounds; in 1783 I weighed not a pound more or less' – riding throughout the British Isles, his horse on a loose rein while he read voraciously. Since he was fascinated by the way his message was received by his hearers, his observations form a quarry for those interested in the psychology of revival and of persecution. He was concerned not merely with conversion, however, but with the problem of forming an organization, or 'connexion' as he called it, and of keeping control of it in his own hands.

It is important not to view these fifty years as a unity. In the 1740s Wesley was a despised open-air preacher; in the 1780s he was a celebrity with so many invitations to preach in churches that he could not accept them all. There was a great difference, too, in his hearers – between, say, those miners at Seaton in Cumberland in 1752, who constructed a kind of outdoor pulpit and provided a cushion of grass for him to kneel on; and the respectable people of Macclesfield in Cheshire in 1787 in their new chapel, enjoying their 'swiftly increasing riches'. The persecution Wesley faced, and the hysteria he provoked, were not constant over the fifty years, either; most of both disappeared in the 1750s. In one way, perhaps, there was little change. The great preacher, though endlessly adapting and perfecting his organization, did not endlessly extend his geographical range. He largely confined his tours to the areas he knew by the 1750s – London, Bristol, and Newcastle formed the points of his great triangle. In this way he strove to strengthen the connexion he had formed, and over which he presided with autocratic control.

The objective of Wesley was the salvation of souls. The method was principally preaching, as many as five times a day, to gatherings large and small. There is a contemporary picture by P. J. de Loutherbourg of John Wesley preaching – a stylized picture, no doubt; with the grouping of the characters and the scenery calculated for effect. Wesley is standing in a makeshift pulpit erected in a large field. A crowd of modest size is disposed around him – its more proletarian members round the pulpit and the more fashionable people showing curiosity from a distance. Such a picture is an aid to the imagination, so long as it does not obscure the variety of places that he preached in and the different ways in which he was received. Some audiences were receptive:

I preached at the Spen [Co. Durham] on Christ Jesus, our 'wisdom, righteousness, sanctification, and redemption'. I have seldom seen an audience so greatly moved, since the time of my first preaching at Bristol. Men, women and children wept and groaned, and trembled exceedingly; many could not contain themselves in these bounds; but cried with a loud and bitter cry. . . . I afterwards spoke with twelve or fourteen of them severally, and found good ground to believe that God had given them the 'taste of the good word, and of the powers of the world to come'.

Some were attentive but uncomprehending:

I preached at Clifton, near Penrith, to a civil people who looked just as if I had been talking Greek.

How was that preaching carried out? Certainly it was not the reading of those pieces which now appear as Wesley's *Collected*

Sermons. Those Professor Outler has described as 'sermonic essays' – the result of preaching on a theme repeatedly and making a mature consideration of it. What actually took place at a field-preaching was the delivery of a sermon without notes, lasting up to an hour, and of a more popular kind than the 'sermonic essay' (A.C. Outler, *John Wesley*, Oxford University Press, 1964, p. 88).

Nobody understood so plainly as Wesley, however, that the effect of preaching was impermanent.

How much preaching there has been for these twenty years all over Pembrokeshire! [he wrote in his Journal in 1763]. But no regular societies, no discipline, no order or connexion; and the consequence is, that nine in ten of the once-awakened are now faster asleep than ever!

It was necessary, then, to have an organization. In Oxford and in Georgia he had already shown an interest in the working of religious societies, and he had observed the Moravian system at work at Herrnhut. After 1739 he improvised and adjusted continually until he had created a connexion. Its object, like that of the religious societies of Restoration London, was to fortify and supplement the work of the Established Church. Due attention to the printed word and to education, and to the collection and composition of a body of hymns, strengthened this connexion and broadened its impact.

At Birstall in the West Riding there survives in the yard of the present St John's Methodist Church a small brick building containing nothing more than a table and some antiquated and assorted chairs. By tradition it was the study of John Nelson, one of Wesley's most famous preachers. It seems to be a memorable piece of ecclesiastical archaeology; a reminder of the class, the distinctive unit of Wesley's organization after 1742.

To join a Methodist society was never difficult, for there were no tests of doctrine. There had merely to be a desire on the part of the intending members to 'flee from the wrath to come, to be saved from their sins'. But the early societies at Bristol and London were large and argumentative bodies with a fluid membership. Their division into classes gave them their spiritual dynamic and enabled Wesley and his helpers to exercise control over them. The first such division, however, was a money-raising device introduced to pay off the debt on the New Room at Bristol in 1742. A Captain Foy suggested that he should take upon himself to visit eleven poor members each week, collecting a penny from each; if they could not pay, then he would make up the sum himself. The class of twelve was almost immediately adapted to serve other purposes. Classes began to meet regularly for prayer, for the settlement of argument, for the consideration of scripture. The ticket of membership became a 'class ticket', issued quarterly and usually on payment of a shilling. A member might easily be expelled without fuss by declining to issue him with such a ticket, and, of course, in that way admission to society meetings and services could be controlled. Class leaders were appointed, not elected; this was one of the many ways in which Wesley maintained his absolute control of the movement. In his eighty-seventh year he wrote:

As long as I live, the people shall have no share in choosing either stewards or leaders among the Methodists. We have not, and never had, any such custom. We are no republicans and never intend to be.

The funds raised by the operation of the classes were variously used for poor relief, buildings, hymn-books, preachers' expenses, and so forth.

The cellular organization of the Methodists was made much more complex by the existence of 'bands' (on the model of the Moravians) from 1738 onwards. These were small groups of members collected according to sex and according to the stage of spiritual development which they had reached. The rules that Wesley drew up for them included questions to be asked of each member at each meeting, such as 'What known sin have you committed since our last meeting?', 'Have you nothing that you desire to keep secret?', and 'What temptation have you met with?'. Besides the classes and the bands, further gradings existed inside the larger societies.

The class system was subject to heavy criticism, and has been

since. Wesley's elder brother Samuel, a conventional Anglican
if ever there was one, complained to Susanna:

Their societies are sufficient to dissolve all societies but their own.
Will any man of common sense or spirit suffer any domestic to be in
a band engaged to relate to five or ten people everything without
reserve that concerns the person's conscience how much soever it
may concern the family? Ought any married persons to be there
unless husband and wife be there together?

Lecky, who quoted this passage, observed:

The members sometimes passed the whole night in the most passionate
devotions, and voluntarily submitted to a spiritual tyranny that
could hardly be surpassed in a Catholic monastery.

In each society there were two important types of official:
stewards and trustees. The duties of stewards mushroomed
rapidly, and ranged from the distribution of offerings for the
poor to the keeping of buildings clean and in good repair; Methodist property was settled upon the trustees.

The local societies had to be held together as a connexion –
not merely by Wesley's own prodigious wanderings, but by the
assistance of other preachers who undertook tours on a smaller
scale than his own, though with the same objectives. The
country was divided into 'rounds' or circuits – seven in England
and Wales by 1746, 114 in the British Isles by the time of
Wesley's death. Inside these large units Wesley's preachers
moved regularly, even daily. Wesley called the preachers
'helpers'; the select ones, given charge of circuits, were called
'assistants'. They depended on their followers for lodgings and
food, though provision was made for their families. Further
help was given to the work by local preachers, who stayed in one
place and combined preaching with their trade in a manner not
infrequently exhausting. Societies inside a circuit were held
together not merely by the work of these various preachers but
by the institution of quarterly meetings, which began experi-
mentally in 1748. These were meetings of society officers inside
a circuit, presided over by the assistant. These institutions could

well have been inspired by the Quaker practice. The business of
the meetings was both financial and spiritual.

It would not be accurate to view the creation of this network
of circuits as a solo performance by John Wesley; in fact he
proceeded in certain areas (to use the engaging phrase of Dr
John Walsh) by a series of takeover bids. He took over existing
little connexions, more loosely held together than his own – for
example, those formed by John Nelson in the West Riding and
by William Darney in the Pennines – and absorbed them into
his own organization. Some indication of how the whole Methodist structure was made up of active cells, each a centre of missionary action, is given in the innumerable small autobiographies which were a considerable by-product of the Revival.
Take, for example, the life of Stephen Brunskill (1748–1836). He
was born at Orton in Westmorland into a background typical
enough of local preachers: his parents were of the Church of
England and inclined favourably to itinerant preachers, and his
wife was a Dissenter. After some few years wandering about the
North of England as a slater he became a tenant farmer in a
small way in various parts of Westmorland; and each stage in his
long career, from the time of his conversion (1772–4) onwards, is
marked by a degree of proselytizing. The family at Orton first
took in travelling preachers, and they ('my father, mother,
brother and sister, with some of the neighbours') formed a
society. Brunskill himself began family worship, and became a
class leader, though with 'a persuasion that the Lord had something more for me to do in his vineyard'. He began to exhort
his class, and then to preach in his own house.

At thirty-five, Brunskill followed Grimshaw, the Vicar of
Haworth and a Methodist, in signing a 'solemn covenant with
God'. To read it is to see the source of much of the local preachers'
energy:

I this day consecrate body, soul and substance, with my time and
talents, to thee. I also cheerfully and willingly engage, through thy
grace, to square my life according to thy Word; to shun every appearance of evil; to lay aside entirely all jesting and foolish talking, all
backbiting and evil speaking, and no more to trifle with thy sacred

name. And I also engage, through thy grace, to confess thee before
men, to call on thee in public and in private and also to reprove
sinners and warn them of their danger as opportunity shall serve.

A room for worship was at length hired in Orton, and there
were signs of Methodism prospering in the village when Brunskill
fell ill and the little society became enfeebled. On his recovery,
he resolved to preach in Kendal twelve miles away, where there
was no Methodist preacher. In 1787, with other Methodist
friends, he journeyed there and preached at the door of the old
playhouse. At intervals over several months they preached in
the open; then the playhouse was taken; and after that an old
chapel formerly used by Lady Huntingdon's Connexion was
purchased by a wealthy supporter. Brunskill took a farm a mile
or two from Kendal in 1790 which he immediately turned into a
centre of Methodist preaching, and he also used an inn room for
the purpose. Every opportunity to attract support – while
delivering milk, making casual acquaintances and accepting
invitations to preach – was taken. At Witherslack, a further few
miles away, he was less successful. In the end, he purchased a
farm at Orton, and a preaching room was again fitted up there
with money provided by a brother-in-law. Three years before
his death he subscribed liberally to the erection of a new chapel
in the village, and he saw 'the congregations doubled, the Sunday
School flourishing, and the society useful and prosperous'. In
such ways Methodism secured a hold in the country (*The Life of
Stephen Brunskill of Orton, written by himself*, London and
Kendal, 1837).

Nevertheless, Wesley regarded the Connexion as his own
organization. The Methodist Conference, afterwards the governing body of Methodism, was first called by him in 1744, but the
role he intended it to play was a subsidiary one – 'I sent for them
to *advise*, not *govern*', he wrote later. The composition of the
Conference was at first only the Wesleys and four other clergymen. Subsequently all the travelling preachers were eligible to
attend, though Wesley limited his invitations as he thought fit.
Conference was first called to the Foundery in London; subsequently it was called annually there, or to Bristol, Leeds, or

Manchester. Its business was 'the promotion of the gospel of
Jesus Christ' but, in particular, to admit new preachers, to
define doctrine, to review the spiritual and financial health of
the Connexion, to introduce new regulations for its government,
and to collect essential statistical information.

As Wesley grew older, both he and his followers grew increasingly concerned for the future of the Connexion. Wesley indeed
designated a successor – one of his most admired sympathizers,
John Fletcher, Vicar of Madeley in Shropshire. But Fletcher
became an invalid, and died some years before Wesley. It was
necessary to make some other arrangements. These involved the
drawing up of the Deed of Declaration in 1784, by which the
Conference became the governing body of Methodism. The
'Legal Hundred' – one hundred preachers chosen by Wesley
himself – was to assume control of the Methodist chapels on his
death. The appointment of the Legal Hundred did little to
modify Wesley's direction. Back in 1773, his letter appointing
Fletcher his successor had quoted (in Greek):

It is not good that the supreme power should be lodged in many
hands; let there be one chief governor.

The great man's autocracy, however, was of a peculiar, if not a
unique, nature; as the 'venerable founder' he enjoyed a moral
authority and prestige inside the Connexion, which, if it did
not exactly temper the dictatorship, made it seem apostolic.
One of the early preachers wrote:

From the creation of the world there never existed a body of men
who looked up to any single person with a more profound degree of
reverence than the preachers did to Mr Wesley.

Such an organization was not held together without proper
attention to the printed word. In the Foundery, the original
London headquarters, the band room was early in use as a
bookstall, and Wesley himself was a compulsive writer. A
'Christian Library' consisting of reprints of spiritual classics in
both the Catholic and the Protestant traditions – often amended,
abridged, and otherwise edited – was issued with the idea of

providing instruction for his preachers. Sermons, letters, and
controversial pamphlets were printed, including a great deal of
matter intended to instruct on political, or at any rate non-
religious, themes. Grammars, Roman history, natural philosophy,
and abridgements of 'improving' poetry by Milton and Young
all appeared from the Methodist Book Room. Medicine was a
particular concern of Wesley, and apart from its being something
of a hobby with him, he clearly regarded the spread of medical
knowledge as part of his mission.

The organization ensured that there was a wide distribution
for such literature, which was usually very cheaply produced.
The *York Courant* of 6 June 1780 accused Wesley of using his
sermons at Halifax and Bingley that year to advertise one of his
pamphlets on the American War – he was hostile to the Colonists
(see p. 86). Indeed, the Government once ordered the issue of
copies of his *Calm Address to the American Colonies* at the doors
of all the London churches. In all publishing matters, as in most
others, Wesley assumed absolute control, and whoever published
or printed without his consent was to be cut off from the Connexion. As late as the August of 1789 he was having second
thoughts about the editor of the official journal, on the grounds
not only that the errata were insufferable, but that the unfortunate man had inserted several pieces without Wesley's knowledge.

Besides the printed word, there was also the written word –
the letter. With their conscious imitation of the practice of the
Primitive Church, it was unlikely that the Methodist leaders
would overlook the example of Paul and others in writing
epistles to their followers. Grimshaw at Haworth began letters
with 'Grace, Mercy and Peace be with you from God the Father
and our Lord Jesus Christ' in the Pauline manner. Such letters
were read out to the societies, who held recognized 'letter days'
for the purpose. Grimshaw introduced one of his letters with a
note to Wesley:

I beg you will present my hearty respects to all your societies, classes
etc. in London or elsewhere, in the following manner . . .

Dr Frank Baker calls these effusions 'sermons *in absentia*' (see his *William Grimshaw 1708–1763*, pp. 216–30). Wesley's correspondence was often pastoral in its intention – one more of his methods of controlling his Connexion.

The Connexion presented in this respect a strange contrast to the Protestant churches then existing inside England and Wales. The Anglicans had, indeed, an elaborate system of church government, but the exercise of episcopal supervision was restricted by the varied nature of the bishops' duties, and, since Convocation was not called (see pp. 13–14; 109), there was no central direction. As for the principal Dissenting groups – the Presbyterians, the Baptists, and the Independents – they were organized by congregations; that is to say, they consisted of separate local communities each with a pastor, but with no appreciable control from the centre. Being newly evolved, too, the Methodist organization did not suffer from the ossification which threatened the Anglican Church. The connection with the State was valuable to the Church of England in giving it a privileged position, but the connection was so close that administrative reform was intolerably difficult. If it became necessary to re-draw the map of Methodist England, to form new societies and circuits, then this was done by local enterprise and by Wesley's fiat; if a new Anglican parish had to be set up, then it took an Act of Parliament to do it.

[8] CHAPELS, SERVICES, HYMNS, THEOLOGY

Chapels

As the government of Methodism became less of an improvisation and more of a rigid plan, the societies made more and more elaborate schemes to house themselves. Field-preaching was all very well for unconverted multitudes; for an organized society, a building was necessary. Nor would a simple preaching-box be adequate: a Methodist chapel required a complex of buildings –

somewhere to preach, somewhere to accommodate the preacher, somewhere to house band meetings, class meetings, and Sunday schools. These buildings rose very rapidly at the original angles of the Wesley triangle – London, Bristol, and Newcastle.

In London, the Foundery in Moorfields was originally a government building for the casting of cannon. It had lain derelict for over twenty years when Wesley gave way to the pressure of his supporters and acquired it. Silas Told, who later became a famous preacher at Newgate Prison, first heard Wesley at the Foundery a short while after its acquisition and described it as

a ruinous place, with an old pantile covering, a few rough deal boards put together to constitute a temporary pulpit, and several other decayed timbers.

As it was developed, it contained a chapel in which men and women sat apart from one another ('as they did in the Primitive Church', Wesley observed); a band room where bands, classes, and a charity school met; a set of rooms where Susanna spent her last days; and additional quarters for assistant preachers and staff. The Foundery was eventually displaced as the head-quarters by Wesley's Chapel in City Road, opened in 1778. In Bristol, the Methodists erected in 1739 a 'society room', the New Room, to which additional living quarters were attached. In Newcastle, the original Methodist centre was the Orphan House of 1743, an even more involved structure of three or four storeys, which appears partly to have been designed to receive widows and orphans, and included quarters for preachers, a band room, society rooms, and a study for the use of Wesley himself.

Before chapels or 'preaching houses' proliferated all over the country there was a kind of Heroic Age when Methodists met where they could. This was often in private houses like Matthew Bagshaw's 'on the right hand side of Crossland Yard' in Nottingham. Bagshaw broke a hole through the floor of the second storey; put the men in the upper room and the women in the lower; and the preacher was able to address both at the same time. Indeed, adapting existing buildings for use as preaching houses became something of a Methodist forte – an old malt-kiln in Warrington, a cockpit at Denholme in the West Riding, a chamber over a smithy at Grantham, and various theatres in Birmingham, were all used. In 1759, when Wesley was in Bedford, he noted that 'the stench from the swine under the room was scarce supportable'.

With the building of more and more chapels, however, the great organizer himself stepped in:

Build all preaching houses, where the ground will permit, in the octagon form. It is best for the voice, and on many accounts more commodious than any other. . . . Let there be no pews, and no backs to the seats, which should have aisles on each side, and be parted in the middle by a rail running all along to divide the men from the women, just as at Bath. . . . Let all preaching houses be built plain and decent; but not more expensive than is absolutely necessary.

This advice was less scrupulously followed than some of his other directions (see G. W. Dolbey, *The Architectural Expression of Methodism; the First Hundred Years*, Epworth Press, 1964).

Making practical arrangements for the erection and maintenance of these chapels involved Wesley in the problem of controlling the premises. For the New Room in Bristol he appointed eleven trustees, but his failure to define their functions adequately led to his being faced with a bill for £150 before long. From that moment he was elaborately concerned with the problems of trustees. It was the responsibility of trustees to see to the upkeep of the chapels; and it was also their business to see that authorized Methodist preachers officiated there, and that they preached accepted Methodist doctrine. Wesley attempted continuously to assume direction over preachers and doctrine – a right which local trustees like those at Birstall were contesting as late as 1782. The issue of the Deed of Declaration of 1784, by which John Wesley, and subsequently Charles, and subsequently Conference, were to be responsible for the selection of preachers, and therefore for the control of doctrine, was brought on by this controversy.

What went on inside the chapels? Here, too, Wesley was a

conscious adaptor and innovator. The Anglican layout of pews
so that the social divisions of the parish were carefully marked
out was abandoned. The notion of class distinction inside the
chapel was evidently repellent to Wesley: his early regulations
for the Foundery, besides insisting (as we have seen) on the
separation of the sexes, also included the requirements that there
were to be no proprietary pews, and that first-comers sat down
first. Indeed there were no pews at all – merely backless benches
for all, rich and poor.

Services

The form and method of conducting services inside the new
chapels, like everything else about the Methodist movement,
took some time to evolve. During Wesley's lifetime the chapel
was not intended to provide all the services; his followers were
at any rate exhorted to attend public worship in the parish
church. In 1766, for example, he was writing:

Some may say 'Our own service is public worship'. Yes, in a sense:
but not such as supersedes the Church service. . . . I advise, therefore,
all the Methodists in England and Ireland, who have been brought
up in the Church, constantly to attend the service of the Church;
at least every Lord's Day.

'Morning preachings' at 5 a.m. were accordingly his rule; he
believed that they were characteristic of the Early Church, and
they avoided competition with Anglican services. At the other
end of the day, the introduction of gaslight enabled him to bring
in something much more permanent – the evening service at 6
or 6.30. Evensong in the Church of England was usually said at
three o'clock in the afternoon. As the practice of attending the
parish church by Methodists began to decline, however, some
form of service was required. Wesley's own prejudice was still in
favour of forms of worship from the Book of Common Prayer;
and he himself prepared an abridgement of it in 1784 which,
though it was never fashionable in village chapels, caught on in
London and the South.

Two forms of service were entirely novel, though Wesley justified them on the familiar ground that they were the practices of the 'ancient Christians': the watch-night service and the love feast. The first watch-night service to be held was in London in 1742, though the idea originated among the miners of Kingswood. Wesley himself described the proceedings:

We commonly choose for the solemn service the Friday night nearest the full moon, either before or after, that those of the congregation who live at a distance may have light to their several homes. The service begins at half an hour past eight, and continues till a little after midnight. We have often found a peculiar blessing at those seasons. There is generally a deep awe on the congregation, perhaps in some measure owing to the stillness of the night.

The love feast was celebrated three times a quarter. The institution was a Moravian one – it was not a fixed form of service, but a meeting in which the 'feast' (of cake and water) was less significant than the relating of spiritual experiences by anyone who chose to speak.

One existing ceremony was carefully used. The funerals of Methodists gave striking opportunities for conversion, and how to 'improve' a funeral (as the expression went) was something to be carefully weighed up – as it was, for instance, when Robert Peck of Loughborough died; and in consequence his obsequies lasted three and a half hours. A funeral oration on the life and merits of the deceased was frequent. So too was a lengthy procession of people – the one following the body of John Nelson was half a mile long – often singing hymns as they proceeded.

Hymns

Hymns played an important part in all their proceedings. They were hymns of a kind, sung in such a manner as the Church of England did not then know. They intensified the emotion of Methodist worship; they drove home the theology the Wesleys preached; and they have provided one of the principal Methodist legacies to Christianity in general. The hymns are conventionally described as Charles Wesley's contribution to the Revival. Charles, four years younger than John, and the original founder of the Holy Club at Oxford, was also an Anglican clergyman, also underwent the experience of conversion, and also became a travelling preacher. He married when he was over forty and eventually settled down in Marylebone. He was a compulsive versifier, writing 6,500 hymns with all kinds of metres. As might be expected, though, it was John who established the details of publication, who directed how the hymns should be sung, and who insisted that they serve to teach his congregations in another way what the sermons had already tried to teach.

The writing, collection, and publication of hymns occupied the Wesleys continuously during their career, from their days in Georgia onwards. The first set appeared from Carolina in 1737, and included John's translation from the German of some Moravian hymns. Groups on specific themes or for specific purposes like *Hymns on the Lord's Supper*, or *Hymns for a Protestant*, or *Hymns for Children*, appeared from time to time; and four standard collections appeared from 1742 onwards, culminating in 1780 in the authorized 525 selected, arranged, adapted, and introduced by John himself: *A Collection of Hymns for the Use of the People called Methodists*.

In content, Wesley claimed that they contained 'all the important truths of our most holy religion, whether speculative or practical', and indeed they are remarkably wide in their scope. Many draw their inspiration from the great festivals of the Church's year. Many are on the theme of the Holy Communion. In concentrating on both these things, Charles Wesley's hymns are notably Anglican, and 'high' at that:

> We need not now go up to heaven
> To bring the long-sought Saviour down
> Thou art for all already given
> Thou dost even now Thy banquet crown:
> To every faithful soul appear
> And show thy real presence here.

Others contain the distinctive emphases of Wesley's teaching. The notion that the love of God is available to all, and not, as Whitefield held, to those predestined by God, appears in:

> Thy goodness and thy grace to me
> To every soul abound;
> A vast unfathomable sea
> Where all our thoughts are drowned.

The idea that a Christian might achieve perfection in this life, not merely in the next – a theme on which Wesley argued for so long – is also present in the hymns.

Concentration on the Evangelical themes of conviction of sin, on the necessity of conversion, on the emotional relationship between man and a personalized God, as well as the now-unfashionable emphasis on blood, on mourning, and death, gave an emotional content to Methodist singing which produced heavy criticism when it was first heard, and does so now. The contemporary *Methodist Hymn Book* (1933) should not be regarded as a guide to eighteenth-century Methodist taste; it admits that changes have taken place.

> Still the fountain of thy blood
> Stands for sinners open'd wide
> Now, even now, my Lord and God
> I wash me in thy side

and

> Ah lovely appearance of death
> No sight upon earth is so fair
> Not all the gay pageants that breathe
> Can with a dead body compare,

though now considered repulsive, indicate important ingredients in the Methodist appeal; and Leigh Hunt at the beginning of the nineteenth century entitled one of his essays *On the Indecencies and Profane Rapture of Methodism*. (For a very hostile view of this aspect of Methodism, and possible sexual interpretations, see E. P. Thompson, *The Making of the English Working Class*, Pelican ed., pp. 402–11.)

The manner of Methodist singing is as important in assessing the appeal of the movement as the words are. John Wesley may not be the author of many of the hymns, but in his passionate desire to see that everything in his movement was effective, he concerned himself very much with tunes and how they were to be sung. Many of the musical practices of the eighteenth-century Church he viewed with contempt. Organs, which obscured congregational singing, were not used in his chapels. Any anthem which contained undue repetition of words was objectionable. At Neath, where in August 1768 the churchwardens of the parish invited him to preach in church, he was

greatly disgusted at the manner of singing. 1. Twelve or fourteen persons kept it to themselves, and quite shut out the congregation: 2. These repeated the same words, contrary to all sense and reason, six or eight or ten times over: 3. According to the shocking custom of modern music, different persons sang different words at one and the same moment: an intolerable insult on common sense, and utterly incompatible with any devotion.

By way of contrast, he noted that he had his own congregation 'at the room' at five o'clock the next morning and 'they sang with the spirit and the understanding also'.

In 1770 he laid down the following directions by way of preface to a collection of hymns:

Sing all. See that you join with the congregation as frequently as you can. Let not a slight degree of weakness or weariness hinder you . . .
Sing lustily and with a good courage. Beware of singing as if you were half dead or half asleep . . .
Sing modestly. Do not bawl, so as to be heard above or distinct from the rest of the congregation.
Sing in time . . .
Above all sing spiritually. Have an eye to God in every word that you sing.

The selection of tunes for the hymns was a matter of some importance to the movement. The variety of metre that Charles Wesley employed (as well as the vigour of manner that John

directed) encouraged the composition of new and lively tunes:
Handel, whose oratorios eventually became a quarry for Metho-
dist tunes, composed three special ones; and a number of minor
composers like Battishill and Lampe contributed many (see
Scholes, *The Oxford Companion to Music*, art. 'Methodism and
Music').

It is clear that music contributed greatly to the success of the
Methodist movement, and that it provoked a great deal of envy
from the Church of England. There was some rather curious
criticism from a clergyman who objected to the labourer taking
'his wife and children from the wheel and other useful employ-
ments in the house' in order to sing hymns, a practice which was
'not infrequently kept up at the expense of fire and candle to an
unreasonable hour'. Secker, the Archbishop of Canterbury,
however, wrote:

Something must be done to put our psalmody on a better footing;
the Sectarists gain a multitude of followers by their better singing.

The contrast between the hymns of the 'sectarists' and the
stock metrical psalms of the Church of England was certainly
very sharp (see p. 33). The conduct of Methodist worship in
general made up a great part of the appeal of the movement. It
is even possible to argue that this changed the movement itself in
a way that Wesley did not intend. If his rules and regulations,
particularly those of the earlier years, are examined, what seems
to emerge is almost monastic in character – a set of moral
requirements. But at the end of Wesley's career, the Sunday
service, a substitute for Anglican worship, had become popular;
and to those Sunday services, attracted by the character of the
singing and the worship generally, came many who were not
society members.

Theology

The theology which Wesley taught in his sermons and writings
is slight and in some ways represents a curious fusion of ideas not
normally found together. Man was in a state of sin, the result of

Adam's Fall in the Garden of Eden. But man could be pardoned his sin, or *justified*, by the grace of God. Faith that Christ died for our sins was all that was necessary for salvation. So far, Wesley was in line with conventional Puritan and later Evangelical doctrine. However, he went on to add that the grace of God was freely available:

For all, for all, my Saviour died

– not, as Calvin taught, restricted to a chosen few. This insistence that grace was freely available was another of the features which made Methodism an attractively 'open' group, in the sense that it was easy to enter. For many years Wesley held that all who were pardoned necessarily felt an assurance that they were saved. Once a man was justified, then he was sanctified – he did not sin. A condition termed 'Christian perfection', inexactly defined by Wesley and modified after much controversy, could be reached by man while he was still on earth; besides being sinless, all his faculties were dedicated to God. The joining together of the idea of conversion with Arminian freewill rather than with Calvinist predestination is strange, and is to be explained by remembering Wesley's Anglican background.

These were the bases of Wesley's teaching. Of course, they were only part of his thought, but they were the distinctive part. The rest he shared with much of Christianity. He could not, of course, escape the influences of the theology and intellectual climate of his own age. He had read, while still a young man at Oxford, some of the standard seventeenth-century scientific works; and the formidable programme of reading which he executed on horseback or in his coach (specially fitted up for the purpose) meant that he was aware of current trends in several branches of science and philosophy. Besides, he was always concerned with medicine and the maintenance of health – 'for six and twenty years, I have made anatomy and physick the diversion of my leisure hours', he once claimed – and he regarded the giving of medical advice to his followers as part of his mission. His *Primitive Physick, or an Easy and Natural Way of Curing most Diseases* was a best seller. For the most part it is a tabulated list of remedies. Others among his books, however, show a more intellectual interest in medical and scientific subjects. Reading Benjamin Franklin gave him a great interest in electricity, and he recommended the merits of shock treatment for a wide variety of disorders. He was conversant with the arguments of seventeenth-century philosophers like Ray, who demonstrated the existence of God by concentrating on the wonders of creation; and the alternative title of his most substantial book on the subject, *The Wisdom of God in Creation*, is the same as Ray's. In his attitude to the Middle Ages, as far as it can be discerned, he has the authentic note of Augustan contempt; St Francis he dismissed as 'a well-meaning man, though manifestly weak in intellect'.

Yet attempts to make Wesley a man representative of his time must fail. Conversion and assurance – his more obvious doctrines – were obvious throwbacks to the previous age. The practice of determining a course of action by opening the Bible at random (which he took from the Moravians) was likewise out of tune with the eighteenth century. Witchcraft he would never reject, and he collected the most circumstantial accounts of witches. Before retailing a lengthy narrative of one Elizabeth Hobson in his Journal for 25 May 1768, he observed:

It is true likewise, that the English in general, and indeed most of the men of learning in Europe, have given up all accounts of witches and apparitions, as mere old wives' fables. I am sorry for it. . . . The wisest and best of men in all ages and nations . . . well know that giving up witchcraft is, in effect, giving up the Bible.

In this last sentence is part of the key to Wesley's narrowness. He was a man of one book, a man with one mission, a man with one set of values; and anything running counter to them was to be condemned out of hand. His reactions on reading Rousseau's *Émile* at the beginning of February 1770 indicate his general attitude exactly:

But how was I disappointed! Sure a more consummate coxcomb never saw the sun! How amazingly full of himself! Whatever he speaks, he pronounces as an oracle. But many of his oracles are

palpably false. . . . But I object to his temper, more than to his
judgement: he is a mere misanthrope; a cynic all over. So indeed is
his brother-infidel, Voltaire. As to his book, it is whimsical to the
last degree; grounded on neither reason nor experience. The advices
which are good are trite and common, only disguised under new
expressions. And those which are new, which are really his own, are
lighter than vanity itself. Such discoveries I always expect from those
who are too wise to believe their Bibles.

[9] WESLEY'S IMPACT ON SOCIETY

The Methodist Revival was flourishing at the same time as the
Industrial Revolution, while the French Revolution was soon
to effect habits of thought. It has therefore always seemed
natural to enquire what connection there was between these
three developments. In Wesley's day and for a generation or
so after, Methodism was criticized on innumerable grounds
(see p. 102–8 ff.), and Wesley himself and his successors as
president of the Conference were extremely sensitive to these
attacks. In defending themselves, they worked out an extremely
complex case. The times were troubled; society was in danger of
disintegrating: the Methodists, so they themselves argued,
helped to mitigate these dangers. The Reverend Thomas Jackson, President of the Conference, prepared a volume in 1839 to
celebrate the centenary of the Revival. As his view has had a
remarkably persistent currency since that time, it is set out in
detail. After observing that 'a more loyal man than John
Wesley never existed', and also that in the early part of the
eighteenth century 'the higher classes were many of them
infidel, and the poor were uneducated, ignorant and grossly
immoral', Jackson went on:

In the English nation thus circumstanced a vast increase of population was about to take place. Wealth, with all its incentives to luxury
and indulgence, was on the point of being everywhere diffused. The

factory system, congregating together large masses of people of both
sexes, and placing them together in a heated atmosphere, was soon
to be extensively introduced. The American War of Independence,
producing temporary scarcity and want, and inviting attention to the
republican form of government, was at no great distance. Then
followed the French Revolution, with its infidel democracy, and
godless theories of social order, inflaming the popular mind, and
endangering every national institution. Had this new state of things
commenced while the elements of evil to which we have just adverted
were in full and unrestrained operation, who can calculate the consequences? By the great mercy of God, there was religious principle
in the country to resist the evils which wealth, revolution and war,
were pouring forth in one mighty tide; but it was religious principle
which, to a considerable extent, was consequent on the rise of
Methodism.

In this view, Methodism was essentially conservative in its
effects. There is however a contrary argument: that Methodism
assisted rather than resisted the process of social change. Wesley,
so it is argued, brought literacy to the lower orders, adjusted
them to the problems of working in industry, and brought them
to political consciousness.

There is something strange in attributing all these social and
political consequences to Methodism. Wesley was a man with
one objective – the salvation of souls. His Journal, his letters,
all his actions, were directed to the one task. As for his views on
politics, they were substantially those of an eighteenth-century
English clergyman of a conservative cast of mind. His views on
society were much as one would expect of someone from the
middle ranks – that is, he showed a prejudice against the lowest
classes of rural society, and a feeling (much more regularly displayed) against the aristocracy. If, therefore, Methodism had
profound social effects, then these effects hardly derive directly
from what Wesley said. It must therefore be argued that a great
deal of the effect of Methodism arose either from the character of
the organization he created, or that he was an unwitting revolutionary in what he did. Both such opinions are tenable.

Consider Wesley's political opinions. Towards the British

monarchy his obedience and even admiration were unvarying.
We have already seen that though the strands that made up
Wesley's religious opinions were varied, his prejudices were often
those of an old-fashioned high churchman of the kind brought
up on texts like 'Let every soul be subject to higher powers'.
These prejudices were translated into eighteenth-century terms.
The God-given rulers were the Hanoverians, and they were to be
admired and obeyed. In 1790, the year after George III recovered
from his first lengthy bout of madness, Wesley was preaching in
the West Riding. The *Leeds Intelligencer* reported:

One evening [he] portrayed the Royal pain in colours most brilliant!
And also dwelt much on the amiableness of the disposition of the
Royal Highness. He spoke very forcibly upon the late indisposition of
his King – and concluded his eulogium with the following emphatic
words, That if the best of Kings – the most virtuous of Queens – and
the most perfect constitution, could make any nation happy, the
people of this country had every reason to think themselves so.

In the great political crises of his age, he rushed to proclaim
his loyalty. In 1745 he rebutted charges that he was a Jacobite.
In 1756, when the Seven Years' War had just broken out, he was
in Bristol and found the city in turmoil. His voice was in a poor
way, so he declined to address the whole of the Methodist Society
there, but he collected those who were voters in Bristol and
'mildly and lovingly informed them how they ought to act in
this hour of temptation'. The threat of invasion roused his
patriotism as far as to offer, in a letter to one of the Joint
Secretaries to the Treasury, James West, M.P., to raise a 'company of at least two hundred volunteers, to be supported by contributions among themselves' ready to act against an invader.
The Wilkes disturbances, and the publication of the *Letters of
Junius* in 1768, brought him quickly into print with *Free
Thoughts on Public Affairs* and *Thoughts on Liberty*. In such a
situation, his thoughts may be guessed: Wilkes was roundly
condemned as much for his bad character as his political views;
the *Letters of Junius* were a villainous criticism of the King; and
the spectacle of mob violence was deplorable.

It was during the American War that Wesley made his most celebrated displays of loyalty and strove his hardest to influence opinion in the country at large. When the War opened he was not altogether unsympathetic to the colonists. On 14 June 1775 he wrote a letter to Dartmouth, who was still Secretary of State for the American Colonies in Lord North's Government. It was a letter of warning – that the colonists had a case, that they might well be a match for British strength, and that in the face of the threat England was open to grave danger from her own weakness and division. Wesley, however, was always liable to be convinced by anything striking that he read, and he was much affected by his reading of Dr Johnson's loyal pamphlet *Taxation no Tyranny*. In any case, the progress of the war soon caused his patriotism to revive. The result was *A Calm Address to the American Colonies* (1775) – a simplification (indeed, a plagiarization) of Johnson's pamphlet, vindicating the legal claims of the British to control and tax America. Wesley was instantly rebuked for his descent into political controversy. The writer of an open letter to him in the *Gentleman's Magazine* that December complained:

You have forgot the precept of your Master, that God and Mammon cannot be served together. You have one eye on a pension, and the other raised upon heaven; one hand stretched out to the King, and the other raised up to God. I pray that the first may reward you, and the last may forgive you.

The entry of Dr Richard Price, the characteristic radical voice of Old Dissent, into the controversy on the other side with his *Observations on Civil Liberty and the War with America* brought from Wesley *Observations on Liberty*, in which he argued that the colonists already had liberty; what they desired was independence, and that was wrong. Democracy he dismissed as impossible to secure. His final shaft was his *Calm Address to the Inhabitants of Great Britain*, an out-and-out attack on the colonists which represents his most influential contribution to the debate. Wesley himself claimed that fifty or even a hundred thousand copies had been sold.

As might be expected from his opinions on these particular issues, Wesley was, in general, an admirer of the existing constitution and spoke and wrote of the liberties enjoyed by Englishmen with a degree of satisfaction characteristic of his time:

What more liberty could one want? We have no claim on us, even as big as a knitting needle.

Like the 'economical reformers' of the seventies and eighties, however, he thought that the electoral system needed cleaning up. One of his most constantly reissued pieces at election times was the *Word to a Freeholder*, originally written in 1747. He wrote there:

I hope you have taken no money. . . . I hope you have received nothing else, neither will receive no entertainment, no meat or drink.

It was of course the preacher writing, and he exhorted his voting readers to vote for a godly candidate – failing that, for 'him that loves the King'. Conference, as early as 1744, instructed preachers to punish those who accepted bribes with expulsion from the societies. In 1774 Wesley instructed the voters in the society at Bristol to 'vote without fee or reward, for the person they judged most worthy'. In 1787 Conference was again ordering:

Read everywhere the *Word to a Freeholder* and disperse it as it were with both hands.

The little autocrat was never more absolute than when it came to imposing his loyalist principles on his followers. Such principles, however, reached their most extreme in the years immediately following Wesley's death, when the official anti-Jacobinism of the Conference rivalled that of the most reactionary. The meeting of 1797 ordered the expulsion of those members who 'maintain and propagate opinions inimical to the civil government and established religion of the country'. Protestations of extreme conservatism remained characteristic of Wesleyan Methodism for a generation.

Clearly, then, Wesley was not in the strictly political sense

the instigator of any connection there might be between Methodism and Radicalism. Bu the was less fatalist in his attitude to the
poor than most of his contemporaries; his concern was deep and
entirely scriptural. The societies helped the poor among their
members – it was one of the duties of the stewards to arrange
such relief. The maintenance of a 'lending stock' by the societies
meant that loans of from one to five pounds could be made to
poor members on the recommendation of the borrower's class
leader. Times of special distress, such as the winter of 1772–3,
were times of special effort for Wesley: that year he wrote to the
newspapers and exhorted the societies to organize visits to the
poor and schemes of relief. That same period of want provoked
him into writing *Thoughts on the Present Scarcity of Provisions*
(1773), an exercise in morals and economics. He attributed the
poverty of the time to distilling – 'that bane of health, that
destroyer of strength, of life and of virtue' – to heavy taxation
arising from an excessive National Debt, and to the growth of
luxury. Among his proposals to deal with the problem were the
discharging of half the National Debt; the abolition of 'useless
pensions, as fast as those who now enjoy them die'; and, since
horses seemed to him a great manifestation of luxury, a tax on
horses to be charged at five pounds a year each.

So far, there is little strange or surprising in Wesley's opinions.
Yet in one particular he did not live up to the image of the perfect conformist so far presented. His distaste for certain sections
of society was very marked. His attitude to the nobility emerges
in his exclamation after a visit to the House of Lords in 1785:

What is a lord, but a sinner born to die!

To be a gentleman was to be concerned with luxury, shallowness,
uselessness:

So much paint and affectation, so many unmeaning words and sense-
less customs among people of rank.

Gentlemen, of course, were not receptive to his message, and he
reached a point where he never expected them to be:

To my great surprise, the mistress of the house, though much of a
gentlewoman, desired she and her family might join with us in prayer.

His irony showed where his sympathies lay after a lifetime's preaching. Appearing at Whitehaven towards the end of his life, he observed that in his congregation were most of the church ministers and most of the gentry in the town, but, he adds, 'they behaved with as much decency as if they had been colliers'. His advice to his preachers included a warning against trying to be gentlemen:

You have no more with that character than with that of a dancing master.

Wesley also had his dislikes elsewhere in society, especially of farmers and of farm labourers; he protested at the conventional views of classical authors and their imitators who praise country life:

In general [the famers'] life is supremely dull; and it is usually unhappy too; for of all the people in the kingdom, they are the most discontented, seldom satisfied with God or man.

The class-conscious character of Methodism, then, may be traced back directly to the founder's writings and actions. The classes he was overwhelmingly concerned with and inclined to from the beginning of his career as a field-preacher were poor, urban, and industrial. He deliberately sought them out.

At seven [he wrote on first visiting Newcastle upon Tyne] I walked down to Sandgate, the poorest and most contemptible part of the town. . . . After preaching, the poor people were ready to tread me underfoot, out of pure love and kindness.

In general, where there was a large working population, there were the Methodists: the West Riding, the Black Country, Cornwall, London, Bristol, Manchester, and Newcastle upon Tyne all provided examples of Wesley's eventual success. Dr Leslie Church has endeavoured to show, however, by making an analysis of various kinds of Methodist literature – early biographies, class lists, trustee lists – that the appeal of Methodism was wider than is normally supposed to be the case, and his gallery of early Methodist people is an attractive one. It includes

Roger Lamb, soldier; prosperous business men like Daniel
Tolkein, the fur merchant, and estimable craftsmen like Melchior
Teulen, the King's hatmaker; bankers like Ebenezer Blackwell
of Lewisham; and Joseph Butterworth, M.P., who led his young
men's class regularly at seven o'clock on a Sunday morning.

As the movement grew, it came to contain quite a cross-section
of society within it. The regular itinerant preachers who had
graduated from the class leader, exhorter, and local preacher
stages did not include any of the professional classes or any from
the higher gradations of society. According to Dr Warner:

The majority of the early Methodist preachers were in that social
grade which includes skilled artisans, small farmers, and tradesmen
in business for themselves in a small way.

The local leadership in the societies – the class leaders and local
preachers – was, however, much more varied in social composition.

The local preachers are in general men of good talents [said Joseph
Sutcliffe in his *Review of Methodism* (1805)]. Being engaged in
business, many of them are opulent, and exceedingly useful. They
frequently ride twenty or thirty miles on a Sunday and preach twice
or thrice without the smallest pecuniary compensation.

(See W. J. Warner, *The Wesleyan Movement in the Industrial
Revolution*, Ch. VIII; and L. F. Church, *The Early Methodist
People* and *More About the Early Methodist People*, Epworth
Press, 1948–9.)

By contrast, the rural areas were neglected, and Wesley's
experiences in them were often unhappy. Many of the southern
counties were visited rarely, and then only briefly. These
counties were 'the Methodist Wilderness'. At the close of the
eighteenth century all Hampshire and great parts of Surrey and
Sussex formed one circuit with its headquarters at Portsmouth.
The total membership in the four counties of Oxfordshire,
Gloucestershire, Worcestershire, and Kent was not more than
two thousand.

Wesley did not often speculate on why his reception was bad
in those areas; at least, not in writing. A brief burst of abuse in

the Journal was usually enough. At Winchester in 1778 he 'had thoughts of preaching abroad, if haply any thing might awaken a careless, self-conceited people'; of Beccles in Suffolk in 1776 he wrote: 'A duller place I have seldom seen. The people of the town were neither pleased nor vexed, as caring for none of these things'. Sandwich in 1777 was 'poor, dry, dead'. The sociologists have often remarked that in communities that were settled, and under the domination of squire and parson, the Methodists had little response. If both were not united against Wesley, one was sufficient. When Wesley was inclined to be specific, he attributed failure either to the society or to the preachers on the spot – at Launceston, for instance, to their failure to preach the doctrine of Christian perfection. He did not grieve long over a poor response – he merely moved to a place where the crowds could be attracted.

Apart from the obvious attractions of having more people, though, why did the cities and the newer industrial areas prove so receptive to Wesley's teaching? To the sociologists, one of the reasons was that they were new conglomerations, destitute of all those influences – agrarian regulation, or the rule of squire and parson – which prevailed in settled communities. It is an attractive proposition, but not easy to demonstrate directly from Methodist literature. To many writers – Dr Wearmouth, for example, or Dr Walsh – some of the success in industrial cities was due to the failure of the Church of England to concern itself adequately with those areas. The absence of a sufficient number of pews in the churches is an example of this. Manchester had a population of 100,459 in 1817, and accommodation in church for 14,850 only. In 1811 there were 60,000 inhabitants in Marylebone and there were seats in the parish church for only 900. It was certainly a very long time before the typical Anglican clergyman became a town parson – if indeed that has ever happened. To the Anglican the ideal was still the rural parish with a resident squire and a resident parson as the agents of social control. The towns presented problems not easy to face – they were one-class parishes without a squire, they were often badly endowed, and they were insalubrious.

In all, the number of British members of the Connexion as given to Conference in the year of Wesley's death was 72,476. Clearly, if the impact of Methodism is to be judged by this figure, then it is not so great as is often argued. The number given, however, is of those holding class tickets, and that is much smaller than the total number attending services at Methodist preaching houses. Furthermore, as will be seen, the influence of Methodism was by that time widely diffused within the Church of England and in some of the Dissenting communities.

The most obvious and spectacular result of Methodism was the growth of respectability (and therefore of political and social consciousness) among the urban classes attracted to it. The change to respectability was one of the obsessions of Wesley in his last years, and is consequently so well documented by him as to have become a cliché. Thomas Bewick, who besides being a celebrated wood engraver was also something of a connoisseur of sermons, observed in the 1820s that the Methodists

took their rise under the able auspices of John Wesley and at that time he did a great deal of good. In this neighbourhood [Tyneside] he greatly civilized a numerous host of semi-barbarian, the pitmen and others employed in the pit-works. These seemed like Cherokees and Mohawks, but they were more wicked.

The picture of pre-Wesleyan workmen as 'Cherokees and Mohawks' is not attractive. The crowds which appear in Wesley's own descriptions were ignorant, credulous, violent. In what ways were they 'civilized' by their religious experience?

In the first place, they were disciplined: Wesley's Connexion, though easy to enter, imposed its own rules; and the great man was determined that it should remain a group of zealots whose job it was to reactivate the Church of England. The rules included the avoidance of a list of evils such as Sabbath-breaking, swearing, drunkenness, 'brother going to law with brother', and so forth; and also a series of positive injunctions to perform charitable acts – sick visiting, prison visiting, supporting fellow-Methodists in business – and to attend the public worship of the

Church of England. The *Directions given to Band Societies* of
1749 banned the drinking of spirits 'except as prescribed by a
physician'; forbade pawnbroking, wearing jewellery, and smok-
ing tobacco; and required attendance at the 5 o'clock preaching
every morning. The Large Minutes of the Conference of 1789
also objected to showy dress, smuggling, gossip, and the marriage
of Methodists to unconverted persons. Those directions were
fortified at various times by more specific advice – *Thoughts on
Dress, Word to a Smuggler*, and so on. As for Wesley's helpers
and assistants, they were subjected to more severe rules which
obliged them to spend from 4 a.m. to 5 a.m. and from 5 p.m. to
6 p.m. in prayer and from 6 a.m. to 12 noon in study. Their
midday meal was to be of potatoes only, and their helping of
meat was to be consumed in the evening.

The enforcement of such rules in such an 'open' society as the
Methodists, with many attenders who did not have class tickets
at chapel on Sundays, presented a difficult problem – and insofar
as Wesley's rules tried to prescribe attendance at the parish
church, an impossible one. The cellular organization, however,
with the class members at any rate 'watching over one another
in love', and the power to withdraw a member's class ticket,
meant that the effort was not entirely vain.

In the second place, Methodists were educated – in an un-
sophisticated way, no doubt, but able to read, write, and consider.
The claims made for Wesley as a contributor to the spread of
education for children of the poor are often over-pitched, as will
be seen later, and the Sunday school movement was becoming
effective only at the end of his life; but in a larger sense he was a
considerable popular educator. His publications were for the most
part cheap; they were on a great variety of subjects; the pressures of Wesley himself, his preachers, and the Conference, as
salesmen were considerable; controversy stimulated sales. It
appears very frequently from the way in which punctuation
marks were distributed and paragraphs numbered in the *Works*
that they were intended for reading aloud and for consideration
by groups. Adults came first in education. 'Not until the Methodist organization for the salvation and reform of the adult was

complete', Miss Jones writes in her study, *The Charity School Movement* (Cambridge University Press, 1937), 'did Methodism turn with enthusiasm to the cause of popular education.' Selina, Countess of Huntingdon and a great supporter of Whitefield, explained to Wesley the reasons for suppressing a school she had earlier founded at Markfield:

A school will never answer the end of bringing forth any of the Gospel fruits of holiness till the parents are first made Christians. The parents must lay up for the children, not the children for the parents.

In the third place, Wesley's specific teaching was not, to say the least of it, directed exclusively to heavenly concerns: 'gain all you can' and 'do not make the care of future things a pretence for neglecting present duty' were injunctions that were powerful to the Methodist. Pointless accumulation of wealth, indeed, Wesley scorned; he condemned the idea of collecting it to leave to one's children, and he was determined to leave nothing himself, in spite of his immense literary earnings. Surplus wealth had to be devoted to charitable objects; wealth was something of which the Christian was only steward on God's behalf.

In the fourth place, the running of the Methodist machine, with its bands and classes, stewards and helpers, gave to many a training in administration which would not otherwise have come their way. The demonstration of this proposition is difficult without, however, combing through the individual histories of innumerable chapels and the little spiritual autobiographies which abound in early Methodism (see R. F. Wearmouth, *Methodism and the Common People of the Eighteenth Century*, Section 3, Chapter II).

The rise of these newly respectable and sometimes well-to-do Methodists had become very clear by the 1780s. In the iron industry, Professor Ashton noted that the Guest family of South Wales, the Walker family of Masborough, and the partners of the Thorncliffe ironworks, were all Methodists. Ridgways, the Hanley potters, were Methodists. Dr Warner, in his analysis of early Methodist literature, *The Wesleyan Movement in the Industrial Revolution*, indicated that it was almost common form

in a Methodist biography to insist that one of the consequences
of adopting the new form of religion was commercial success.
The rules of conduct made them desirable employees:

Actuated by interest [wrote Joseph Sutcliffe in 1805], proprietors of
factories . . . chose sober and pious men for their freemen and over-
lookers.

Prosperity brought with it problems. In Macclesfield (where
the Methodists were uncommonly successful in business, and
subsequently in municipal affairs) Wesley wrote of 'a people
still alive to God, in spite of swiftly increasing riches'. So acute
an observer was dubious, though. In his sermon 'Concerning the
Inefficacy of Christianity', dated from Dublin in 1789, he
remarks:

The Methodists grow more and more self-indulgent, because they
grow rich. Although many of them are still deplorably poor . . . yet
many others, in the space of twenty, thirty or forty years, are twenty,
thirty, yea, a hundred times richer than they were when they first
entered the society. And it is an observation which admits of few
exceptions, that nine in ten of these decreased in grace, in the same
proportion as they increased in wealth. Does it not seem (and yet
this cannot be) that Christianity, true scriptural Christianity, has a
tendency to destroy itself?

Historical judgements on the social effects of the Revival have
been elaborated steadily since Wesley's death, though different
conclusions have been drawn from the same evidence. The
obituary notice which appeared in Woodfall's *Diary* for 17
June 1791 spoke of Wesley's work in conventional terms:

He penetrated the abodes of wretchedness and ignorance, to rescue
the profligate from perdition; and he communicated the light of life
to those who sat in darkness and the shadow of death. He changed the
outcasts of society into useful members; civilized even savages, and
filled those lips with prayer and praise that had been accustomed to
oaths and imprecation.

Robert Southey, whose critical account of Wesley was issued
in 1819, the year of Peterloo, was still concerned with the social

utility of the Methodist movement. He was willing to admit that conversion might have a great effect in improving the morality of the individual person, and commended Wesley's insistence on strict control over personal expenditure and avoidance of personal indulgence. Lecky, who was strenuous in attacking the Methodists for their irrationality and for their spiritual tyranny, developed these arguments in a more sophisticated way. England, he argued, was saved from anything like the French Revolution by many things, but among them was the new religious enthusiasm,

which had enlisted in its service a large proportion of the wilder and more impetuous reformers, and which recoiled in horror from the anti-Christian tenets that were associated with the Revolution in France.

The Industrial Revolution, he argued, created a wide gulf between rich and poor, and therefore a dangerous situation, but the religious revival did something to avert the danger – the morality of the poor was strengthened, and the philanthropy of the rich was stimulated.

The speculations which originated in the platitudes of an obituary notice became more and more involved. Halévy, in the early part of this century, was more positive than ever in explaining why it was that England escaped revolution and sudden change:

The élite of the working class, the hard-working and capable bourgeois, had been imbued by the evangelical movement with a spirit from which the established order had nothing to fear.

He also indicated that it was a characteristic of social change in England that it took religious forms:

Nonconformity . . . tended to become a transitional creed, a stage in the history of an English family. The unskilled workman becomes in turn a skilled workman, an artisan, the head of a small business, a business man possessed of a modest capital, and as he rises out of the barbarism in which the working class was plunged, he becomes a

Nonconformist. If he himself rises still higher on the social ladder, or if his children rise after his death, he or they go over to the Church of England.

Recently there has been a revival of this type of speculation. E. P. Thompson, in his *Making of the English Working Class*, has taken the view that the effect of the Methodists on the development of that class was disastrous in three senses. First, he argues, working-class Radical activity was inhibited by the Methodist 'insistence on submissiveness'; secondly, Wesley insisted on the virtues of work and played into the hands of the industrialists; and thirdly, that Methodist concentration on the emotions had harmful psychological effects. Thompson explains the subsequent participation of the Methodists in working-class activity by proposing the theory that such activity was a natural and despairing reaction to the autocracy and conventionalism of the Wesleyan leaders. Professor Harold Perkin, in his *Origins of Modern English Society 1780–1880*, has developed Halévy's observation on the connections between a man's rise in social status and his change of religion. In the birth of the modern class structure, he sees religion as the 'midwife', in the sense that it enabled men to escape from dependence upon the gentry, and that it gave them 'a model of class organization'. There is another sense in which Nonconformity eased the process of class change:

not so much by passive teaching of patience as by active example of the benefits of non-violent organization, to influence class conflict in the direction of non-violence.

Philanthropy was the rage of the century, and Wesley shared it, often with motives more powerful than most of his contemporaries. Something could be done. There were, however, several limitations to Wesleyan philanthropy. It was widely diffused, certainly, because each ticket-holder was enjoined to undertake active charity; but as Dr Warner has complained:

The failure of the movement . . . was its inability to translate this habitual mood into anything more than personal and ameliorative activity. Its philanthropy was characteristically individual and local, not organized and curative. It is an interesting spectacle. A great social movement which owed its existence to efficient organization more than any other one factor, creates an unparalleled philanthropic disposition and permits it to dissipate through lack of organization!

No new method of philanthropy was devised, though all the characteristic eighteenth-century forms of it were supported: charity schools, hospitals, dispensaries, and so forth.

The judgment of Lord Mansfield in the Somersett Case in 1772, that the state of slavery could not exist in England, brought the whole issue of the slave trade and of negro slavery into public notice. Before this, it appears, Wesley had no strong views on the matter: he baptized a slave owner and two of his slaves in 1760. But in 1772 Wesley read the attack on the trade made by Anthony Benezet, a Quaker. It stirred him to his most energetic language, and the trade became to him 'that execrable sum of villainies' which infinitely exceeded in barbarity 'whatever Christian slaves suffer in Mahometan countries'. He entered the controversy with his *Thoughts on Slavery* in 1774, an attack on the entire system of slavery. His view of the life of an African before capture might have been rather romantic, and his account of the Africans' capture and of the horrors of the Atlantic crossing in a slave ship might have been highly coloured; but he had clearly studied the details of the slave trade before putting pen to paper.

The next stage in the development of the campaign was the formation of the Committee of Twelve for the purpose of agitating for the abolition of the trade. Wesley wrote expressing his enthusiastic approval of its being set up, and wrote later to Granville Sharp, its chairman, deploring the slave traffic. Wilberforce undertook to raise the problem in the Commons in 1788, though illness delayed his plans. Early in March that year, when slavery was a general topic of public discussion, Wesley preached at Bristol his sermon on 'God shall enlarge Japheth'. His packed congregation of 'high and low, rich and poor' was disconcerted by a storm, which struck in the middle of the sermon, and

Wesley was happy to explain it in supernatural terms: 'Satan fought, lest his kingdom should be delivered.'

We set Friday apart as a day of fasting and prayer [he continues in his Journal] that God would remember these poor outcasts of men; and (what seems impossible with men, considering the wealth and power of their oppressors) make a way for them to escape, and break their chains in sunder.

Wesley's letter at the end of his life to Wilberforce, commending his 'glorious enterprise', ended his personal contribution; but just as Wesley transmitted political subservience to many of his followers, so he also transmitted his intense hatred of slavery.

His admiration for Wilberforce was paralleled by his admiration for the prison reformer John Howard. The two men met in Ireland in June 1787, and Wesley considered him 'one of the greatest men in Europe'. Wesley had been known for very many years for his insistence on prison visiting as a Christian duty. The programme of the Holy Club at Oxford included such activities – the principal prospect, of course, was the salvation of the prisoners – and the Conference of 1776 enjoined the preachers to visit prisons. Wesley himself, however, did not spend much time visiting them in later life, but the curious career of his preacher Silas Told succeeded in identifying the movement with prisons. Told had been converted in 1744, and began preaching, often in Newgate and other prisons. A famous print by Hogarth shows him, finger pointing heavenwards, accompanying a condemned criminal on his way to the gallows. His autobiography was published in 1786, with a note by Wesley. But though Silas Told expertly described criminals at Newgate, claimed many conversions, and even set up a Methodist society among the debtors, there is no evidence that he urged prison reform in the accepted sense of making some physical improvement in the prisoners' lot – and the same may be said of Wesley himself. Indeed, one is tempted to observe that they found that the threat of execution hanging over criminals' heads was the greatest aid to their work of conversion. Horace Walpole took this accusation several stages further in 1768 in a letter to the Rev. William Cole:

I hope the Methodist, your neighbour, does not, like his patriarch Whitefield, encourage the people to forge, murder, etc., in order to have the benefit of being converted at the gallows.

Silas Told, at the time of his conversion, gave up his excellent job as a clerk in Wapping at the earnest insistence of Wesley, to teach the children at the Foundery School. There he

collected three score boys and six girls; but the society being poor, could grant me no more than ten shillings per week. This, however, was sufficient for me, as they boarded and clothed my daughter. Having the children under my care from five in the morning till five in the evening, both winter and summer, sparing no pains, with the assistance of an usher and four monitors, I brought near forty of them into writing and arithmetic. I continued in the school seven years and three months, and discharged two hundred and seventy-five boys, most of whom were fit for any trade.

The association of Wesley with education is often pointed out, though the nature of the association is difficult to define. Popular educator and publisher of improving literature he certainly was, as has been shown; but in that impressive series of movements which produced thousands of day schools for the instruction of poor children in the eighteenth century, Wesley's place is significant rather than predominant. In two senses Methodist influence was positively retrograde. In the words of M. G. Jones, it 'deflected public interest from the schools'. Moreover, Wesley's opinions on the instruction of children were those of his mother: a child was a sinful creature whose will was first to be broken.

It is difficult to describe the Methodist contribution to schooling as being more than merely following fashion – first in the founding of charity schools, and then the founding of Sunday schools. In the days of the Holy Club, with its insistence on philanthropy, attempts were made to set up prison schools, and members of the Club taught children their catechism in parishes round about Oxford. Whitefield, as the moving spirit of the Holy Club after Wesley left Oxford, took charge of several charity schools in the neighbourhood, and became for a time a famous preacher in aid of charity schools. But in the course of the actual Revival, Wesley did not make great efforts to found schools. Kingswood he originally set up to instruct the Bristol miners' children, and afterwards the children of his preachers. But the rules were fiendish; children at Kingswood were not to be taken away for even one day, and they were to rise at four in the morning. His Newcastle Orphan House had similarly severe regulations – no child was to speak in school – but there Wesley's charitable intention of having forty poor children educated seems never to have been carried out.

In the 1780s the idea of the Sunday school was being put into practice, notably in Gloucester by the Anglican newspaper proprietor, Robert Raikes, and in Windsor by Sarah Trimmer. The Sunday school, financed by the contribution of the middle classes, was an attractive proposition at the time in a number of ways. It did not interfere with work; it kept the poor children off the streets on the Sabbath (they irritated the respectable town dweller); and it was cheap. It therefore attracted great attention both among churchmen and Dissenters, and became almost a *sine qua non* in every parish. The Sunday schools were at this early time often interdenominational. Wesley took a year or two to recognize their significance and usefulness; after 1784 he commended the scheme to the societies. In a famous Journal entry he wrote of his visit to Bingley in 1784, where he saw two hundred and fifty children being instructed in Sunday school – though its aims and achievements were to his mind very limited:

So many children in one parish are restrained from open sin, and taught a little good manners at least, as well as to read the Bible.

At Bolton in 1788, where he was cheered at the sight of nine hundred or a thousand Sunday-school children, their achieve-

ments were social and spiritual (as Wesley wished) rather than
academic. The children's 'usual diversion' was

> to visit the poor that are sick (sometimes six, or eight, or ten together)
> to exhort, comfort and pray with them. Frequently ten or more of
> them get together to sing and pray by themselves; sometimes thirty
> or forty; and are so earnestly engaged, alternately singing, praying,
> and crying, that they know not how to part.

There are not the signs of great educational achievement here.

[10] OPPOSITION TO METHODISM

Wesley's calm endurance in the face of physical attack, and his
courtesy in replying to literary attack, have often been the subject of remark. Indeed he imagined a parallel between his own
position and that of the Christians of the Early Church, and drew
inspiration from it, considering that persecution was the lot of
the Christian. He felt himself under the particular protection of
providence, and needed such consolation during the first dozen
years of his field-preaching, since the variety and degree of
attacks on him were considerable. Some of his attackers, no
doubt, were looking round for convenient and topical offensive
labels in accusing him of Jacobite leanings, or of Popery. Others,
well-bred and rational, disliked the emotions he played on and
provoked. The crowds he collected caused social comment.
Actors found an obvious subject for their talents, and authors
some obvious 'copy'. The Church of England clergymen, who
had most reason to criticize him, disliked his manner, his theology,
and his threat to church order. This large miscellany of critics all
found him a splendid subject for gossip. Wesley withstood it all
and defended himself from it. So did many of his nineteenth-
century apologists – they were even more obsessed with the persecution Wesley endured than was Wesley himself.

When he defended himself, though, it is hard to resist the

conclusion that his own view of what he had done was remarkably narrow. He congratulated himself frequently on the spiritual results of his work, and prided himself, too, on his loyalty to the existing political framework. But the threat he produced to church order and to the social order was either ignored or not understood by him.

The more extraordinary attacks on him may easily be dismissed. The attempt to make him out a Jacobite in 1745 – there was even a rumour that he was with Charles Edward in Edinburgh – was sufficient to provoke him into effusions of loyalty addressed to the Mayor of Newcastle, to the soldiers there, and to his societies; to investigate the state of the cannon defending Newcastle; and even to declare that he would 'rejoice to serve, as he was able, his King and Country'. As for Charles Wesley, he provided a suitable hymn for singing at the Foundery on the day of thanksgiving for victory over the Jacobites:

> Jehovah quelled their boastful might
> And knapped their spears, and broke their swords.
> And showed – the battle is the Lord's.

Popery was a more enduring charge, though no better based than the charge of his being a Jacobite. In a scare of 1744, during which Papists were ordered to leave London, Wesley felt obliged to write a loyal address to George II from the 'societies in England and Wales, in derision called the Methodists', though the address was never sent. One of the most influential attacks on Methodism was made by George Lavington, Bishop of Exeter – his *Enthusiam of Methodists and Papists compared* (1749–51). Lavington (who was nothing if not exhaustive, and even suggested that drugs were administered to Methodists to induce hysteria) complained that a Methodist had

high pretences to piety; which is to consist of unscriptural peculiarities, whimsical strictnesses, and bitter zeal against innocent and indifferent things

and compared Wesley with the great founders of Catholic orders, Dominic and Ignatius.

The contents of Wesley's 'Christian Library' display his strong interest in Catholic mysticism; but on the political position of the Papists, as on many another subject, his views became very conventional and amounted to approval of the situation as it existed – that is, no open persecution. The Gordon Riots of 1780, however, provoked the Wesleys into an anti-Catholic outburst or two. Charles wrote:

> Let the blind sons of Rome bow down
> To images of wood and stone.

John objected to the Saville Act of 1778 by which some of the Penal Laws were lifted. He supported the Protestant Association. Lord George Gordon, the leader of the riots, was put in the Tower, where he asked to see Wesley. The two talked of Popery, and Wesley was clearly sympathetic to Gordon's views. General opinion inside the societies followed Wesley in this. Lecky, weighing up the results of the Methodist Revival, was concerned at the encouragement that Methodism and Evangelicalism gave to anti-Catholic sentiment, and indeed anti-Catholicism was the standard attitude of nineteenth-century Methodism.

Not all attacks on Wesley came from outside his movement: the internal squabbles of Methodism were devastating and distasteful. The greatest of theological controversies, that between free will and predestination, was played out inside the movement. Wesley, as an Arminian, maintained the first position, a position which became his high-church origins, and Whitefield, as a Calvinist, the second. The two maintained friendly and courteous relations with one another, but when Whitefield died in 1770, his patroness, Lady Huntingdon, acted immediately against Wesley and his doctrines. Fletcher of Madeley, the head of Lady Huntingdon's college for preachers at Trevecca, was dismissed as a Wesley sympathizer. The controversy continued intermittently for years, being led from the Calvinist side by Rowland Hill and Augustus Toplady. The latter – the author of 'Rock of Ages' – could coin striking abusive phrases: he once called Wesley 'a low and puny tadpole in divinity'. 'I do not fight with chimney sweepers', Wesley observed of Toplady; 'he is too dirty a writer for me to meddle with; I should only foul my fingers.'

The hysterical phenomena associated with conversion provoked some criticism for a long time, though the phenomena themselves were characteristic of the earliest period of the Revival – only, as Sidney Dimond observed in his sympathetic study in 1926, between 1739 and 1742. An experience of conversion – the 'New Birth' was the most usual phrase for it – was an essential part of Methodism. The address of the preacher convinced the hearer that he had sinned and was damned. Then, or perhaps after some time, he became convinced that Christ died for his sins. Finally the subject became convinced of his being forgiven. Each of these stages could be accompanied by noisy and spectacular actions – groaning, falling down, convulsions. Wesley had a clinical interest in them all, and recorded the details fully. The case of John Haydon, a weaver of Bristol, is not typical, since Wesley himself admitted that he 'never saw one so torn of the Evil One', but it illustrates what is meant. Haydon came to a meeting out of curiosity to see the strange fits into which people fell. He left after the meeting, and went about to his friends deploring the 'delusion of the devil'. Somewhat later, however, when reading a sermon on 'Salvation by Faith', he 'changed colour, fell off his chair, and began screaming terribly, and beating himself against the ground'. Wesley was called, to find him surrounded by his neighbours, and later reported the situation fully in his Journal:

He then roared out 'O thou devil! thou cursed devil! yea thou legion of devils! thou canst not stay. Christ will cast thee out. I know His work is begun. Tear me to pieces if thou wilt; but thou canst not hurt me.' He then beat himself against the ground again; his breast heaving at the same time, as in the pangs of death, and great drops of sweat trickling down his face. We all betook ourselves to prayer. His pangs ceased, and both his body and soul were set at liberty.

The physical violence which greeted Methodist preaching, and the causes of the violence, are a problem in several senses. Like most of the phenomena popularly associated with Methodism, the violence is most characteristic of the early years. By 1747, Wesley was writing in Cornwall that 'wherever we went we used to carry our lives in our hands; and now there is not a dog to wag his tongue'. It was not over everywhere by 1747, however. Some of Wesley's most circumstantial pages are given to describing the extraordinary attempts at Cork to break up Methodist meetings and to terrorize Methodists by a crowd led by 'King' Nicholas Butler in 1749 and 1750. Nor must the evidence be artificially confined by referring merely to John Wesley's Journal; violence was more lasting and more widespread than appears from that source. Wesley's assistants were as much exposed to it as he was himself, and the experience of John Nelson and others less significant in their local communities was severe.

Why were there such disturbances? Various reasons have been advanced. The sympathy of the Church of England clergy towards the violence is certainly evident from time to time: Dr Borlase, an Anglican clergyman, stimulated the crowds to mob Wesley in the West of England; and the Vicar of Wednesbury in Staffordshire was provoked by the language of the preachers into opposition. But much of the violence is without any kind of religious explanation. It is the horseplay of an ignorant crowd in search of sport, a crowd inadequately controlled by the creaking machinery of law and order. The Justices of the Peace – the peace-keeping authority – were often accused of being anti-Methodist; so they were, if only on the ground that the presence of Methodist preachers in a town offered for some years the possibility that order could not be maintained. Some of the classic accounts of disorder in Wesley's Journal may best be explained by such arguments.

The Wednesbury disturbances of 1743–4 show Wesley as the subject of war between rival bands of toughs. A crowd summoned him from where he was staying, and he accompanied them to the homes of two local J.P.s, who both refused to see him. The most prominent person they saw was a J.P.'s son, who enquired what was the matter. 'Why, an't please you, they sing psalms all day; nay, and make folks rise at five in the morning.' To such an accusation the magistrate's son could only reply by

telling the crowd to go home and be quiet. Unsuccessful in their
approach to the magistrates, they proposed to take Wesley
home. A second hostile crowd, from Walsall, then appeared and
seized him. He showed his usual composure – 'from the beginning
to the end I found the same presence of mind as if I had been
sitting in my own study' – and his courage won over the former
leader of the crowd, who secured him safe passage into Wednesbury again. Wesley was somewhat put out to read later that the
two magistrates who declined to see him issued a circular to the
local constables stating that:

Several disorderly persons, styling themselves Methodist preachers,
go about raising routs and riots, to the great damage of His Majesty's
liege people, and against the peace of our Sovereign Lord the King.

To accuse them of raising a riot was doubtless a little strong; but
their presence was certainly an invitation to disturbance in the
area, which was troubled intermittently from June 1743 to
February 1744. Wesley showed the same incredulity when the
authorities of Cork were plainly not enthusiastic about his
presence there.

Attacks on Wesley and on the movement generally were, of
course, more than merely physical. The language and gestures of
Whitefield, for example, were obvious materials for an actor like
Samuel Foote:

If [Whitefield] is bit by fleas, he is buffeted by Satan. If he has the
good fortune to catch them, God will subdue his enemies under his
feet.

The ignorance, the low social station, and the emotional sermons
of the Methodist preachers were made the theme of Richard
Graves's novel *The Spiritual Quixote* (1776). The amorous ter-
minology of some of the hymns, the familiarity with which
'Jesus' and 'Christ' were used, and the theological terms the
Methodists used (particularly the 'New Birth') provoked some
ribald criticisms. To the *beau monde*, the spectacle of one of
Wesley's meetings offered innumerable grounds for comment.
Horace Walpole's celebrated and characteristic letter from Bath
(10 October 1766) details the music:

I have been at one opera, Mr Wesley's. They have boys and girls with
charming voices, that sing hymns, in parts, to Scotch ballad tunes;
but indeed so long, that one would think they were already in eternity,
and knew how much time they had before them

– the furnishing and the preacher:

Behind the pit, in a dark niche, is a plain table within rails; so you
see the throne is for the apostle. Wesley is a lean elderly man, fresh-
coloured, his hair smoothly combed, but with a *soupçon* of curl at the
ends. Wondrous clean, but as evidently an actor as Garrick. He spoke
his sermon, but so fast, and with so little accent, that I am sure he
has often uttered it, for it was like a lesson. There were parts and
eloquence in it; but towards the end he exalted his voice, and acted
very ugly enthusiasm

– and the congregation, from a strictly social point of view:

Except a few from curiosity, and some *honourable women*, the congregation was very mean. There was a Scotch Countess of Buchan, who
is carrying a pure rosy vulgar face to heaven.

[11] WESLEY AND THE CHURCH OF ENGLAND

The Church of England, of course, was the principal critic of
Methodism; yet it did not set out to destroy the movement or
drive it outside the fold. The observations and activities of a
few bishops are well known: Lavington's abusive comparisons
between Popery and Methodism; Gibson's legal strictures; and
the refusal of Pretyman Tomline, Bishop of Lincoln from 1787
to 1820, to grant Methodist preachers a licence. The opposition
of the lower clergy was often (as has been seen) at the level of
prejudice alone. But Charles Wesley indicated another side to all
this in a letter to John in 1785:

I do not understand what obedience to the bishops you dread. They
have left us alone, and left us to act, just as we pleased for these fifty

years. At present, some of them are quite friendly towards us, particularly towards you.

The lack of concerted action by the bishops against Methodism is something of a puzzle. In part it was a consequence of the absence of machinery through which to act. Convocation had been suspended in 1717, and apart from one attempt in 1741, did not debate at all until 1852. The attitude of Church leaders to this suspension varied. At one extreme Edmund Gibson complained bitterly, and urged that Convocation should be revived. However, the Governments of George I and George II were unwilling to disturb the Dissenters (their devoted supporters) by permitting an increase in the Church's power. At the other extreme, the Archbishop of Canterbury from 1758 to 1768, Secker, urged the merits of letting things alone. The revival of Convocation would lead to the enemies of the Church – atheists, Dissenters, and Papists – uniting against the Church. In arguments which appear ludicrously timid but which in view of the earlier history of Convocation were well founded, he pointed out that if little resulted from the debates of Convocation, or if there were great divisions of opinion, the Church would appear ridiculous. Secker's views henceforth prevailed, and the occasional gatherings of bishops for social and ceremonial purposes were not bodies which could take decisive action on Methodism or on anything else (on this point see N. Sykes, *From Sheldon to Secker*, Ch. VI).

The failure to act is not to be explained entirely by the absence of appropriate machinery. Not everything about Methodism could be brushed aside and condemned; much about it extracted (sometimes rather grudging) admiration. In the great features of Christian theology, it was orthodox. Secker, addressing his own clergy, observed that their only 'complete vindication' would be

to preach fully and frequently the doctrines which we are unjustly accused of casting off or undervaluing.

He also commended to them, rather obliquely, the example of the conduct of the Methodists:

Those who are forming new separations gain and preserve a surprising influence among their followers by personal religious intercourse.

In one great respect the Methodists did inaugurate a revival in Anglican practice – in the more frequent taking of Holy Communion. It was then customary to celebrate it three or four times a year. The Reverend William Grimshaw, a strange hybrid who was perpetual curate of Haworth between 1742 and 1763, and a Methodist of great influence and power at the same time, appeared before Archbishop Hutton of York in 1748. He stood accused of preaching outside his own parish. His report, however, that hundreds regularly presented themselves for Communion at Haworth brought the answer:

We cannot find fault with Mr Grimshaw, as he is instrumental in bringing such numbers to the Lord's Table.

Wesley, of course, exhorted his followers to take the sacrament at the parish church and on a number of occasions shepherded them there with immense satisfaction to himself. In Dublin in July 1789 he

desired as many as chose it of our society to go to St Patrick's [Cathedral] . . . and we had such a company of communicants as, I suppose, had scarce been seen there together for above a hundred years.

Nevertheless, Anglican criticism of Wesley is comprehensible, though it was often not so to Wesley. His movement upset the law, upset the Anglican way of doing things, tried to divert the current slant of Anglican theology, and even threatened what appeared to Anglicans to be the bases of society. The argument that souls were to be saved, and a confidence in the workings of Divine Providence, were doubtless sufficient to convince Wesley that he was right; they were not equally convincing to his critics. In this situation, Wesley's decisiveness deserted him. He foresaw a break between his societies and the Church, but he declined to anticipate it. Many influences – his upbringing, loyalty, and appreciation of tradition, and the markedly Anglican views of Charles – created in him a prejudice in favour of maintaining the links with the Church of England. Pressure from below, inside his own societies, pushed in a contrary direc-

tion. In refusing to face a breakaway, he was ignoring the
realities of the situation, and leaving behind a problem which
the Methodist Connexion was unable to solve for some years
after his death.

Bishop Gibson was the most distinguished ecclesiastical lawyer
to indicate the challenge that Methodism offered to the existing
law – as indeed he was to indicate the challenge it offered to
much else – in his *Observations upon the Conduct and Behaviour
of a Certain Sect usually distinguished by the Name of Methodists*
(1744). He pointed out that field-preaching was contrary to the
Conventicle Act of 1662. He noted their refusal to license their
preaching houses under the provisions of the Toleration Act of
1689, which would have given them legal protection – but as
Dissenters. Wesley was in a quandary here. His societies often
needed legal protection. J.P.s in some areas chose to operate the
law and break up unlicensed meetings; informers in some areas
obliged them to act. For Wesley to admit that the Connexion
was outside the Church of England was, however, for long very
objectionable. At length, in July 1790, Wesley tried to persuade
Wilberforce to speak to the Prime Minister, Pitt the Younger,
about this legal difficulty. It is not, however, known whether
this contact was made, and certainly nothing came of it.

Wesley also questioned the accepted conduct of worship in the
Church of England. He indeed venerated the Book of Common
Prayer – though that did not prevent his making a drastic
revision of it in 1784 – and for many years tried to insist that the
time of Methodist meetings did not coincide with the time of
services in the parish church. But what might now be regarded
as the inessentials of Anglican worship – and which in fact give
it so much of its character – were attacked directly, or at any
rate by implication, in the way he himself conducted things at
Methodist meeting houses. (Compare the account of the conduct
of services in church, p. 33, with that of services in chapels on
pp. 75–80.) The Anglican modes of singing hymns he considered
an insult to common sense. Wesleyan hymns were far different
in content from the familiar metrical psalms. The prepared and
read sermon of the Church of England clergyman was in sharp

contrast to the ecstatic utterances of Wesley's followers (if not
to those of Wesley himself). 'Enthusiasm', a frequent charge
against Methodism, was not essentially a question of manner.
It was 'a vain belief of private revelation; a vain confidence of
divine favour or communication.' Wesley understood it in this
way; so did Bishop Butler in his famous rebuke to Wesley:

Sir, the pretending to extraordinary revelations and gifts of the Holy
Spirit is a horrid thing: yes, sir, it is a very horrid thing.

Methodist emphasis on the sinfulness of man and his need for
redemption was unfashionable, and sharply in contrast with the
thought of that guide to all eighteenth-century clergymen,
Tillotson. Indeed, the revival of Puritan doctrines from the
previous age made many uncomfortable; so did Wesley's
credulity, which led to his retailing many stories of witches and
ghosts both in his Journal and in the *Arminian Magazine*.

'I look upon the whole world as my parish' is the most hack-
neyed of Wesley's quotations, but it needs to be considered not
merely as an example of his evangelical zeal, but as the major
reason why he was criticized by the Church of England. He
attacked the basic unit of Anglican organization. To Wesley a
resident incumbent was deeply objectionable on grounds of
ineffectiveness:

Be their talents ever so good, they will ere long grow dead themselves,
and so will most of them that hear them [he wrote to Samuel Walker
in 1756]. I know, were I myself to preach one whole year in one place,
I should preach both myself and most of my congregation asleep.
Nor can I believe it was ever the will of our Lord that any congregation should have one teacher only. We have found by a long and
constant experience that a frequent change of teacher is best. . . .

Once Wesley had decided this – and he assumed it for himself
from 1739, partly basing his legal right to preach in any parish
on his Fellowship of Lincoln College – then he became in one
sense a professional nuisance to the Anglican clergy, as did his
predecessors and imitators in the practice of itinerancy. Where
such men were Church of England clergymen – like Griffith Jones
at Laugharne, or Grimshaw at Haworth – they were summoned

before the ecclesiastical courts on the grounds of intruding in other parishes. The Wesleyan insistence on their followers attending Communion at the parish church caused particular difficulty. As it stood in the Book of Common Prayer, the Holy Communion was essentially a parish activity supervised by the incumbent. The rubrics at the beginning of the form of service assume his acquaintance with his parish, since they direct him to exclude 'evil livers' and those who live at enmity with one another. Clearly an incumbent could not stand in such a relationship with the Methodists flocking in from other parishes.

In a larger sense, Wesley was attacking the structure of society as well. Visibly, the Methodist meeting – either outside or in one of the new chapels with the sexes segregated and seated on benches on the principle of first come, first seated – was in as sharp a contrast as could be imagined to the hierarchically ordered congregation at the parish church, surrounded as it was with hatchments, memorials, and decorated pews. Less obviously, the attack on the parish was also an attack on the elaborate complex of property rights in which clergy and landowners shared (described on pp. 11–12). It was natural that the squires of England should resist Methodism, though their resistance seems to have been at the instinctive level of the squire of Pebworth in March 1768. Wesley wrote in his Journal:

The Vicar of Pebworth had given notice in the church on Sunday that I was to preach there on Friday. But the squire of the parish said 'It is contrary to the canons and it shall not be.' So I preached about a mile from it, at Broadmarston, by the side of Mr Eden's house.

The appointment of lay preachers, which Wesley undertook reluctantly from 1739 onwards, was necessary to the survival of the societies, since insufficient numbers of Church of England clergymen joined him. This step led to a series of difficulties which were insoluble without a division with the Church. In the first place it left him open to attack for employing illiterate men. Most Methodist preachers, Lackington wrote,

are very ignorant and extremely illiterate: many of these excellent spiritual guides cannot even read a chapter in the Bible.

This is a biased view, but Wesley felt the force of it, and tried to eliminate the criticism by laying down for his preachers a most rigorous course of training. In the second place, the appointment of laymen who had no previous strong connection with the Church of England and who could scarcely comprehend Wesley's entrenched pro-Anglican attitude was bound to lead to demands for secession. Warner has analysed the origins of sixty-three first-generation Methodist preachers: twenty-six of them were of Church of England background, but the overwhelming majority of them had in fact graduated from Methodist societies, and had been class leaders first, then exhorters, then local preachers, then itinerants.

Wesley strove to ensure that the functions of a lay preacher were confined to preaching and teaching and burying only. This careful restriction could never last, for two reasons: the demands of the rank and file Methodists themselves, and the demands of the preachers. Robert Currie has acutely observed (in *Methodism Divided*, 1968) that in the movement

the vertical chains of command, from member to leader, to preacher, to Wesley, became entangled with a horizontal pattern of Methodist life and Methodist chapels . . . the Methodist people created an earthly 'lasting city' of their own, the chapel, and increasingly regarded Wesley's proselytizing theocracy as a destruction or intrusion.

Many Methodists objected to attending the parish church if their reception was cool. Moreover, they often objected to receiving Communion from a man whose conduct they disliked in some particular. The wishes of the societies coincided with the natural professional desires of the preachers to extend their functions, especially in the matter of administering Holy Communion.

This pressure from below was visible not merely in the last few years of Wesley's life, but from the middle 1750s. In 1754 a preacher, Charles Perronet of Shoreham in Kent, administered the Communion in London to Methodist preachers and ordinary society members. John Wesley, who held Perronet in very high regard as a scholar, was not inclined to take action, and indeed seemed prepared to ordain preachers if they wished it. Charles, always the more resolute Anglican, was alarmed and sought support against his brother's position – in particular from Grimshaw of Haworth (the whole story is told by Frank Baker, *William Grimshaw*, Ch. 17). Grimshaw rehearsed the arguments against permitting lay preachers' administration of the Lord's Supper in a letter to one of his regular correspondents, Mrs Gallatin:

It is not expedient: because few of the clergy deny this sacrament to our people; nor is the reception of it from a carnal minister's hand any objection thereto; or any obstruction to the communicant's blessing, provided he receive in faith.

He furthered argued that such a step would result in a 'manifest rupture with the Established Church' which as a loyal minister of the Church he could not countenance.

In 1755 the Methodist Conference was called to Leeds, and was a victory for Charles and for Grimshaw. John briskly noted the result in his Journal with a certain lack of commitment. As to separation from the Church of England:

We were all fully agreed in that general conclusion, that (whether it was *lawful* or not) it was no ways *expedient*.

The issue did not rest there. Charles realized that John was not entirely to be depended upon, and continued to marshal his supporters; in particular Samuel Walker of Truro, and Grimshaw. The matter recurred in 1760 in a form similar to that of 1754–5. In that year, three lay preachers at work in Norwich, Paul Greenwood, Thomas Mitchell, and John Murlin, administered Communion. Charles, however, in a meeting of the London leaders, secured their enthusiastic support for remaining inside the Church, and the matter was dropped before the 1760 Conference at Bristol.

The critical decision in ensuring the breakaway has long been thought to be Wesley's appointment of a 'superintendent' and two 'elders' for service with his societies in America in 1784. Wesley, a priest, took it upon himself to appoint a man with the function of bishop (Coke) and two men with the function of priest (Whatcoat and Vasey). In doing so, he was assuming the functions of a bishop. He had long accepted the arguments of two earlier Anglican authorities, Stillingfleet and King, that the distinction between priest and bishop did not exist in the Primitive Church. In the crisis situation that was brought to Wesley's attention in 1784, however, he acted consciously against the rule of the Church of England.

When it could not be avoided without sacrificing some real good [wrote his admiring biographer Richard Watson in 1831], he did violate the established order, thinking that this order was in itself merely prudential.

A letter of Wesley from Bristol, dated 10 September 1784, set out the pressing circumstances which led to the appointments. The United States of America was newly independent; there were now no English bishops with any jurisdiction there. (Previous to Independence, the Bishop of London ordained clergymen for the colonies.) Methodist preachers had met with success in America, but now they had nobody to carry out baptism or administer Holy Communion. Wesley wrote:

Here therefore my scruples are at an end; and I conceive myself at full liberty, as I violate no order, and invade no man's right, by appointing and sending labourers into the harvest.

Anglicans have been increasingly preoccupied ever since the Oxford Movement with the problem of the validity of their orders, and hence with the details of ordinations; and unnecessary concentration has been given to these events of 1784. For one thing, they did not alter Wesley's own general practice in England, although he did appoint preachers to administer the sacraments in Scotland and in the colonies. In spite of pressure he normally refused to make such appointments for England:

I have still refused not only for peace's sake, but because I was determined as little as possible to violate the established order of the national church to which I belonged.

For another thing, the Church of England did not act against him in consequence of what happened in 1784. At the death of

John Wesley in 1791, therefore, the Connexion was still where he would have wished: inside the Church of England. Once his overwhelming authority was gone, the pressure to separate soon made itself felt. This pressure had been visible for more than forty years. John Wesley was not, as Halévy once wrote, 'driven from the Church of which he was an ordained priest'; at least, not by the Church. The Church did not like him; but the desires of his supporters, his own wish to preserve his movement, and his expressed and implied criticism of Anglican thought, habits, and procedures brought on the breakaway.

(See in particular on this problem N. Sykes and G. Rupp in *Conversations between the Church of England and the Methodist Church: an Interim Statement*, S.P.C.K. and Epworth Press, 1958; A. W. Harrison's lecture *The Separation of Methodism from the Church of England*, Epworth Press, 1945; E. W. Thompson, *John Wesley, Apostolic Man*, Epworth Press, 1957; and F. Baker, *John Wesley and the Church of England*, Epworth Press, 1970, especially Ch. XV.)

Further Reading

The *Pelican Guide to Modern Theology*, Vol. II (1969), pp. 302–6, gives an admirable critical bibliography on the theme of this chapter; it is compiled by J. H. S. Kent

Frank Baker, *William Grimshaw 1708–1763*. Epworth Press, 1962.
    John Wesley and the Church of England. Epworth Press, 1970.

R. Davies and G. Rupp, eds., *A History of the Methodist Church in Great Britain*, Vol. I. Epworth Press, 1966.

R. Davies, *Methodism*, Pelican, 1963.

M. Edwards, *John Wesley and the Eighteenth Century*. Epworth Press, 1934.

V. H. H. Green, *John Wesley*. Nelson, 1964.
    The Young Mr Wesley. Edward Arnold, 1961.

E. Halévy, *History of the English People in the Nineteenth Century*, Vol. I, Part III, Chapter I. Originally, in French, 1913; in English, Ernest Benn, 1924.
    The Birth of Methodism, ed. Bernard Semmel. University of Chicago Press, 1971.

I regret that this appeared after the present book was written. Professor Semmel has performed a great service by translating and republishing Halévy's articles, which appeared originally in the *Revue de Paris* in 1906, but which have not generally been taken into account by historians since. Halévy's articles are principally remarkable in their rather laboured attempt (pp. 62–73) to show that a political and economic crisis coincided exactly with the beginning of the Revival. Professor Semmel's introduction points out that the notion of Methodism as an antidote to revolution was not only elaborated in England from the 1790s onwards (as I have indicated on pp. 95ff.), but also asserted by French nineteenth-century writers like Taine and Guizot. It would, therefore, be well known to Halévy before he began his work in England.

R. Knox, *Enthusiasm*. Oxford University Press, 1950.

W. E. H. Lecky, *History of England in the Eighteenth Century*, Vol. III. Longmans, 1878.

David Martin, *A Sociology of English Religion*. S.C.M. Press, 1967.

Harold Perkin, *The Origins of Modern English Society 1780–1880*. Routledge, 1969.

M. Schmidt, *John Wesley: A Theological Biography*, Vol. I. Epworth Press, 1963.

R. Southey, *Life of Wesley (1819)*, ed. M. H. Fitzgerald. Oxford University Press, 1925.

E. P. Thompson, *The Making of the English Working Class*. Gollancz, 1963; Pelican, 1968. The Pelican edition has an important postscript.

W. J. Warner, *The Wesleyan Movement in the Industrial Revolution*. Longmans, 1930.

R. F. Wearmouth, *Methodism and the Common People of the Eighteenth Century*. Epworth Press, 1945.

Bryan Wilson, *Religion in Secular Society*. Pelican, 1966.

Note on Wesley's own Works

Wesley's *Journal* has appeared in many editions: the standard (but least portable) one is edited by Nehemiah Curnock, 8 vols., Epworth Press, 1909–16. His *Works*, substantially as edited by Thomas Jackson, were last printed in Michigan in 1958 (Zondervan, 14 vols.). His *Sermons* were edited by E. H. Sugden (Epworth Press, 2 vols., 1921) and his *Letters* by John Telford in 8 vols. (Epworth Press, 1931).

The Origins and Development of Methodism (to 1791)

The Notions of 'Societies'

The formation of societies within the Church to invigorate spiritual and philanthropic life – which, in some senses, Methodism was – began during the period of the Restoration

1678. Anthony Horneck instituted a society in London for Anglicans resolved on 'a holy and serious life'

1680. *The Country Parson's Advice to his Parishioners* advertised the merits of these societies

1699. The Society for the Reformation of Manners established The Society for Promoting Christian Knowledge instituted for the circulation of Christian literature and promotion of schools

1701. The Society for the Propagation of the Gospel – particularly in the colonies

The Insistence on Conversion and New Forms of Evangelistic Preaching

These were not characteristic of Methodism alone and appeared variously in Wales, in the American Colonies, in Germany, and in England. By 1739 some links had been made between similar movements in all these areas

1710. Griffith Jones, curate of Laugharne, began itinerant preaching

1727. Conversion experiences among the Moravian Brethren at Berthelsdorf, Saxony; their missionary activity began in England (1728) and in Georgia (1735)

1728. William Law's *Serious Call to a Devout and Holy Life* – it had considerable effects in stimulating conversion

1734. Beginning of Jonathan Edwards' Revival in Northampton, Massachusetts

1735. Conversion of George Whitefield in Oxford, of Daniel Rowland in Cardiganshire, and of Howell Harris at Talgarth, Brecon
The Wesleys departed for Georgia – and met the Moravians

1738. John Wesley returned from Georgia
John Wesley converted

1739. Whitefield began field-preaching

The Evolution of Methodism in John Wesley's Lifetime

1739. Wesley began field-preaching at Moorfields, Bristol, at White-field's invitation. First lay preacher appointed

1742. Introduction of the system of 'classes' at Bristol – groups of twelve formed, originally as a means of fund-raising, but rapidly adapted by Wesley for religious and social purposes

1744. First Methodist Conference – a body merely to advise Wesley. It met anually and its duties were further defined by the Deed of Declaration in 1784

1746. The first six 'rounds' or circuits existed

1748. Beginning of Quarterly Meetings

1755. The Leeds Conference made the first decision on whether to permit Methodist preachers to administer Communion or not – against

1760. Greenwood, Mitchell, and Murlin (Methodist preachers in Norwich) administered Communion. Condemned by Charles Wesley and the London leaders

1774. Wesley's *Thoughts on Slavery*

1775–83. American War of Independence
Wesley's attitude was anti-American: *Calm Address to the American Colonies*, 1775; *Observations on Liberty*, 1776; *Calm Address to the Inhabitants of Great Britain*, 1776

1780. *A Collection of Hymns for the Use of the People called Methodists* (Collections had appeared at various times since 1737)

1784. Deed of Declaration
Wesley was by 1784 faced with two major problems: that of the succession to himself, and that in the future trustees of individual chapels might choose preachers who would not have been approved by him. By this Deed, Wesley constituted a 'Legal Hundred' to form the Methodist Conference and under-take specific duties, including the approval of preachers and expulsion of members where necessary

1784. Wesley appointed a 'superintendent' and two 'elders' for service with his societies in America. This is held by some to be the decisive break between Methodism and the Church of England, though Wesley did not regard it as such, and justified the 'ordinations' on ground of necessity

1791. Death of John Wesley

PART III
The Rise of Evangelicalism

Methodism burst the essential framework and order of the Church of England, and under the government of John Wesley assumed an orthodox Arminianism in doctrine. Not all the eighteenth-century revivalists took these directions. Many of them, Church of England clergymen converted by contact with Wesley and Whitefield, or by reading, or by their acquaintances, chose to stay inside the Church and therefore to operate inside their own parishes. This confinement to working inside one parish was a rule of church order on which the bishops were usually prepared to insist. Another mark of an Evangelical Church of England clergyman was his resistance to the employment of lay preachers, especially in the administration of Communion. Many, following their own or Whitefield's convictions, were Calvinist; and indeed what was called 'moderate Calvinism' was the standard doctrine of the Church of England Evangelical. In some senses, both theologically and socially, they were uncommonly conservative – they insisted that their doctrine was that of the Reformation, and referred frequently to the Prayer Book, the Thirty-nine Articles, and the Book of Homilies, the official sermons produced for the Elizabethan clergy. The very fact that they had chosen to work within the existing parochial system, so very much under the control of the gentry, meant that they had to control any tendency to social radicalism or do without any kind of preferment. They were at first thinly scattered over the country and depended on pious laymen for their advancement. At length, towards the end of the eighteenth century, this hitherto insignificant group secured both lay and clerical leadership of great influence, wealth, and determination. With Wilberforce in Parliament, and Charles Simeon at Cambridge – both of them in their respective places for a generation – the movement became a powerful element in politics, a 'party' in the Church of England, and the propagator of most of the essentials of Victorianism. Its rise from obscurity to dominance is the theme of this section.

[12] THE EARLY EVANGELICALS

Names of pioneer Evangelical clergymen are usually linked with the parishes they served – Berridge of Everton, Adam of Winteringham, Walker of Truro, Haweis of Aldwincle, Newton of Olney, and so on. The obscurity of the parishes reflects the obscurity of the men. There was no indication until the 1780s that their movement would emerge from this position. It did not even possess a uniformity of view, save in holding the doctrine of justification by faith. Most were Calvinist; but Adam of Winteringham (1701–84) was an Arminian. Samuel Walker of Truro was adamant in staying inside the bounds of his parish, and objected to any notion of the Methodists of permitting lay preachers to administer Holy Communion; but John Berridge (1716–93), a Cambridge don who accepted the living of Everton in Bedfordshire in 1755, was equally insistent that to save souls he had to be a 'riding pedlar' called by his Master 'to serve near forty shops [parishes] in the country beside his own parish'.

Conventionally the inspiration and founder of this group of churchmen is considered to be Wesley, and if not Wesley, then Whitefield. George Whitefield, born in the Bell Inn at Gloucester in 1714 and after leaving school 'a common drawer' at the inn 'for nigh a year and a half', was educated at Pembroke College, Oxford, and converted in 1735. He was a late entrant to the Holy Club, and was ordained deacon by the Bishop of Gloucester in 1735, and priest in 1739. He immediately established himself

as a popular missionary preacher. Having been dissuaded from
joining Wesley in Georgia in 1736, he at length set out for the
colony in 1738 just as Wesley was returning. In Georgia, Whitefield was eminently successful, and the setting up of an Orphan
House and its maintenance and expansion in Savannah became
one of the main aims of his life. Henceforth, he was celebrated
both in the British Isles and in the American Colonies – he crossed
the Atlantic thirteen times – and died in America in 1770.

His position in the history of the Evangelical movement is
difficult to estimate. It is easy to show that he anticipated Wesley
in many of his techniques: he preached outdoors (in February
1739) before Wesley did; he issued an instalment of his Journal
(in 1739) before Wesley issued his; he began the publication of a
regular periodical, his *Christian History*, in 1740; he called his
first Conference of Calvinistic Methodists at Caerphilly in 1743,
the year before Wesley's first. Whitefield was indeed the man
who did most to create the image of the Methodist preacher. It
was 'Dr Squintum' – measles in childhood had left him with a
squint – with his great voice, the simplicity of his manner, his
dramatic effect, his vanity, and his constant appeals for money
for his tabernacles or his orphanage, who attracted the satirists.
He shared some of Wesley's social attitudes, and expressed them
with great simplicity and force.

Nothing tries my temper more [he said in his sermon on 'Soul Prosperity'] than to see any about me idle; an idle person tempts the devil
to tempt him . . . if anybody says the Methodists teach to be idle, they
injure them. We tell people to be at their work early and late, that
they may redeem time to attend the word. If all that speak against
the Methodists were as diligent, it would be better for their wives
and families. What, do you think a true Methodist will be idle?

On other things he disagreed. Wesley, as we have seen, was
instinctively anti-aristocratic; Whitefield was not. On the title
pages to his various works, Whitefield appears as 'Chaplain to
the Rt Hon. the Countess of Huntingdon'. This was Selina
Hastings (1707–91), and the acquaintance of the two was an
important one for the future of Evangelicalism. First, Selina was

a countess, and could appoint chaplains; in that way she supported a number of the new 'enthusiasts' like William Romaine and Henry Venn, as well as Whitefield. Secondly, she had money and could start ecclesiastical foundations. Her theological college, Trevecca, was founded in 1768; she also built chapels in places deliberately chosen to attract the more fashionable classes – at Brighton, Tunbridge, and London, for example. It was her proposal to build one in Spa Fields in 1779 that was successfully opposed in the Consistory Court of the diocese of London and obliged her and her connexion to seek the protection of the Toleration Act – to go over into Dissent. Thirdly, she launched from her drawing room a mission to the fashionable world, which came to hear her chaplains preach. Her successes were modest, but her methods remained as an indication of how a future generation would secure greater successes for Evangelicalism.

Whatever inspiration Whitefield might have given to the early Evangelicals, he was not a good model to those English parochial clergymen who sympathized with him. In England, in the American Colonies, and in Scotland, Whitefield repeatedly refused to be bound by any rule which obliged him to preach in a particular church or to be bound by a particular liturgy.

I do not care whether you go to church or meeting [he said in his sermon on 'Spiritual Baptism']. I am, I confess, a member of the Church of England, and if they will not let me preach in the church, I will preach anywhere; all the world is my parish, and I will preach wherever God gives me opportunity, but you will never find me disputing about the outward appendages of religion; do not tell me you are a Baptist, an Independent, a Presbyterian, a Dissenter; tell me you are a Christian, that is all I want . . .

Bad models or not, Wesley and Whitefield both had a critical impact on the Evangelical Revival, even if they did not begin it. They were the principal exponents and publicists of its methods; they inspired and to a certain extent unified its activities; they were national figures. The Journal and the correspondence of Wesley indicate quite clearly that he was an observer of the whole Revival in England, in person or by collecting others' accounts; that he encouraged many of the preachers and was in

controversy with others; and that he often took over the converts
and societies that others had made. But how did Evangelicalism
spread inside the Church of England?

The answer to this problem is ordinarily given in biographical
terms, working on the principle of James Stephen in his celebrated essay *The Evangelical Succession*:

The history of all the great moral renovations of any large bodies of
mankind is indeed nothing else than a series of the biographies of men
bearing a general resemblance to John Newton.

The exercise of bringing together all the Evangelicals and giving
a potted biography of each has several times been attempted
since Stephen's time, and from such work it is possible to discern
a solution.

The process of individual conversion (which all these clergymen shared) came about partly by reading contemporary works
like Law's *Serious Call*, as Thomas Adam had done, or works
by seventeenth-century Puritans, like Owen's *On Justification*,
on which Grimshaw had depended. More usually it was a matter
of personal contact. Conon, a schoolmaster of Truro, converted
Samuel Walker. George Thompson, Vicar of St Genny's in
Cornwall, converted his near neighbour, John Bennett of
Tamerton. Henry Venn was converted after undertaking a
preaching tour with Whitefield. Sometimes a personal crisis
produced the appropriate frame of mind – James Hervey was
recuperating from illness in 1738. It could be a combination of
all these circumstances. John Newton (who as Curate of Olney,
1764–80, and Rector of St Mary Woolnoth, 1780–1807, enjoyed a
more influential role than many of his Evangelical contemporaries) was impressed first by reading Thomas à Kempis and
afterwards sought advice from Wesley, Whitefield, Grimshaw,
and Berridge. Nor was conversion necessarily an instantaneous
procedure. Grimshaw was first affected in 1734, but did not
reach a condition of full assurance until 1744. First of all he was
ashamed of some vain advice he gave to parents whose baby had
died – 'get into company and divert yourselves'. Five years later
he suffered great emotional distress and inclination to suicide on

the death of his first wife. His tension was relieved and his faith restored by turning to Owen's *On Justification*. He is said to have felt a flash in his face as he picked up the book, and another on opening it. Finally, in 1744, he was taken ill at a religious meeting, and in a state of semi-consciousness saw Heaven and Hell.

Conversion provided the essential dynamic; but as with Methodism, so with Evangelicalism – organization mattered. The Evangelical clergymen reinvigorated the church life of their parishes by a great number of institutions and devices, and often by unremitting hard work. Preaching is always regarded as the great *sine qua non* of Evangelical practice. Energy and eccentricity made some of the early leaders into legends. Grimshaw at Haworth used 'market-language', or homely expression, to impress his congregations:

They who have this God for theirs shall never want a pound of butter for eightpence or three pints of blue milk for a halfpenny as long as they live.

Berridge at Everton had the same plainness; Lecky's judgement of him was that he was 'eccentric almost to insanity'. Great eloquence was not uniformly characteristic of the Evangelicals; an account of Berridge and his colleague Hicks, quoted in Wesley's Journal, observes that 'neither of these gentlemen have much eloquence, but seem rather weak in speech', though Wesley himself admitted that Berridge's 'word was with power'. John Venn's son thought that his father 'had no address as a public speaker' and that 'his delivery wanted animation and relief'. John Newton, on the evidence presented by Sir James Stephen, is said to have

appeared perhaps to least advantage in the pulpit, as he did not generally aim at accuracy in the composition of his sermons, nor to any address in the delivery of them. His utterance was far from clear, and his attitudes ungraceful.

The author of these critical remarks also said of Cadogan of Reading that he had 'a scowling sort of aspect' and that his utterance was 'rather indistinct, and at times unpleasantly monotonous', though his sermons had some passion and urgency.

Nevertheless, good preachers or bad, the Evangelicals set aside a great deal of time for preaching.

Preaching, however, is a time-honoured method: the innovations were more striking. When Newton became curate of Olney, he initiated early-morning prayer meetings, Bible classes, 'classes for young people and enquirers', children's meetings 'to reason with them and explain the scriptures in their own little way', as well as meetings in various houses of the parish. When Henry Venn, after a zealous incumbency of Huddersfield between 1759 and 1771, moved to Yelling in Huntingdonshire, he held 'kitchen meetings' in the parsonage; and the opening up of family prayers to parishioners became a common practice among Evangelicals. In visiting parishioners (and having parishioners visit them) many of these men set incredibly high standards. At Clapham, with Henry Venn's son, John, as rector (1792–1814) and a distinguished coterie of lay sympathizers resident in the parish, a Society for Bettering the Condition of the Poor of a very sophisticated kind was set up in 1799. The society consisted of thirty members, who met monthly to drink tea in each other's houses, and to determine the business of the society. The parish was divided into eight districts. Visitors operated in each of these and they met regularly to determine the aid which should be given, and in what form, to those who needed it. The society even undertook the vaccination of the entire parish in 1800, just after Jenner introduced the process.

Two features familiar to students of Methodism also account in part for the rise of Evangelicalism: concentration upon hymn singing, and the energetic writing and circulation of devotional literature. John Newton introduced a new hymn at each of his Tuesday evening prayer meetings. Some he wrote himself, but many were written by his diffident parishioner, William Cowper, whose *Olney Hymns* originated in this way. Berridge emphasized the strategic importance of hymns in a letter to Wesley in 1759. He was writing of those 'with convictions'.

At first they only sing; afterwards they join reading, and prayer to singing; and the presence of the Lord is greatly with them. . . . At Orwell two people were broken down in one night, only by having a few people sing hymns. At Grandchester, a mile from Cambridge, seventeen people were seized with strong convictions last week, only by having a few people sing hymns.

John Venn at Clapham collected and published various versions of the psalms as well as hymns. The literature of Evangelicalism became immense: sermons by their leaders were reprinted regularly for a century, and works like Thomas Adam's *Private Thoughts on Religion*, Henry Venn's complete *Duty of Man*, and Scott's *Force of Truth* appeared by the thousand to ensure the continuance of Evangelical attitudes.

The early Evangelicals were conscious of their isolation and consequent weakness. Some of them indeed were not afraid of travelling huge distances for spiritual comfort. Samuel Walker once went from Truro to the south bank of the Humber to discuss his perplexities over the burial service with Thomas Adam at Winteringham. The normal solution to the problems of isolation, however, was to form a club. Walker's Clerical Club of 1750 seems to have been the first. Some half-dozen clergymen in West Cornwall, of similar opinions, came together monthly. These clubs for 'gospel ministers' were to be found afterwards in various parts of the kingdom, and it became *de rigueur* for an incoming Evangelical minister to form such a group. Henry Venn formed one during his time at Huddersfield in 1767, which was transferred to Elland by his former curate and is still extant as a society for the encouragement and financing of ordination candidates. The subjects were much concerned with increasing the efficiency of the parochial ministry – preaching, the formation of religious societies, and the visiting and 'inspection' of parishioners were standard subjects of discussion. These 'serious' clubs were in contrast with meetings of Anglican clergy generally. The commonest such meetings, for official visitations, were legal in intention and often convivial in practice, as may be seen in Woodforde's *Diary* or, more satirically, in a famous essay in Goldsmith's *Citizen of the World*. (Michael Hennell has a good account of clerical societies in his *John Venn and the Clapham Sect*, pp. 83–8 and Appendix B.)

Whitefield found himself an aristocratic patroness, and he

thereby indicated to his sympathizers another important way forward. The landed gentleman who was 'saved' had livings to fill and influence to exert. The Hill family, predominant in Shropshire, placed Fletcher at Madeley; the Earl of Dartmouth, one of the Countess of Huntingdon's converts, secured Huddersfield for Henry Venn, Leicester for Robinson, Hotham for Stillingfleet, Dewsbury for Powley, and Olney for Newton. The revivalist clergymen themselves were sometimes not without aristocratic relations: Cadogan was preferred to St Giles's, Reading, by the Crown in 1774, and by his grandfather, Lord Cadogan, to St Luke's, Chelsea, in 1775. Though he caused consternation by immediately dismissing his Evangelical curate at Reading, he himself became 'serious', and his funeral sermon was preached by Charles Simeon.

The first generation of Evangelicals, however, scarcely did more than make a slight entry into high society. When Berridge stayed in London at the Countess of Huntingdon's invitation, he 'expounded' every morning and evening for her, and spoke also at the houses of Lady Gertrude Hotham and Lady Fanny Shirley; but when he was at home in Cambridgeshire, his audience and helpers were more rustic. He reported to his fellow-Evangelical Martin Madan that:

My squire swears he will do my business; and last Lord's Day evening when I came from church, he stopped me and called me by the usual names of enthusiast etc., etc. Today I hear that the Squire has sent for such tenants as are disposed to hear the word of God, and has given them warning to leave their farms directly.

A report of 1812 suggests that Berridge had other supporters than tenant farmers:

in a barn at Waterbeach . . . was a numerous seminary of the disciples of Mr Berridge of Clare Hall, called from him 'Berridges', and who to this day send out preachers, gardeners, collar-makers, shopkeepers, etc., into many of the adjacent villages.

Georgian Evangelicals, in fact, appealed to the high and the low; Victorian Evangelicalism principally to the middle.

By the 1780s, then, it is possible to discern the aggressive principles on which the Evangelicals would act. As yet, though, there were two weaknesses: their temptation to strain at the parochial discipline of the Church of England (as has been observed), and the difficulty of ensuring that once a 'serious' incumbent was dead his message would be carried on. Canon Charles Smyth, in his *Simeon and Church Order*, and especially in his account there of Cadogan of Reading, has elucidated this point. If the continuity of a 'gospel ministry' could not be guaranteed, the congregation was tempted to go outside the Church of England in search of it. The Reverend William Talbot had already established Evangelicalism at St Giles's when Cadogan succeeded him in 1774: Cadogan was not then a sympathizer. The congregation therefore dispersed, to seek sermons more to their liking, and to set up a chapel in the Countess of Huntingdon's Connexion. Cadogan at length re-established an Evangelical tradition, and all was well until his death in 1797. Again, a considerable section departed and set up another chapel. Developments of this kind were sufficiently widespread to make it clear that continuity was a major problem, and that a drift towards Dissent was possible. In the next generation, these and other questions facing Evangelicalism were to have their solution.

[13]   THE CLAPHAM SECT

In *The Newcomes* Thackeray pictured an Evangelical at the time of the Napoleonic Wars: Sophia Alethea Newcome, who had been christened by Whitefield. Her father was a cloth factor, and she was worth a quarter of a million. She lived in a 'serious paradise' at Clapham, surrounded by lawns and gardens, pineries, graperies, aviaries, luxuries of all kinds. Her concerns were with business and good causes:

to manage the great house of Hobson and Newcome; to attend to the interests of the enslaved negro; to awaken the benighted Hottentot to a sense of the truth; to convert Jews, Turks, Infidels and Papists; to arouse the indifferent and often blasphemous mariner; to guide the washerwoman in the right way; to head the public charities of her sect; and to do a thousand kindnesses that none knew of. . . .

These causes are those associated with the Clapham Sect – a group whose historic functions were not merely the abolition of slavery, but also (building upon the foundations already laid) to impose upon much of English society a new set of governing ideals. This group of second-generation Evangelicals differed from the first in a variety of ways: they were wealthy, they were close to those with political power, they were unbelievably well-informed on the subjects they took up, and they understood the techniques of political persuasion. The changes in political thought brought about by the Revolutionary and Napoleonic Wars assisted them enormously. At the same time, their attitudes and achievements depended greatly on those of the first generation. Whitefield had sought to reach the higher ranks of society; Whitefield and Wesley had created a public, and Wesley had provided a national organization on which the great campaigns of the Clapham Sect could depend for countrywide support. Most of the early Evangelicals had demonstrated the need for machinery – for societies at every level – to make their work effective. Above all, the dynamic was the same – conversion and conviction. To attribute the success of the Clapham Sect merely to acumen, influence, money, or lack of scruple (which has been done from their own day to ours) is a misreading of history and a distortion of their motives.

The Clapham Sect was a group which collected round Henry Thornton, a celebrated banker. In 1786 Thornton met William Wilberforce (1759–1833); both were young M.P.s, and Thornton's father, John, was Wilberforce's uncle. Thornton took up residence in Clapham (where his boyhood had been spent) in 1792. He enlarged his house, Battersea Rise, and built two houses adjoining. Battersea Rise – with its oval library, constructed to the design of Edward Elliott, Pitt's brother-in-law – became the Sect's strategic headquarters. Other principal members were Charles Grant, Sir John Shore, Zachary Macaulay, James Stephen, Thomas Clarkson, William Smith, and John Venn, the Vicar of Clapham. These men were only the nucleus of the group, however. Others with close sympathies and ties included a parliamentary block of about twenty, known as the 'Saints'; Thomas Gisbourne, a Staffordshire clergyman; Isaac Milner, President of Queens' College, Cambridge, and Dean of Carlisle, who had converted Wilberforce; Thomas Babington of Rothley Temple, Leicestershire; Hannah More, once an ornament of London literary society and now concerned with more serious pursuits; and the ageing pioneer of the anti-slavery campaign, Granville Sharp.

Together they formed a group of considerable influence and range. Their wealth was huge, and at the service of Evangelical causes. Thornton gave away up to £7,500 a year before his marriage, and between two and three thousand pounds a year after it. Wilberforce, who married the daughter of an Evangelical banker of Birmingham and was himself the head of a large commercial house of Hull, had an income which at its height was as much as £30,000 a year. Their range of interests was considerable, and was reflected in the causes they championed. John Shore, who became Lord Teignmouth, had succeeded Cornwallis as Governor-General of India. Charles Grant made his name in India and became Chairman of the Court of Directors of the East India Company in 1794. Stephen had practised as a lawyer in St Kitts, and in Barbados had seen a negro tried and burned alive; Macaulay had been the overseer of an estate in Jamaica.

The political power of the group, and its identification with what Cobbett called the 'Pitt System' was obvious. Wilberforce was a close friend of Pitt, and, after Wilberforce's conversion, it was Pitt who suggested that he take up the abolition of the slave trade – though he knew the inclination was already there. As well as having the ear of the Prime Minister, Wilberforce had obvious advantages. He was M.P. for Yorkshire from 1784 to 1812. His oratory was impressive, and probably more remarkable on account of his appearance, accurate accounts of which are not easy to come by. Sir James Stephen wrote of his body being 'but a caricature of the human frame divine'; and the French visitor Louis Simond in 1811 wrote that he was 'as thin as a shadow and drawing one side of his body after him as if paralytic'. His contacts in society were with the very highest, even if conversion made him set out to big houses with the deliberate intention of using 'launchers', as he called them – that is, contrived openings to divert the conversation to serious subjects. Some gifts associated with the success of his campaigns Wilberforce personally did not have. Though the author of an astonishingly successful pamphlet, he wrote only with great difficulty; he appears also to have been extremely disorderly in the keeping of his papers. These defects were made good largely by Zachary Macaulay and Thomas Clarkson, whose skill in collecting information and in clerical work was amazing.

Inevitably, the work of the Clapham Sect has been viewed as a conspiracy. The frequent 'cabinet councils' at Battersea Rise, the care taken over matters of timing in their campaigns, the deliberate stating of aims, the distribution of money and propaganda, all support this impression. 'Well, Henry, what shall we abolish next?' Wilberforce asked Thornton when they were chatting at the end of the last debate of the anti-slavery struggle. The latest interpretation of the 'Age of Wilberforce' views them very much as plotters (see Ford K. Brown, *Fathers of the Victorians*).

The aims of the Clapham Sect might be thought of as those Wilberforce expressed as his own in 1787:

God Almighty has set before me two great objects – the abolition of the slave trade and the reformation of manners.

At that time, he was specific. The attack on the trade was about to be launched. He had just secured by his influence a Royal Proclamation against Vice and Immorality, and had formed a Proclamation Society to put the proclamation into effect by attempting to check indecent literature, enforce Sunday observance, and so on. But the Evangelical scheme was much larger. Earlier that year Wilberforce had written:

There is needed some reformer of the nation's morals, who should raise his voice in the high places of the land, and do within the Church, and nearer the throne, what Wesley has accomplished in the meeting, and amongst the multitude

– a scheme which he was eminently fitted to carry out. The progress of events, and the interests of the various members of the Sect, added other planks to their platform: the conversion of the heathen (especially, perhaps, in India); the propagation of 'gospel Christianity' among the lower orders as well as among the upper; a measure of church reform, largely against pluralism and non-residence; limited schemes of philanthropy and education; and an aggressive programme to strengthen the Evangelical party inside the Church of England.

The conservative political climate brought about by the French Wars greatly conditioned their aims and assisted their activities. The general approval of the early events of the Revolution was sharply checked by the appearance of Burke's *Reflections on the Revolution in France* in October 1790. Burke was no Evangelical, of course, but the *Reflections* contained a defence of the Established Church as a partner in the Constitution, a partner necessary to consecrate the workings of the State. The later proceedings of the revolutionaries strengthened this (as well as many other) arguments of the book, and the governing classes were disposed to look more favourably upon Christianity and upon the existing Establishment. But the church Burke defended was the unreformed Church of England, whose doctrines appeared so cool to the Evangelicals. Wilberforce set out to win the support of the governing classes for 'vital Christianity' – at a time when Britain appeared to be in maximum danger. In 1797, he produced his *Practical View of the Prevailing Religious System of Professed Christians in the higher and middle Classes in this country, contrasted with Real Christianity*. The timing of it was not accidental. Wilberforce had long contemplated such a book, but had declined to publish anything of the kind since the classes he meant to impress would not then have liked it: 'The dread of an over-righteous man would deter people from co-operating with me for national reform.' When the book did appear, it had a huge sale. It recommended itself to the 'higher and middle classes' by rejecting at least the externals of Methodism:

There will be no capricious humours, no moroseness, no discourtesy, no affected severity of deportment, no peculiarity of language, no indolent neglect, no wanton breach, of the ordinary forms and fashions of society.

Christianity also had a social function attractive to Wilberforce's readers:

moderating the insolence of power, she renders the inequalities of the social state less galling to the lower orders, whom also she instructs.

The doctrines commended in the *Practical View*, however, were those of the Evangelical Revival. The crisis of society, it was argued, was moral rather than political. All were 'frail, corrupt and fallen creatures'. A kind of religious radicalism was therefore allied to political conservatism – an accusation Wilberforce had often to bear. The object of his activities was conversion, and the French revolutionaries, in a paradoxical way, were his allies. As V. Kiernan observes: 'Jacobinism, which abolished the Christian calendar in France, helped to establish the Victorian Sabbath in England' (see his article, 'Evangelicalism and the French Revolution', in *Past and Present*, February 1952).

[14] SLAVERY

In the public mind, the victorious anti-slavery agitation was the principal achievement of the Clapham Sect. The campaign was launched in 1787; the abolition of the slave trade in the British Empire was accomplished in 1807; the abolition of slavery itself followed in 1833. In establishing the fame of Wilberforce, in asserting the influence of Evangelicalism, and in determining the essential direction of Evangelical thought in relation to the Empire, it was decisive. The triumph of the campaign is not only to be accounted for by the talents and contacts of Wilberforce and the Sect. It was in part the result of skilful and dedicated publicity on an increasingly receptive public, in part the result of profound economic change in Great Britain and in the West

Indies, and in part the result of increasing difficulty in administering the West Indies. The success of the campaign in fact coincided with the decline of the West Indian interest.

The trade which was destroyed was impressive in its volume, in its importance to the whole economy, and in its parliamentary weight – at any rate in the 1780s. The trade was part of the 'triangle' linking Great Britain, West Africa, and the West Indies. Textiles, beads, gunpowder, iron, and alcohol were exported to West Africa. Slaves were taken on there for the 'Middle Passage' to the West Indies, where, if time permitted, sugar and rum were taken on for the voyage to Britain. About thirty-five thousand slaves a year were being taken to the West Indies in the 1780s. The prosperity of Liverpool, and, less exclusively, of Bristol and Glasgow, was closely involved. Indeed, the interests concerned were incredibly wide – the sugar refiners (whose plant was in Britain) obviously enough, but also the textile manufacturers of the North, the gunsmiths of Birmingham, the iron manufacturers, the bankers, and slave owners as various as the Society for the Propagation of the Gospel and Lord St Vincent. (Dr Eric Williams has traced these ramifications in great detail: see his *Capitalism and Slavery*, paperback edition, André Deutsch, 1964, pp. 85–107.) The trade was defended by Nelson and Rodney as a 'nursery of seamen' – though the Middle Passage was hard on white seamen as well as negro slaves. Anything which expanded the total volume of shipping was to be excused. Moreover, other European countries found the trade profitable; it would, as many government apologists for the trade were to declare, be putting Britain in a weak position *vis-à-vis* her competitors to abolish it without their doing the same. As powerful as all these things was the legal and conventional attitude which made property – even if it was human – sacred.

Slavery was already a public issue when Wilberforce took it up on the advice of Lady Middleton and with the encouragement of Pitt. Granville Sharp had been successful in securing a judgment in the Somersett Case (1772) which made slavery in Britain unlawful; Wesley, Adam Smith, and Dr Johnson had all discussed the matter; the Quaker Committee of Six had been formed in 1783 and was already circulating tracts; Thomas Clarkson had already written his university prize essay on slavery, his principal obsession. Across the Atlantic, the sugar planters faced a deepening crisis after the American War. The great plantations in the older sugar islands like Jamaica were becoming exhausted, and their sugar more expensive to produce in comparison with that grown on the more recently developed French plantations of Saint Domingue. In 1775 Jamaica had 775 plantations; by 1791, out of every hundred of these, twenty-three had been sold for debt, twelve were in the hands of receivers, and seven had been abandoned. The British West India planters were twenty million pounds in debt. In 1788, Saint Domingue's exports were double those of Jamaica. The independence of the United States left the British West Indies trade pattern in confusion. Normally, the British islands had exported molasses to New England, and in turn depended upon the Thirteen Colonies for necessaries like grain and fish. Now the Americans – with the Navigation Laws operating against them – conducted their trade principally with the foreign West Indian islands.

In Britain, investigations began in 1787. Clarkson visited the slave ports; Pitt instructed the trade committee of the Privy Council to report on the slave trade. The introduction of the matter into Parliament, at first delayed by Wilberforce's severe illness, took place after the trade committee reported in 1789 – but no progress was made then, or in 1791, towards abolition. The rejection of 1791 stimulated the campaign which initiated so many of the techniques of modern political persuasion. The agitators had the advantage of an incredibly emotional subject. Pamphlets appeared by the thousand. The appropriate parliamentary debates were reprinted. Wedgwood produced a cameo for the campaign bearing the figure of an imploring negro and the inscription 'Am I not a man and a brother?', which also appeared on hairpins and snuffboxes. Corresponding Committees were set up. Petitions were organized and timed to arrive at Westminster as the subject was renewed in Parliament; 312 came in from England, and 187 from Scotland. Clarkson travelled the country, as became usual with him. He encouraged sympathizers to boycott West Indian sugar, and claimed that three hundred thousand gave up using it in 1792.

The debates of 1792, and afterwards, were like all else affected by the progress of the French Revolution. Wilberforce, both emotional and statistical in his speeches, could not (in spite of Pitt's support) counter the alarm provoked by violent slave disturbances inside French colonies. Clarkson faced considerable suspicion, as he was by no means anti-Jacobin in his views, and had spent some time in Paris in 1789, impressing his opinions on slavery on Mirabeau. His consorting with the London Corresponding Society caused Pitt to send an anguished little message to Wilberforce: 'What business had your friend Clarkson to attend the "Crown and Anchor" last Thursday?' The changes in Pitt's administration in 1794, bringing in the Portland Whigs, also stiffened the opposition to Wilberforce. Nothing, in wartime, could be allowed to weaken the mercantile marine. The volume of the slave trade was in any case diminishing as the war progressed: 26,971 slaves were taken to the West Indies from Africa in 1792: by 1795 the figure was 7,157.

Some of the changes which took place during the war, however, played into Wilberforce's hands. The Act of Union of 1800 brought in Irish members who sympathized with him. The capture of Caribbean islands from foreign countries meant that the British West India planters had an ambivalent view of the slave trade; fresh supplies of slaves would develop rival islands. Trade in all goods taken together increased during the war – but the slave trade was a less significant part of the whole. Moreover, the anti-slavery movement was not an exclusively British phenomenon, and there was a prospect that the whole traffic might be ended by international agreement at the next peace congress. Even the death of Pitt early in 1806 was an asset to the movement. Despite his personal commitment, he never agreed to make the issue government business; and certainly the appearance of Fox and Grenville, both dedicated abolitionists, resulted in the rapid introduction and passing of the Act (1807) which abolished the trade from 1 January 1808.

The ultimate achievement of 1833 – abolition of slavery by statute – was not contemplated in 1807. A number of circumstances kept the issue alive, however. The Act of 1807 had to be enforced, and the Evangelicals acted as watchdogs. Their aspirations for the negroes were in any case wider than just the securing of a statute from the British Parliament: they wanted international abolition at the peace conference. And all along, their intention was missionary – to save the Africans' souls by the agency of the Church Missionary Society and the British and Foreign Bible Society. The Clapham Sect had also (from 1787) its own colony of Sierra Leone, which became a Crown Colony in 1808. It had served originally as a refuge for destitute slaves freed in England; after 1808 it became a refuge for the victims of pirate slavers.

The African Institution, set up in 1808 with the Duke of Gloucester (always the Evangelicals' royal figurehead) as chairman, was officially to promote civilization in Africa, but it soon concerned itself principally with the enforcement of the Act of 1807, which was strengthened several times. To compel the registration of slaves in the West Indies appeared to be the best safeguard against illicit traffic, and Registry Bills were promoted by the Institution from 1812 onwards.

In 1814–15 the Sect put forth its best efforts to impress European diplomats and potentates, and their activities then illustrate not merely their extraordinary vigour but the international standing which Wilberforce in particular had attained. When Tsar Alexander I came to England in 1814, he expressed a wish to see Wilberforce; a meeting which Wilberforce used to propagate his views. At the time of the first Treaty of Paris in 1814, the Sect was determined to prevent the French from reviving the trade, and wished this to be written into the treaty. Stephen was sent as their 'ambassador' to brief Castlereagh – but the attempt failed. (Napoleon, however, declared against the trade on his return from Elba.) In order to secure a declaration by the Congress of Vienna, Wilberforce again adopted the methods of 1792, and as many as eight hundred petitions poured in to Parliament. The Treaty of Vienna contained at any rate a

statement by the powers condemning the trade and affirming
their determination to abolish it as soon as possible.

The positive decision to work for the total abolition of slavery
inside the Empire was taken in 1821. By this time the planters'
position had weakened further. Competition from other and
more recently developed sources was potentially very severe.
The East India Company had taken to sugar growing after 1787,
and since it claimed that its sugar was not tended by slaves,
abolitionists commended its use. The growing of sugar beet had
started seriously in Europe during the Napoleonic Wars. Cuba
and Brazil were producing sugar cheaply and in vast quantities.
In these circumstances the old West Indian monopoly was hard
to defend, and in any case economic theory and practice had
turned against the mercantilist ideas under which the West
India interest had once flourished.

Increasingly, too, the West India problem was becoming a
problem of order, and an insoluble one. The planters' enemies –
ministers and other missionaries – were well entrenched in the
Islands. The Westminster Government's policy was 'ameliora-
tion' of the slaves' condition. It was difficult to interpret and
to enforce. The planters thought themselves beleaguered and
misunderstood, and attempted stern repression. The slaves,
denied promised improvements and constantly anticipating
emancipation, rebelled – thirteen thousand in Demerara in 1823.
John Smith of the London Missionary Society endeavoured to
moderate their activities, but he was tried for incitement and
died in jail of consumption. Fifty thousand slaves rose in
Jamaica in 1832.

The abolitionists, on the other hand, were in a stronger position. Their personnel was changed. Wilberforce, an invaluable
figurehead still, but now inclined to forget his speeches, handed
over the leadership to Thomas Fowell Buxton in 1822 and
withdrew from Parliament in 1825. Some of the original Clapham
Sect were dead – Henry Thornton and John Venn among them –
though Clarkson and Macaulay were still able to show their skills
in propaganda. The country had undergone a campaign of re-
education since 1787, and the Anti-Slavery Society was able to

muster a huge number of respectable names. The spread of the Evangelical party in the Church of England and the development of Methodism meant that a vast number of churches and chapels could be regarded as abolitionist centres. The Methodist Conference in 1830, 1831, and 1832 insisted that Methodist voters should exact a promise from the parliamentary candidate for whom they voted to agree to abolition. The techniques of agitation developed further in the twenties. The Anti-Slavery Society – not merely a London pressure group, but made up of local branches – had 1300 affiliated societies by 1832. The *Anti-Slavery Reporter*, the compilation of which was virtually a one-man performance by Zachary Macaulay, was their journal. The now-elderly worthies of the African Institution were rather timid, but the cause was strengthened by radical abolitionists like George Stephen and the Agency Committee, who employed paid lecturers primed with prepared notes, and staged a mass meeting at Exeter Hall on the eve of abolition with sixty-six M.P.s who were ready to vote at Stephen's command. Every indiscretion of the planters was made the occasion for the publication of posters, statistics, and eye-witness accounts. The particularly widespread slave rising in Jamaica in 1832 was used to bring pressure on the Government. When Goderich was replaced by Lord Stanley as Colonial Secretary in March 1833, the Government accepted abolition. The legal status of slavery was to cease within a year. Existing slaves over six years old were to have the status of 'apprentices' – for six years if field labourers, and for four years otherwise. Compensation of twenty million pounds was offered to the planters.

[15] IMPERIAL ATTITUDES

At the same time as the battle against slave traders and plantation owners was being waged, the Sect was deploying its energies in an agitation which indicates more clearly the mainspring of

Evangelical action. During the eighteenth century the East India Company had established itself as the principal political power as well as the principal trading interest in India. Clive, Hastings, and others had secured control over the lives of millions of Indians. Recurrent financial and administrative crises in the affairs of the Company had compelled some government intervention, notably the Acts of 1772 and 1784. The latter established dual control by the Company and by the Board of Control, whose president was a member of the Government. The opportunity for statements of policy towards India came in 1788 with the impeachment of Warren Hastings; in 1793, when the Charter of the East India Company came up for renewal; and in 1813 when it came up again.

In the 1780s and 1790s the standard nineteenth-century attitudes towards India crystallized. The passing of Pitt's India Act in 1784, and the subsequent appointment of Cornwallis as Governor-General, were intended to establish a tradition of incorruptibility in the administration of Indian affairs. The speeches of the Opposition managers of Hastings' impeachment (and most notably those of Burke) expressed a respect for Indian rulers and civilization, and insisted that the British had a duty as trustee of the Indians. The views of the Clapham Sect, first clearly enunciated in the struggle over the renewal of the Charter in 1793, incorporated the trusteeship idea, but narrowed it to a mission to convert the heathen, and to a refusal to see any merit in Indian religions or culture. Since some practices – thuggee, suttee, and female infanticide – were abominably cruel, their campaign was able to take on an emotional and humanitarian tone. Missionary concern did not only extend to Indians; the conduct of Europeans in India by no means reached Evangelical standards.

For Christian missionaries to secure a foothold in India was difficult. They had to be licensed by the East India Company, but the Company resolutely declined to admit them, considering it no part of its business to upset existing Indian culture. In 1784, while Charles Grant was still in India, there was some slight attempt at Methodist penetration there. Dr Thomas Coke wrote him a letter asking that Christian missions be established; but the suggestion was dropped. William Carey, the Baptist shoemaker, went to India in 1792 with the backing of the Baptist Missionary Society, but his legal employment was as manager of an indigo plantation, and the headquarters of his missionary enterprise was at Serampore, a Danish settlement near Calcutta. In 1793 the policy of Wilberforce and Grant was to secure the official appointment of chaplains and schoolmasters by the Company. The Company, however, prevented the insertion of these clauses in its Charter, and Wilberforce deplored the leaving of 'our territories in Hindustan, twenty millions of people included . . . in the undisturbed and peaceable possession, and committed to the providential protection of – Brama'.

This failure by the Sect led to a contest of power and a political campaign which eventually succeeded in 1813. Sir John Shore (subsequently Lord Teignmouth, a member of the Sect) became Governor-General in 1793. Grant became a director of the Company and used his influence to have chaplains appointed. The London Missionary Society ('for Missions to Africa and the East') was set up under Evangelical direction in 1797. A war of pamphlets took place after one of Grant's nominees, Buchanan, wrote a book urging an ecclesiastical establishment in India. As the date for the next renewal approached, Wilberforce interviewed the Prime Minister, Spencer Perceval, and wrote an article for the *Christian Observer*. 'Cabinet councils' were called at Clapham. Thomas Babington stimulated the submission of 837 petitions. The Company continued its resistance, but its position was weaker than it had been twenty years before. Many wished its trading monopoly to end; its finances were not healthy. Wilberforce's clauses were inserted. Ten thousand pounds were to be spent annually on Indian education. If the East India Company declined to issue a licence to a missionary, than an appeal might be made to the Board of Control. (In fact, there was free entry after 1813.) An ecclesiastical establishment was set up in India – a bishop and three archdeacons – though its ministrations were to the Company's servants. Wilberforce again commended to Parliament in 1813 a policy of Anglicization and

Christianization. It was not the entire philosophy of British administrators in India in the next generation, but an important ingredient of it. Its basic anti-Indian feeling was fortified a few years later in James Mill's *History of India*. Mill the rationalist was as contemptuous towards Indian civilization as was Wilberforce the Evangelical. In India – and it was not the only sphere of action where they combined – Benthamism and Evangelicalism allied to produce what they both aimed to do. Under the direction of the thorough-going Benthamite Lord William Bentinck as Governor-General (1827–34), thuggee and suttee were abolished, western rather than oriental knowledge became the recognized content of education, and English was the acknowledged medium of instruction. With the arrival of Macaulay – Zachary's son – as a member of the council in 1834, English not only became the language of education, but also of the higher courts and of the administration.

The Indian and anti-slavery causes, and with them the foundation of the London Missionary Society and the Church Missionary Society, created an enormously powerful interest in colonial affairs for several generations. The secretary of the Church Missionary Society was a figure to be reckoned with in government circles. Two second-generation Claphamites ensured the continuance of Evangelical pressure: Sir James Stephen was Permanent Under-Secretary for the Colonies between 1836 and 1847; and Charles Grant, Lord Glenelg, was Melbourne's Colonial Secretary between 1835 and 1839. Evangelical attitudes became standard – that is to say, the civilization of native populations by missionaries was not to be obstructed by the intrusion of European settlers. This policy was calculated to lead to the exasperation of European developers on the spot and of rival interests in London.

In South Africa the policy was particularly explosive, since it was combined with poor execution of the Act abolishing slavery. The Great Trek was the result. In 1828 the Fiftieth Ordinance gave the Hottentots equality with the white men, which meant in practice that blacks could sue whites for ill-treatment. The Boers regarded this as an impossible situation, since they were unable to discipline their own servants; and they immediately attributed the ordinance to the Evangelicals. In 1833 there were in South Africa about thirty-nine thousand slaves, valued at between two and three million pounds. Under the terms of the Abolition Act, however, only one and a quarter million was offered in compensation. The actual payment was made in London, where the Boers had no agents – they were therefore obliged to sell their claims to speculators on the spot, with consequent financial loss. In 1834, the new Governor of the Cape, Sir Benjamin D'Urban, occupied a piece of Kaffir territory by way of reprisal for a Kaffir attack. The area was thrown open to the Boers – and there was an immediate outcry by English missionary interests. Sir Benjamin gave in, and put into force standard missionary policy; the Kaffirs were given reservations. It was too late; Glenelg, without knowing this, ordered D'Urban to leave. The Boers shortly afterwards set out on their trek across the Vaal.

A similar contest between rival interests was visible in New Zealand. Gibbon Wakefield on one side, and Stephen and Glenelg on the other, were the contestants. Wakefield wanted planned and large-scale colonization by a corporation. His opponents, with the 1837 Report of the Aborigines Committee backing them, insisted that European intrusion – other than missionary intrusion – on the aborigines was harmful. Only when Glenelg left public life in 1839 was there hope for Wakefield. The operation of his New Zealand Committee was finally permitted in 1841.

[16] THE PROGRESS OF EVANGELICALISM IN THE CHURCH AND SOCIETY

The Evangelicals' attitude towards the Established Church was in many ways ambivalent. It was worthwhile for them to capture it, they thought, as a kind of guardian of morality and as a provider of religious education. On the other hand, they were usually friends of Dissenters, whose overriding aim – salvation – was the same as their own, and with whom they worked through agencies like the British and Foreign Bible Society and the Lancasterian (or British and Foreign Schools) Society in providing popular education. Moreover, their Calvinist doctrine could destroy harmony at the parish level if an Evangelical incumbent placed a great gulf between those who were converted and those who were not, or if one or more traditional views kept the 'serious' part of the congregation at arm's length. (George Eliot, the best-informed and most acute observer of religion and society among the Victorian novelists, produced *Janet's Repentance* on this theme. Her account of the havoc that Mr Tryan, with his Sunday evening lectures and his doctrine that 'good works are not necessary to salvation', produced in the parish of old Mr Crewe who 'in a brown Brutus wig delivered inaudible sermons on a Sunday' may be found in *Scenes of Clerical Life*.) Despite all the disharmony, Wilberforce and Simeon were determined to see their cause advanced within the Establishment. They were the creators of the first of the modern 'parties' in the Church of England. According to Professor Owen Chadwick, the politicians in whose hands the appointments to bishoprics and deaneries lay did not consider labels (apart from Whig and Tory) until quite well on in the nineteenth century. It began to occur to Lord Aberdeen somewhere about 1853 that the bench ought to be representative of the various church parties. It is therefore rather vain to add up lists of Evangelical dignitaries at this early period in order to calculate their strength or weakness.

When Wilberforce began to attempt to use his influence to secure high preferments for his sympathizers, he was not greatly successful. Pitt, though a friend, was unaffected by 'vital Christianity'. All Wilberforce secured was the deanery of Carlisle for Isaac Milner, the man who had converted him. More than this might have been expected from Spencer Perceval, 'our first really devout Prime Minister', but nothing more was forthcoming. An attempt was made in 1820 to persuade his successor, Lord Liverpool, to appoint more Evangelicals to high places, but

Liverpool replied expressing his distaste for Calvinism. By 1815, in fact, only Ryder of Gloucester was an Evangelical among the bishops, and he was the brother of a cabinet minister.

The real penetration of the Church was done by other means, and was not directed at merely securing top appointments. At Cambridge, Charles Simeon (1759–1836) was the decisive Evangelical personality. A complex character, passionate, ill-tempered, wealthy, almost foppish in his costume, and utterly dedicated to his mission after his conversion in 1779, he used his immense influence as Fellow of King's and Vicar of Holy Trinity (1782–1836) for the invigoration and entrenchment of Evangelicalism. He saw that the undergraduates before him were potential carriers of 'gospel Christianity' to the entire kingdom:

Many of those who hear me are legions in themselves, because they are going forth to preach, or else to fill stations of influence in society.

Professional training for potential ordinands was then nonexistent. Simeon supplied the need at Cambridge with his 'sermon classes' and Friday evening 'conversation parties' in his drawing room at King's, with instruction not only in the content of sermons, but also in elocution. His example probably encouraged the institution of the first specialist theological colleges at St Bees in 1816 and Lampeter in 1828. Besides, his administration of his own parish, with its apparatus of prayer meetings and societies already familiar in Evangelical parishes, served as a model to his hearers. He was much concerned with the supply of suitable ordinands: the Bristol and Elland Societies had his backing, and he founded the London Clerical Aid Society in 1799.

When the candidates were ordained, there was the problem of placing them in livings, and particularly of ensuring that there was a continuity of 'gospel ministers' in a living. To this end Simeon's own funds were largely dedicated – his father was a wealthy attorney in Reading and his brother was a director of the Bank of England. The idea of a corporation or trust to secure advowsons was one which had first been operated by John Thornton, Henry's father. Simeon began his Trust in 1817 with the purchase of the patronage of Cheltenham. His most spectacular purchases, which depended on the success of appeals to his sympathizers, were in consequence of the Municipal Corporations Act of 1835, which compelled the corporations to disgorge their patronage. Under this he and his successors secured Bath, Derby, Macclesfield, Bridlington, Beverley, and St Thomas's and St Martin's in Liverpool. He was conscious to a greater degree than many of his contemporaries of the need to secure a foothold in those towns with a sharply rising industrial population.

Prejudice and conviction made Simeon very conscious of the need to operate within the bounds of the Church of England. In his twenties he had worked with Dissenters; on his visits to Scotland he worshipped in Presbyterian churches; opposition from his own churchwardens compelled him, between 1783 and 1790, to operate what was in fact an 'illicit conventicle' in a room just outside his own parish on Sunday evenings. But the insistence of earlier Evangelicals, like Berridge, that the commission to preach the gospel to every creature meant that they could override parochial boundaries, he disliked. His insistence on church order, as the Reverend Charles Smyth argues at length in his *Simeon and Church Order*, probably averted the danger of the Evangelicals leaving the Established Church altogether.

Simeon, then, considerably advanced the Evangelical cause among the clergy. But how, directly, did a similar process affect the laity? The influence of the 'Saints' among the leaders of society played some part; but the nationwide penetration was done much more systematically. Ford K. Brown, in his *Fathers of the Victorians*, has suggested that the two foremost missionary societies connected with the Revival, the British and Foreign Bible Society (1803) and the Church Missionary Society (1799), of which Wilberforce assumed the chair in 1811, independently of the success they enjoyed outside Britain, played a great part in extending influence inside Britain. The object of the Bible Society was extraordinarily simple and apparently could do nothing but good – the dissemination of bibles without note or comment. Clearly this accounts for much of its astounding success. By 1825 it had issued four and a quarter million bibles. Non-Evangelical churchmen, however, did not like it; they emphasized the importance of the Book of Common Prayer as well as the Bible, and disliked the co-operation with Dissenters that the Society encouraged. The extension of the Society involved the setting up of sectional associations and local auxiliaries – by 1825, there were 859 auxiliaries in England and 2,000 associations – and thus the recruitment of Evangelical cadres in each area, and the securing of as many influential and titled names as was possible. (This last was not a distinctively Evangelical habit, and everybody from a sports meeting organizer to an agricultural show committee did the same thing.) Sometimes the setting up of an auxiliary led to a severe test of strength, and the institution of one at Cambridge in 1811 was only achieved by the combined energies of Milner and Wilberforce, who brought the Duke of Gloucester to attend the meeting. The Bishop of Ely (Dampier) and most of the University were hostile.

The campaign of the Church Missionary Society in 1813–14 also met with great success in attracting support for the Evangelicals. In that season preachers were sent out in pairs all over the country. They preached only in churches, and some of their greatest successes were in the cities of the West Riding. When the Rev. Leigh Richmond appeared to preach at Sheffield, his congregation was 3,500 strong but crowds were left outside. They were also well received in some big houses.

Much has been observed already about the Evangelicals of the Age of Wilberforce being wealthy men: but they were as determined to appeal to the 'lower orders' as the preachers of the Age of Whitefield were. By the 1790s, however, in the face of the threat of revolution, there was a much clearer determination to keep the lower orders in their place. Evangelical methods were not so much based on preaching as on the Sunday school and the Tract. Hannah More (1745–1833) used both these, and is the most famous of the Evangelicals in this work.

The More sisters, Hannah and Martha, were originally proprietors of a successful school in Bristol. Hannah became a considerable figure in literary London in the 1770s, but it was not until she heard a sermon by John Newton in 1787 that she became a recruit to Wilberforce's cause. She first tried to do what Wilberforce later intended: to convert the rich by pamphlet. Her very successful *Thoughts on the Importance of the Manners of the Great to General Society* (1788) was for a time believed to be by Wilberforce. He also financed her attempts to 'educate' (if that is the right word) the working population of the Mendips, which she directed from Blagden, a village which 'excelled in wickedness, if possible, anything we had taken in hand'. By 1800 there were about thirteen or fourteen hundred children under instruction in nine parishes, besides adults attending meetings in the evening. The instruction was meagre – it did not include writing, and one of the teachers indicates his aims for his pupils thus:

A thorough knowledge of religion, and of some of those coarse warts [*sic*] of life by which the country may be best benefited, includes the whole stock of instruction which, unless in very extraordinary cases, I should wish to bestow.

The object, in fact, was conversion. Because of her employment of a Methodist teacher in this scheme, Hannah became involved in a lengthy controversy. She was not successful, but a great deal of publicity was attracted, some of it (especially Cobbett's) memorable in its vituperation.

Hannah More's attempts to convert the poor also included the writing and distribution of what were called Cheap Repository Tracts, which she started in 1795 and intended to be read by adults. Henry Thornton was the treasurer for this venture, and Macaulay was the agent; the authors enlisted to write tracts included both those men, John Venn, and (most effective) Leigh Richmond. In planning this series Hannah More was responding in particular to the alarm of the governing classes at the circulation of Tom Paine's *Rights of Man* and *The Age of Reason*, which were sold in (very) cheap editions. Two years after it was written, *The Rights of Man* had sold two hundred thousand copies; and Miss More observed that these 'pernicious pamphlets' were 'dropped, not only into cottages and in highways, but into mines and coalpits' (E. P. Thompson has some good examples of its vast circulation: op. cit., Pelican ed., pp. 117–18). All the tracts – there were 114 of them, and in one year at any rate the circulation exceeded two million copies – had the same Evangelical and conservative intention. They were not all stories: they included poems and collections of prayers. They were distributed by every means that could be devised, not merely through booksellers, but by pedlars, hawkers, and friends. Bulk purchase and free handing-out partly explain the enormous circulation figures.

Thus the Evangelicals in the era of the French Wars directed their attentions at all sections of society. Wealth, social and political contacts, and the very evident crisis in society provoked by Revolutionary ideas, assisted them to inculcate their ideas among the highest classes; the anti-slavery campaigns and the British and Foreign Bible Society mobilized the middle classes (including many Dissenters), who could collaborate heartily in both; the Cheap Repository Tracts were intended as wholesome fare for the working population. The involvement of the middle classes is not surprising – they had Puritan virtues long before the 1790s – but the penetration of the upper and lower levels is. It is an important step in the 'Victorianizing' of society (see Part IV).

[17]   POLITICAL AND SOCIAL ATTITUDES

The 'Saints' were both political conservatives and political innovators; this paradoxical combination has baffled commentators from that day to this. They were nearly all dependable followers of Pitt, and supported his repressive measures; yet they preserved their right to criticize him. Many of their views on the poor display insufferable contempt, and if the poor felt like Cobbett, their tracts were repellent rather than attractive; yet they were humanitarians. They were alarmed at popular discontent; yet they were experts at moulding and using popular opinion for their own purposes. They were prepared to countenance some parliamentary reform, and Roman Catholic Emancipation. Morality – or what they considered the Christian attitude – was the test, and consequently they laid themselves open to the charge of hypocrisy.

Anti-Jacobinism was characteristic of the Evangelicals as a body. James Bean, the author of *Zeal without Innovation* (1808), observed of their ministers that:

> They have not only remained uncorrupted, but have often availed themselves of their situation as ministers to stem the tide of sedition. It deserves notice, that in the most threatening periods of Revolutionary mania, these men spoke out very decidedly from the pulpit, in defence of our enviable constitution. In some places, their zeal was such, as to make many conclude, that in the event of an insurrection, they would be among the first to be sacrificed.

Simeon, their leader (whose official position was 'I do not think clergymen have much to do with politics'), in fact assisted in launching *The Anti-Jacobin* in 1799. In 1796 he had preached on 'Beware of false prophets', and the false prophets in fact turned out to be Dissenters, whose doctrine 'had a manifest tendency to make people factious, or disturbers of the public peace'. Henry Venn and Isaac Milner shared Simeon's views (on this point, see Smyth, op. cit., esp. pp. 295–8).

> It was well known that the set of politicians, ironically called the Saints, were the main prop of the Pitt System. It was well known that under the garb of sanctity, they aided and abetted the worst things that were done. . . . They were never found wanting at any dirty job; and invariably lent their aid, in those acts, which were the most inimical to the liberty of England.

Cobbett was the most virulent of the Evangelicals' critics, and his charges have been repeated many times up to the present day – often with particular reference to Wilberforce.

Wilberforce was very close to Pitt, of course, and he was alarmed at the danger of the spread of revolutionary and anti-religious ideas. His attitude towards the Government's repressive legislation during the Revolutionary War and in the years after Peterloo has been thoroughly charted. He approved of the sentence on Palmer for sedition in 1793. He was consulted by Pitt on the Treasonable Practices and Seditious Meetings Acts of 1795. (He defended them as 'a temporary sacrifice by which the blessings of liberty may be transmitted to our children unimpaired' and journeyed rapidly to Yorkshire to scotch opposition raised by Wyvil and others.) The Combination Laws of 1799–1800 he was partly responsible for. He considered the unions politically dangerous and economically disastrous, since they would force up wages and prices so as to threaten the trade of the country. Though the Combination Laws were not in practice so much of a hindrance as was once thought, Wilberforce has nevertheless a black reputation with historians of labour. In the years following the Napoleonic Wars, he approved of the suspension of habeas corpus (1817) and the Government's actions after Peterloo (1819). He was easily frightened, and wrote at that time:

Seldom has a boy returned on a black Monday with more reluctance than I to St Stephen's. I dare not be too confident that we may not witness scenes of something nearer to civil war than this land has exhibited since 1646.

There are qualifications to be made to all this. First, there is no sign that Wilberforce was ever muzzled by his friendship for Pitt. The Prime Minister had to face some very uncomfortable home truths from Wilberforce: that desire for French West Indian islands was one of his reasons for continuing the war with France, or (most devastating of all) that Pitt's minister and crony, Melville, should be impeached for permitting embezzlement in his department. Second, Wilberforce was concerned for parliamentary reform. He supported Pitt's abortive proposals for reform in 1784, and remained attached to the general idea. Curwen's Act of 1809 he supported because it forbade the sale of parliamentary seats, and after 1822 he rather tepidly supported a general measure of parliamentary reform since it would improve electoral morality. Third, alongside his own huge campaigns, Wilberforce remained interested in other humanitarian causes. He was an opponent of the severe Game Laws. There was some suggestion that he should assume Romilly's place at the head of the campaign to reform the Penal Code when Romilly committed suicide in 1818, but Wilberforce pleaded physical incapacity. Bentham's original proposals for prison reform attracted him. So did the work of Elizabeth Fry and Fowell Buxton in the prisons. He supported (as he might have been expected to) the Health and Morals of Apprentices Act of 1802, and spoke in favour when Peel's 1818 Factory Bill originally appeared. He attempted to modify both bills in a more humanitarian sense. He repeatedly supported Bennett's bills (1817–19) to end the practice of sending boys up chimneys (see R. Coupland, *Wilberforce*, esp. pp. 411–35).

All this seems a very equivocal record; how is the equivocation to be explained? Partly it was simple anti-Jacobinism, allegiance to Pitt and Sidmouth, ordinary laissez-faire ideas. There are, however, more telling explanations. Moral considerations mattered – they gave a standard of judgement. Thus Melville should be punished – even if Pitt, the friend of a lifetime, were to lose what prestige and strength he had left. Parliament must be reformed – because that was the obvious way to improve electoral conduct. Morality was also the first objective in dealing with the problem of the poor. Cobbett complained that Wilberforce's philanthropy did not operate

in behalf of more than a million paupers in existence in England. One eighth of our population! But they were not slaves. Say, rather, they were not black; a thing which they might seeing the preference given to that colour, have well regarded as extremely unfortunate.

It was never Wilberforce's belief that material prosperity should be man's major concern. He wrote:

I declare my greatest cause of difference with the democrats is their laying, or causing the people to lay, so great a stress on the concerns of this world as to occupy their whole minds and hearts, and to reserve a few scanty and lukewarm thoughts for the heavenly treasure.

Moral improvement had to be somehow instilled into them – by Sunday and other schools, and by tracts, as well as by the means intended for all classes – abolition of cruel sports, Sabbatarianism, and so forth. (Sabbatarianism he always justified on social as well as religious grounds – as a relief to the industrial workers. He characteristically observed that Pitt might not have met his early end, and Castlereagh might not have committed suicide, if they had not worked Sundays and weekdays alike.) The task of moral improvement was an uphill one; according to Hannah More's sister, Martha, the poor had 'so little common sense and so little sensibility, that we are obliged to beat into their heads continually the good we are doing them'. It is not surprising that the contrast between the opulence of Clapham and the poverty of the Mendip Hills, and the condescension of one to the other, have brought down so much obloquy on the Saints.

In one sense, the Evangelicals contracted the concerns of politics to the single issue of morality. In other senses they widened the whole sphere of politics. The techniques of agitation were developed enormously under their direction. Pressure groups like the Dissenting Deputies, the East India Company directors, or the West India planters, were familiar in the eighteenth century; but national societies, journals, and other mass publications were not. The Evangelicals saw a way of harnessing the new moral and religious sentiment in Britain; they formulated new colonial and philanthropic attitudes, and thus they became a striking feature of the nineteenth-century scene.

Further Reading

G. R. Balleine, *A History of the Evangelical Party*. Longmans, 1908, etc.

G. F. A. Best, 'The Evangelicals and the Established Church in the Early Nineteenth Century.' *Journal of Theological Studies*, Vol. X (April 1959).

Ford K. Brown, *Fathers of the Victorians. The Age of Wilberforce*. Cambridge University Press, 1961.

A controversial work which plays down the religious motive and exaggerates the conspiratorial aspects of the Clapham Sect; but some very valuable information is collected, especially on the Missionary Societies and on the Cheap Repository Tracts. Brown's view of Wilberforce is a useful corrective to Coupland's.

R. Coupland, *Wilberforce. A Narrative.* Oxford University Press, 1923.
Coupland never made large claims for his book, which is largely derived from the official biography by Wilberforce's sons, and is therefore over-friendly to its subject. The book, however, has not yet been displaced.
The Anti-Slavery Movement. Home University Library, 1933; repr. Frank Cass, 1964.

M. Hennell, *John Venn and the Clapham Sect.* Lutterworth Press, 1958.

E. M. Howse, *Saints in Politics.* University of Toronto Press, 1952.

M. Jaeger, *Before Victoria: Changing Standards and Behaviour, 1787–1837.* Chatto and Windus, 1956; Penguin, 1967.

V. Kiernan, 'Evangelicalism and the French Revolution'. *Past and Present*, Vol. I., 1952.

A. O. Pollard and Michael Hennell, eds., *Charles Simeon.* S.P.C.K., 1959; paperback edition, 1964.

C. Smyth, *Simeon and Church Order.* Cambridge University Press, 1940.

James Stephen, *Essays in Ecclesiastical Biography*, Vol. II. (Many editions: last repr. Longmans, 1907)
Stephen was the son of James Stephen of the Clapham Sect and Permanent Secretary at the Colonial Office; the essays include one on the Evangelical Succession, one on Wilberforce, and one on the Clapham Sect. They were written 1838–44.

E. Williams, *Capitalism and Slavery.* First published 1944; André Deutsch, 1964.
Dr Williams is hostile to the 'traditional' interpretation of Wilberforce's campaign presented by Sir Reginald Coupland. Dr Williams traces the economic importance of the West Indies in the eighteenth century and its subsequent decline. The decline coincided largely with the abolitionist campaign.

Evangelical Achievements, 1780–1833

1782. Charles Simeon became Fellow of King's College, Cambridge, and Vicar of Holy Trinity (to 1836). In this position he trained a whole generation of Evangelical clergymen and deployed his own and other Evangelical wealth to put the patronage of many livings permanently into Evangelical hands

1784. William Wilberforce, a close personal friend of Pitt the Younger, became M.P. for Yorkshire

1785. Wilberforce was converted to Evangelicalism and persuaded to take up the cause of abolishing the slave trade

1786. Wilberforce first met Henry Thornton, M.P. – the two formed the nucleus of the Clapham Sect. Thornton later resided at Clapham, and his group had a great variety of parliamentary and colonial influence. It included Charles Grant, John Shore, Zachary Macaulay, James Stephen, and John Venn

THE AIMS OF THE CLAPHAM SECT

The Abolition of the Slave Trade and of Slavery

1787. Opening of the campaign

1807. Abolition of the slave trade in the British Empire

1814–15. Campaign to check slave traffic by other countries – produced a declaration against it in the Congress of Vienna

1833. Abolition of slavery in the British Empire

Stimulation of Missionary Activity

With the Evangelicals' encouragement:

1787. Sierra Leone founded

1803. The British and Foreign Bible Society was founded – an organization which enabled the Sect to extend its influence in Britain, and to 'organize' its supporters

1813. On the revision of the East India Company's Charter, India was provided with a religious Establishment for the first time

The Conversion of the Governing Classes and the Stemming of 'Jacobin' Feeling

1788. Hannah More published *Thoughts on the Manners of the Great*

1797. Wilberforce's *Practical View of the Prevailing Religious System of Professed Christians*

Both commended 'vital religion' as a social duty for the great

1795. Beginning of *The Cheap Repository Tracts* – Hannah More and others produced these Evangelical alternatives to Paine's *Rights of Man* (1791), then circulating in cheap editions among the lower orders

PART IV

The Early Nineteenth Century

[18] THE IMPACT OF THE CHURCHES: SOME PROBLEMS

When the details of the Census taken in 1851 were revealed nearly three years later, they were subject to more than customary scrutiny – on at least three grounds. The first was the obvious one, the continuing rise in population: the total for the United Kingdom was twenty-seven millions, sixteen millions more than it had been at the beginning of the century. The second was that for the first time ever more people lived in towns than in the country. The third was that it included a novel (and never-repeated) religious census, with an analysis by Horace Mann, who was in charge of it. The census numbered attendances at a place of worship on 30 March 1851. The figures for England and Wales were: Church of England, 5,292,551; main Nonconformist Churches, 4,536,264; Roman Catholics, 383,000. The total population of England and Wales was 17,927,609. Every sort of cavil has been made at these figures. (The most exhaustive analysis, by W. S. F. Pickering, is 'The Religious Census – A useless Experiment?' in the *British Journal of Sociology*, 1967.) Mann himself tried to make his statistics reliable by making deductions for young children, invalids, child minders, and some at work on Sunday; he said that fifty-eight per cent of the population could have attended worship, that is, about ten million people. But his figures were of attendances, not persons. The number of persons who attended is therefore a matter for refined guesswork. Dr Pickering's estimate

is seven million people, or about thirty-six per cent of the population, more or less equally divided between Anglicans and the
rest. Notwithstanding all the difficulties of analysis, there are
some firm observations which can be made. Vast numbers of
people stayed away – most obviously the lowest classes of the
great towns, who were apparently outside the range of church
and chapel influence altogether. The Church of England could
no longer claim with so much certainty as before to be the
national Church. It remained the strongest in the counties round
London and in eastern England, but in some northern and
western areas – notably Newcastle upon Tyne, the West Riding,
and Cornwall – the chapelgoers were in a majority (on the
religious census, see also K. S. Inglis, 'Patterns of Worship in
1851', *Journal of Ecclesiastical History*, Vol. X, 1960; and O.
Chadwick, *The Victorian Church*, Part I, pp. 363–9).

The conclusions to be drawn from the 1851 Census – not merely
the religious part – prompt many questions. Not all of them are
the same as the shocked Victorian commentators asked. Numerically and socially the churches were a powerful complex of
interests. Change in the first half of the century was rapid beyond
all example. The structure of society became more subtle as a
new industrial working class and a new commercial and industrial
bourgeoisie emerged. Entire new industrial communities erupted.
Observers as diverse as Engels, Mrs Gaskell, and Disraeli were
obsessed during the 1840s by the divisions in society. In the
1830s and 1840s a spate of legislative reforms made changes in
Parliament, in local government, in the Poor Law, in education,
in the Church of England itself. Chartist agitation, factory disturbances, violent agricultural discontent, and anti-Corn Law
campaigns all made their mark. In all this did the churches do
anything to fix political attitudes? What was their contribution
to a changing society?

Generalizations cause great difficulties here. It is often assumed
that Church (of England) means Tory, and that Chapel means
Whig (or, in due course, Liberal). This is a good rule when
writing about the seventeenth century, and is generally valid for
the last quarter of the nineteenth century: it does not help much

when considering the early nineteenth-century situation. Equally misleading is the assumption that there existed a necessary connection between Methodism and the political aspirations of the working classes. This notion is a product of the period of elaborate concern with social issues, stretching from about the 1880s to the 1930s, when the writings of Dr R. F. Wearmouth and Rev. H. B. Kendall, both Primitive Methodists, took back into the Methodist past the concerns of their own times.

Political attitudes were determined in a more casual and pragmatic way than these generalizations indicate. Many political issues of the period were essentially religious in their nature – Roman Catholic Emancipation, the problems of education, and all matters relating to the administration of the Church of England, from new churches to church rates – and a 'party line' could be expected. Evangelicals inside the Establishment and their sympathizers in the sects (as has already been observed) broadened the content of politics with their elaborate concern for philanthropy and for the heathen, so that colonial matters became their particular preserve. But feelings towards other issues could not be formed so easily. Members of particular churches did not form fixed opinions on Chartism or on trade unions according to their religious affiliation. The Church and the Chapel – particularly the Chapel – were not there to lay down political opinions or determine social attitudes. They usually immersed their active members in the affairs of the class meeting, the quarterly meeting, or the chapel trust, and not infrequently concerned their members for the salvation of their souls. There were other determinants of their political conduct. Church and Chapel had one positive solution to the troubles of the time: to provide more churches and more chapels, as others were providing more drains, more workhouses, and every other kind of social utility.

[19] THE INSTITUTIONAL HISTORY OF THE CHURCHES

The Church of England

The unreformed Church, like the unreformed Parliament, survived very uncomfortably after Waterloo; but the Church as it stood by 1850 was revolutionized in its constitutional relationship with the State, in its administration, and even to some degree in its theology. All three aspects are closely related. The changes turned the Church into a tolerably efficient machine which would bear the scrutiny of its critics more easily, and the clergy into a profession with raised standards but much narrower interests. Behind the changes was the challenge presented by the industrialization of the country.

Like the members of the unreformed Parliament, the clergy of the unreformed Church had their own elaborate defence of the status quo. In many respects the views of both coincided. Their property rights were to be defended at all costs. They were not accountable to the public. They had, as established institutions, a prescriptive right to authority. The Church, however, was unable to maintain such arguments for long, for a variety of reasons. First of all, the Church was not united in holding them. Critical opinion, whether it came from the Evangelicals or from inside the mainstream of the Church, or from the laity, concentrated on the reform and reinvigoration of the parish (see p. 178 ff.). Such changes could not take place while so many anomalies existed: non-resident clergy, poor curates, parish boundaries which ignored changes of population, shortage of church accommodation. The solution of many of these problems lay in a redistribution of income – and therefore an attack on the inflated revenues and establishments of cathedrals. This possibility caused a deep rift among the clergy. Secondly, by the Act of Union in 1800, the Church of England and the Church of Ireland were united. It became necessary to reform the gross abuses and alter the political position of the Church of Ireland. As one suffered, so the other Church was threatened. Thirdly, since the Church of England had no governing body of its own, it had to depend upon Parliament, and therefore on party politicians, for its reform; and though the Church might be aloof from public opinion, the politicians were not. There was scarcely a Member of Parliament who would accept the unreformed Church's case. Peel was the nearest thing to a friend the Church had – but he disliked the vast wealth and staff of the cathedrals; he accepted the repeal of the Test and Corporation Acts; he introduced the Catholic Relief Act; he sealed the fate of the unreformed Church with the setting up of the Ecclesiastical Commissioners. It was he, in short, who executed the constitutional and administrative revolution. In such a situation, with all bastions evidently falling, Oxford found a limited theological defence for the Church: the Tractarian Movement.

By a series of instinctive but ill-judged actions, the Church identified itself with extreme Toryism and alienated public opinion in the 1820s and 1830s. Criticism of some features – like the collection of tithe – was ages old; but it was with Peterloo in 1819 that the Church became a favourite target for Radical abuse. The action of the Home Secretary, Lord Sidmouth, in congratulating the magistrates for their handling of Peterloo, in which so many were killed and injured, stimulated liberals to hold meetings and sign declarations criticizing the Government. Such meetings were held, among other places, in Durham. The endowments of the cathedral and of the bishopric of Durham were enormous, and nothing there was calculated to win public support. The clergy of Durham dissociated themselves from the liberal critics of the Government, and a lengthy war of words ensued between one of the canons, Henry Philpotts, on one side, and the Whig leaders in the North-east, Lord Grey and Lord Lambton, on the other. By 1823 the quarrel had become a national issue with *The Times* and the *Edinburgh Review* weighing in on the Whig side.

The events of 1828 and 1829 showed the Church how little it could expect from its political friends. With the Duke of Wellington as Prime Minister and Peel as Home Secretary, the Test and Corporation Acts were repealed, and the Catholic Relief Act was passed. (A minority of enlightened bishops was found to vote for both measures.) The special relationship which had ensured an Anglican Parliament was at an end: Dissenters and Roman Catholics would now participate in legislation affecting the Church.

The long crisis over parliamentary reform which convulsed political life between 1830 and 1832 further tarnished the reputation of the Church. Criticism of it mounted to its height, and pamphlets on church reform were showered on the public. Twenty-one bishops voted against the second of the Reform Bills introduced by the Whigs during the crisis; they were not blind to the importance of their vote, but they grossly misjudged public opinion. In the autumn of 1831 the bishops were fearful of making public appearances, and the most strident of the reactionaries, Philpotts, by then Bishop of Exeter, was afraid to stay in Exeter and was hanged in effigy in Durham. Blomfield, the Bishop of London, tried to undo the damage on a subsequent vote, and secured eleven episcopal supporters for the third bill – but the damage was done as far as the Church was concerned. The identification of the Church with reaction was complete. (See the account of the bishops and the Reform Bill in R. A. Soloway, *Prelates and People: Ecclesiastical Social Thought in England, 1783–1852*, pp. 242–55.)

One work from the controversies of 1832 attained particular influence as a solution to the Church's problems. Lord Henley, Peel's brother-in-law, an eminent lawyer and an Evangelical, produced his *Plan of Church Reform*. It suggested the commonplace idea of evenly distributing the Church's revenues – to take the excess away from the cathedrals, the collegiate churches, and some of the bishops, and transfer it to the parish clergy. Where the *Plan* impressed was in suggesting a method by which this could be done: a body of commissioners should be set up who would be responsible for receiving the money and administering it. When William IV dislodged Lord Melbourne and the Whigs, and appointed Peel (November 1834–April 1835), this was the proposition which attracted the new Prime Minister.

The Church, fearful of Whigs and Nonconformists, accepted Peel's Government with relief, though if Peel was regarded as a friend of the Church, he was a remarkably candid one. He publicly accepted the need for reform in the Tamworth Manifesto, with the proviso that church revenues should not be diverted to non-ecclesiastical uses. An Ecclesiastical Duties and Revenues Commission was set up in 1835, dominated at first by Peel himself, and after his resignation by Bishop Blomfield and the Commission's secretary, Charles Knight Murray. This body produced its reports in 1836, when it was transmuted into the Ecclesiastical Commissioners, a permanent body charged with the reform of the Church's structure. This included equalizing the boundaries of existing dioceses and creating new ones; equalizing bishops' revenues (1836); placing severe restrictions on pluralism (1838); and suppressing excess revenues of cathedrals for distribution among those with greater need (1840). These changes, though profound, were not all: in Lord Melbourne's second administration, the Tithe Commutation Act of 1836 did away with tithes in kind and substituted money payments calculated on the average price of grain over the preceding seven years. The Registration Act of 1836 put the work of registering births, marriages, and deaths in the hands of a civil official and not of the Church of England incumbent. The Dissenters' Marriage Act of 1838 ended the obligation of Nonconformists to marry in an Anglican church. In every way, then, the thirties were revolutionary.

The Church's most curious defence against such a continuous attack was the Oxford Movement. The recognizable beginnings of it were in 1833, and despite interesting attempts to discover its origins in some remote continuity from the seventeenth century, or in the personalities and eccentricities of its founders, or in romanticism, it was basically a protest against the Whigs, whose relations with the Church were so bad. 'Damn it; another bishop dead!' Melbourne once cried. It was their radical attack on the Church of Ireland in 1833 which brought matters to a head. The Irish Establishment was pruned; two archbishoprics and eight bishoprics were abolished, making available about a hundred and fifty thousand pounds. At first the Whigs intended to distribute it as Parliament should decide, and

O'Connell even hoped that it would go to pay Roman Catholic priests; but the clause to divert funds from the Church had to be withdrawn. The close connection of Church and State was now seen as an enormous obstruction; there was no advantage to be gained from it. The Church had somehow to establish its authority on quite a different footing, and it did so by asserting its *divine* authority. The bishops were not merely the nominees of the Prime Minister, they were in a direct line from the Apostles; episcopal ordination was necessary for proper ministry. The most influential propagators of these views were Oxford dons: Newman, Keble, Froude, and Pusey.

The movement's tracts, and the arguments conducted in the columns of the sympathetic *British Magazine* and the hostile *Christian Observer*, publicized their views, which constituted a case, altogether, for the essential catholicity of the Church of England. Eventually their influence in clerical circles was very great. The standards of efficiency and decorum of the clergy had been rising perceptibly ever since the appointments made by Spencer Perceval and Lord Liverpool; now clergy acquired a stronger sense of vocation. (Evangelicalism in a different way also provided this sense.) Eventually, though not in its first phase, the Tractarian Movement, by its concern for the history and traditions of the Church, stimulated great changes in the conduct of public worship and in the design of churches. In its time, the influence of the movement was in some ways dubious. It was little concerned with the pressing industrial and social problems of the age, and in spite of Pusey's own concern over (and expenditure on) godless industrial parishes, it was in the later Victorian period that high-church priests and slum parishes became closely associated. Moreover, the movement exacerbated the divisions between the Church and the Dissenters. Even the Wesleyan Methodists, constitutionally inclined to pro-Anglican attitudes, were outraged by the 'Popery' of the 'Puseyites'.

Methodism

It does not seem reasonable to doubt Wesley's greatness as an organizer. The developments inside Methodism in the generation after his death in 1791, though, make the description a questionable one. So many problems, left unsolved or even unforeseen in 1791, had then to be worked out with painful results. There was the problem of relations with the Church of England, which was already approaching crisis point in the 1780s; there was the difficulty over licensing Methodist preachers and chapels; but most of all there was the conflict which could be seen developing between the pretensions of Conference and its president on the one hand and the interests and aspirations of the rank and file on the other. The shadow of Wesley was a long one, and all the participants in the struggles which preoccupied the movement claimed to be operating inside his tradition. The Conference, made up of preachers only, and its dominant figure, Jabez Bunting (1779–1858), continued to hold Wesley's autocratic and clerial views, and to share his essential political conservatism, but they distrusted the revivalist techniques he had used. Those who questioned the autocracy continued to praise revivalism and to operate it. Compared with these tensions in the movement, both national and local, the issues of politics were often of slight interest to the members.

Contention arose immediately in 1791. The first problem, of course, was over the leadership. Dr Thomas Coke, an Anglican priest whom Wesley had made a 'superintendent' in 1784, would probably have liked to assume Wesley's mantle, but his missionary activities on the other side of the Atlantic, his deeply clerical views, and his want of capacity as an administrator, disqualified him. He became secretary of the Conference in 1791. Of the other preachers, Adam Clarke already had a distinguished reputation, but he was only twenty-nine. In the event, the presidency of the Conference was occupied by a series of respected elder preachers who endeavoured to quieten controversy by postponement and by diplomacy.

The next argument was over the administration of the Lord's Supper. 'Church Methodists' – often the respected trustees of chapels in the big cities – objected to the administration of the sacrament by preachers in chapels, and wished to continue their attendance at parish churches for the purpose. Many thought the opposite, and, in spite of a ban imposed on the sacrament in chapel in 1792, they very soon won. A circular from Conference the next year admitted as much:

You see clearly from hence, dear brethren, that it is the *people* in the instances referred to who have forced us into this further deviation from the Church of England.

The solution proposed at the Manchester Conference in 1795, the Plan of Pacification, permitted the administration of the sacrament in chapels where the trustees at one meeting, and the stewards and leaders at another, agreed to it. Conference had also to approve. A similar procedure was to be used to determine whether services should be permitted at the same time as those in the parish church.

At the same time the leadership faced for the first time an obvious criticism of the Methodist structure. This was the absolute control of the Connexion by the preachers, both in the Conference and in the circuits. What share should laymen, who financed the chapels, have in the process of decision making? Demands that they should have a greater say came from Cornwall, where a meeting was held at Redruth in June 1791, and from Alexander Kilham in the North-east. Conference acted more decisively on this problem than on the others. It gave laymen some standing in the localities by allowing them to act alongside the minister in choosing lay officials, in considering the admission and ejection of members, and in the disciplining of members. They were not, however, admitted to the Conference, which soon gave indications that it intended to retain absolute control. Meantime, it elaborated still further the organization of Methodism by grouping circuits into districts on the analogy (at least in Coke's mind) of Anglican dioceses, and by calling assistants in charge of circuits 'superintendents'.

The problems Wesley had faced over licensing chapels and preachers soon came up for resolution in a manner which Halévy singled out for particular description and described as the Nonconformists' 'most brilliant victory'. In 1803 the Methodists formed the Committee of Privileges to defend their interests in

Parliament and in the courts; in 1811–12 they faced a challenge from both. In Parliament, Lord Sidmouth introduced a bill stating that nobody should be given a preacher's licence whose form was not signed by six reputable householders. The Methodists parried this with a brisk agitation which led to the dropping of the bill. In the Court of King's Bench, a ruling that a man seeking a licence to preach had to show that he had a particular congregation was a blow directly at intending Methodist preachers, since, unlike Dissenting ministers, they were tied to no congregation. To this threat the Committee of Privileges (working with the Dissenters' Committee of Three Denominations) responded. The Prime Minister, Perceval, drew up the bill which became the 'New Toleration Act'. By this Act the Five Mile and Conventicle Acts were repealed, and several clauses were specifically inserted to benefit the Methodists. All exemptions which clergymen enjoyed by law were granted to the itinerant preachers; no person need relinquish his attachment to the Church of England to bring himself under the protection of the bill; places of worship need not be certified before a preacher preached inside them – though they had to be certified eventually; and a preacher could operate before taking an oath, though he could be required to do so at any time by a magistrate.

Triumphant as this achievement might be, and remarkable though the increase in membership was, the internal tensions of the movement grew steadily more critical. Over the next half century, Methodism became a group of churches rather than one; the parent Wesleyan Methodists were surrounded with breakaway movements. Some are styled 'offshoots': they were concerned at the developing respectability of the Connexion, and at its increasing hostility to old-style evangelism. Of these the most celebrated were the Primitive Methodists, led by Hugh Bourne. They introduced, directly on the model of American evangelists and (as they might and did claim) indirectly on the model of Wesley himself, large outdoor rallies called 'camp meetings'. The practice incurred the censure of Conference and the expulsion of Bourne in 1808. (This effective and class-conscious group had important social effects: see pp. 199–213.)

The Bible Christians of the South-west were a group of a similar kind.

Others are called 'secessions'. They were breakaways from the main Wesleyan body – mainly as protests at the excessively clerical and autocratic nature of the government of the Connexion. The first of the secessions was led by Alexander Kilham. His protest at the control exercised by the ministers led to his expulsion in 1797 and the creation of the New Connexion. Its basic units of administration, though going under the same names as the parent body, included ministers and laymen in equal numbers. The tendency to further secessions of this kind increased during the long rule of Jabez Bunting. Bunting, the son of a Manchester tailor, could easily demonstrate that most of his attitudes, which were absolutist, clerical, and conservative, were those of the founder. He became assistant-secretary of the Conference in 1806, secretary in 1814 (annually re-elected), and permanent general secretary of missionary activities in 1833. He was at the head of a considerable propaganda machine, and he controlled the Stationing Committee which placed ministers in their circuits. In other words, he was in control of all the rewards and punishments available to the ministers. He ran the Conference absolutely, and such power corrupted considerably if not completely.

He used his power, for example, to attempt to break up the strongly revivalist Methodists of Leeds. They were led by a schoolmaster called James Sigston, who fell foul of the Buntingite superintendent Edmund Grindrod. A majority of the trustees of Brunswick Chapel decided in 1827 to instal an organ; they were, however, defeated at a District Meeting. Conference (which had not the power to do so) overruled the District Meeting; the organ would be fitted. A further District Meeting was then called to try the opponents of the organ. Bunting himself appeared, and many of the opponents resigned or were expelled, as Bunting intended. But the dissidents formed the Protestant Methodists. At length, three men – Robert Eckett, Samuel Warren, and James Everett – backed by many sympathizers in the chapels, brought about the significant secession of the Wesleyan Reformers (1850). The Reformers, besides wishing a return to the simplicity and fervour of the early movement, were concerned to assert the near-independence of each circuit, to give laymen control over their own chapels, and to substitute democracy for autocracy. Eckett, a Yorkshire stonemason, was the originator of the demand for greater independence of the circuits. Warren, a minister, established his reputation as an anti-Buntingite by his opposition in 1834 to Bunting's scheme for a Theological Institution. The Reverend James Everett embarrassed Bunting by a whole series of satires, by setting up rival newspapers, and probably by writing *The Fly Sheets*, four attacks (1844–8) on Bunting and his system: he was expelled in 1849. Buntingism was very costly. Those who had taken any part in the agitation for Wesleyan reform were ruthlessly expelled or forced to resign, and no less than one hundred thousand members were lost in this way between 1849 and 1855. (The most sympathetic, analytical, and illuminating accounts of Bunting are by John Kent; see his *Age of Disunity*, esp. Ch. 4; also R. Currie, *Methodism Divided*, Ch. 2.)

The mass departures of the early fifties should not be allowed to detract from the magnitude of the Methodists' success in the first half of the century. It was during this period that it was established as a mass religion. In 1801, the Wesleyan Methodist membership was 90,000; in 1850, it was 358,227. In addition, the various offshoots numbered about 152,000 by the middle of the century. Horace Mann gave his opinion that the number of those attending some form of Methodist activity was about three times the number of communicants – that is to say, about two millions. In fact, there were altogether about eleven thousand Methodist chapels by 1850, with seating for 2,194,248 (see R. F. Wearmouth, *Methodism and Working Class Movements in England 1800–1850*, esp. pp. 15–17).

How the Methodists retained this dynamic has been the subject of considerable speculation. Dr Hobsbawm has tried to relate it to the vigour of popular agitation (see his article 'Methodism and the Threat of Revolution in Britain', in *History Today*, February 1957), and has concluded that the periods of rapid rise (more than nine thousand a year) coincide with years of political activity: 1793–4, 1831–4, 1837–41, 1848–50. The only exception was the 'good years' of 1820–4. E. P. Thompson has tentatively stated what amounts to the opposite view: that the defeat of political ambitions provoked an immediate despairing reaction to Methodism. This is in line with a theory he propounds that counter-revolution produces a psychic effect; the frustrated revolutionaries are (as it were) laid open to religious frenzy. In support of this theory he adduces some of the more bizarre revivals of the Napoleonic War period, like Joanna Southcott's. This, too, is a difficult argument. Both exclude strictly internal and ecclesiastical reasons for fluctuating numbers. The success of Wesleyan Methodism as a missionary institution *over the whole period* is more satisfactorily explained by more straightforward causes than this. Rapid growth was always expected by the preachers – one of them, Stoner, observed in a prayer 'I am thankful for one soul, but oh! I want thousands' – and revivals bringing in thousands at a time were characteristic of second-generation Methodism. The organization of the Connexion was such as to admit new nembers and chapels easily, and the improvement of communications strengthened both the circuits and the Connexion. In the circuits the superintendents directed the itinerants so as to attend effectively to the needs of each society. The way in which rapid evangelizing took place is illustrated best by Bishop Wickham's examples in Sheffield (*Church and People in an Industrial City*, pp. 78–81). Large and respectable Wesleyan chapels, with most of their pews rented, were built as the city expanded; but the Wesleyans and the New Connexion Methodists continued also to preach in houses and barns, and to erect chapels wherever there were preachers and a congregation. In his list for 1841, Wickham notes, besides the four great Wesleyan Methodist chapels in the city, no less than twelve more Wesleyan, six New Connexion, two Protestant Methodist, and two Primitive Methodist chapels. Such rapid chapel-building created some difficulties, but it was a sign of extraordinary vigour (on this, see also E. R. Taylor, *Methodism and Politics 1791–1851*, pp. 98–103).

Old Dissent

The success of the Evangelical Revival was also visible among the Presbyterians, the Congregationalists (or Independents), and the Baptists. The victorious Methodists had four advantages – political conservatism, theological orthodoxy, effective organization, and emotional and aggressive preaching. The most important of the old sects, the (English) Presbyterians, virtually disappeared under the shock, and re-emerged as a completely different entity; the Congregationalists had to compromise on their cardinal idea of church government, the independence of each congregation. This was also a vital part of Baptist order, but it had to give way.

English Presbyterianism as it existed when the Revolutionary Wars broke out was numerically in decay. Once it was easily the majority group among the Dissenters, but by the 1790s it formed only a twentieth part. Politically, its leaders, if not its rank and file, were sympathetic to the ideas of the French Revolution. Theologically it was Unitarian; that is to say, it accepted the divinity of God only. Along with its calm rationalism, this proved its overwhelming weakness. The Independents and Baptists, who remained orthodox Trinitarians, accomplished an astonishing takeover of Presbyterian meeting houses. Halévy (*History of the English People*, Vol. I, pp. 417–18) gives some figures. In 1796 there were only 15 Presbyterian congregations, as compared with 33 Independent and 18 Baptist congregations, in London. By 1796, 20 Presbyterian chapels had been closed in Devonshire. In 1812, only 2 Presbyterian chapels remained in Hampshire, whereas there had been 40 in 1729.

This seizing of empty or struggling chapels produced at length a legal struggle over the endowments of the Presbyterians. The Wolverhampton Case of 1816 arose because the minister of a Unitarian chapel, found to be a Trinitarian, refused to be ejected by his congregation. The congregation met elsewhere, and sued for the endowments. The Toleration Act of 1689 excluded Unitarians from its benefits: they could only worship in strict legality after the Act of 1813. Endowments made before 1813, therefore, could only be made to Trinitarians. The Wolverhampton minister therefore secured the decision – which threatened all Unitarian endowments. A further case, brought by the Independents in 1830 and not fully resolved until 1842, made this clearer than ever. Lady Howley's Charity (a fund for the maintenance of preachers in the six northernmost counties) could only be distributed to Trinitarians. A number of other cases were pending. Peel's Government had to resolve the problem in an Act of 1844 (which caused a storm among the orthodox) by permitting usage over the past twenty-five years to determine the fate of the endowments unless the trust deed of the chapel specified otherwise.

Unitarianism was thus able to survive, though in some ways as a curiosity. By descent it should have been calm, intellectual, questioning, and interested in the problems of this world. As will be seen, there were Unitarians of this type, and the general atmosphere of freedom of thought attracted philosophical converts like Arthur Clough. But Unitarianism did not escape the prevailing Evangelicalism and romanticism: their greatest luminary, James Martineau, read the Anglican Evangelicals in his youth, and his hymn-book (1840) showed it – though there were Roman Catholic hymns in it as well. In one sense, however, the Unitarians were untouched by the Revival; they were not actively missionary, and their numbers were constant. In the 1851 Census they had 229 meeting houses.

Some Presbyterians who still believed in the Trinity were left after the flight to Unitarianism, but they were rescued in their weakness by the Church of Scotland, and in general the Presbyterians in England in the nineteenth century were Scottish exiles or descended from them.

Independency (or Congregationalism) was gaining ground at the beginning of the century. There were then 1,024 Independent congregations. Their orthodoxy was, as we have seen, a major reason for their expansion. Other, more accidental, reasons could account for their rise. Bishop Wickham details the setting up of five Independent chapels in Sheffield between 1774 and 1790 by a process of secession provoked largely by disagreement between sections of congregations. The principal development of the early nineteenth century was to remedy these basically anarchic procedures. For waging Dissenters' political campaigns, for founding new chapels, for administering endowments, and for missionary activity, especially through the London Missionary Society, some central organization was necessary. The term 'Congregational Union' was a clear contradiction in terms to a body which held that individual congregations were the units of government and the determinants of doctrine; but it was set up in 1831 and it issued a declaration on doctrine and government in 1833. But its income by 1839 was only £117 and its expenditure £574. It was saved by its publications: a very successful hymn-book (1836), and three newspapers.

To form a Baptist Union was harder still. The principal difference between the Baptists and the Congregationalists was their belief in adult rather than in infant baptism; otherwise, they both held that the opinions of individual congregations were decisive. The varying attitudes towards Calvinism within the sect kept them divided among themselves. The most rigid predestinarians were the Strict and Particular Baptists; the less rigid, the Particular Baptists; the Arminians, the General Baptists. (There were also some Unitarian Baptists – the Old General Baptists.) One further cause of dissension was the attitude to be taken to the problem of 'open Communion': that is to say, whether all holding generally Evangelical opinions should be admitted to Communion, or merely those baptized as adults. A form of union did emerge – at first among the Particular Baptists in 1832 – though it was not able to finance itself from publications with such success as the Congregational Union did, and in consequence remained weak. The most eminent of all Baptist preachers, Charles Haddon Spurgeon, did not begin his London career until 1853. Most of the Baptist pastors were very obscure men. The total numbers of Baptists are hard to come upon. Professor Horton Davies quotes a figure of 708 congregations at the beginning of the century. In 1851 there was a total of 2,222, most of them Particular Baptists. 366,000 went to the best-attended service at Baptist chapels on 30 March 1851.

[20] THE CHURCHES AND SOCIAL AND POLITICAL PROBLEMS 1791–1850

The Church of England

The response of the Church to the twin problems of the French Wars and industrial change was in some ways oblique. The romantic flight into medievalism, and the continued hankering of the English clergyman after a country parish, represented a revulsion from the new society. The most characteristic form of social action in the Church was the erection of thousands of churches and the invigoration of parochial life – the cure for every form of disaffection, and the pre-eminent objective of many of the great administrative reforms. Nothing approaching a social programme emanated from the Church except for the collection of humanitarian interests and prejudices of Lord Shaftesbury, the cloudy and rather apologetic Christian Socialism of Maurice and Kingsley, and some acute observations by Dr Arnold. This is not to say that the Church was not involved in politics – it was. Peel, Goulburn, and Graham on one side, and Melbourne and Russell on the other, were concerned from day to day with matters which had an ecclesiastical dimension and required them to consider increasingly the balance of church and chapel interests and opinions.

Most of the social attitudes of the early Victorian Church were formulated in the years between the outbreak of the French War and Peterloo. The opinions of churchmen in general during that period require no great space to set down. A Whig like Richard Watson, the Bishop of Llandaff (whose superb intelligence on political, ecclesiastical, and agricultural matters is usually obscured by concentration on the details of his absenteeism), underwent the expected changes of opinion as the Revolution progressed. The fall of the Bastille and the Declaration of the Rights of Man pleased him, and appeared to portend the general spread of liberty. The later events, however – the increasing activity of the French 'populace', the fear of social strife in this country, and the rise of Napoleon – changed his mind. Other

bishops expressed their anti-Jacobinism with varying degrees of
enthusiasm: Samuel Horsley (1733–1806), successively of St
David's, Rochester, and St Asaph, wanted the clergy to form an
armed militia in 1798, and at St Asaph had a volunteer force
exercising on the parish lawn. For some years in the middle of
the war the belief that there was a general conspiracy against
Christianity exercised the imagination of some of the bishops.
The appearance of works by the émigré Abbé Bruel and by the
Scots Professor John Robison in 1797 seeking to demonstrate
that the Revolution was a result of a conspiracy by Freemasons
and their sympathizers like Voltaire and Diderot gave the
bishops their arguments.

Mainly, however, churchmen were concerned with the possibility of internal upheaval. From them all came the view that
the Church was the appointed instrument for securing social
cohesion, for maintaining existing ranks and degrees, for ensuring
happiness in the next world if not in this: opinions which (except
for the last) were shared by Napoleon and his most strenuous
opponents on the English episcopal bench. There was a general
consciousness of guilt, of vice or idleness, among the upper class,
which set a bad example to the lower orders. This notion is often
associated with the Evangelicals, but it was not their exclusive
property. John Bowdler, a high-church layman, in his *Reform or
Ruin* (1797) complained that:

Luxury, Corruption, Adultery, Gaming, Pride, Vanity, Idleness,
Extravagance and Dissipation prevail too generally. (R. A. Soloway,
Prelates and People, p. 27)

There was, too, a sense of guilt inside the Church itself: that the
machine was rendered inefficient by pluralism, non-residence,
top-heavy cathedral establishments, and bad distribution of
stipends. Plenty of voices, of course, justified these things in the
obvious way. Samuel Horsley explained:

They arise from the nature of our calling: in part from the corrupt
manners of a world at enmity with God; but primarily, from the
mysterious councils of Providence.

But the pressure of the Evangelicals and the social alarms of the period set all that aside. It appeared that a well-ordered and efficient parochial life was the best guarantee against revolution. If that were so, then the Church was not doing its job. Arthur Young (whose sympathies were mildly Evangelical) turned to the sociology of religion at the end of his *General View of the Agriculture of the County of Lincoln* (1799) to observe that he 'found upon the Wolds a neglect of public worship which ought to receive animadversion'. The neglect arose mainly from smallness of stipends, and as a result

the people, abandoned to Sundays of mere idleness, without religious instruction, necessarily resort to the alehouse, and become depraved and licentious. National prosperity depends on the industry of the common people; industry on good morals; and as good morals amongst the poor are nursed only by the Gospel being preached to them, it must be clear to every considerable mind, that the most important of the national interests must suffer by a neglect of public worship . . . I know of nothing better calculated to fill a country with barbarians ready for any mischief, than extensive commons, and divine service only once a month.

A report compiled in that county by some parochial clergy in 1800 revealed most alarmingly that in a population of 15,000, something under 5,000 had nothing to do with the Church. Less than one-sixth of the adult population were communicants, and there was little in the way of family religion.

In other senses the Church appeared guilty of neglect. The rise and shift of population meant that the available churches in many parishes would not seat anything like the available population. It had also neglected the education of the poor.

The Church's solution to the social evils of the time was therefore to increase the efficiency of the parish. As a legal entity, the parish was involved enough; as a pastoral unit it became more and more so, as commentators and practitioners of every shade of opinion added their requirements. A resident clergyman and a resident squire were necessary to its working. It had to be of workable size, and have endowments to provide a reasonable living for the clergymen. In the course of the war period a school became a necessity for the inculcation of 'right principles'. Southey, in 1817, in his *Letter to William Smith* insisted that the children of the poor

must be taught to 'fear God and keep his commandments, for this is the whole duty of man'. Mere reading and writing will not do this: they must be fed with the milk of sound doctrine, for states are secure in proportion as the great body of the people are attached to the institutions of the country.

(This was not, however, Southey's only argument for education.) Later, various other devices, particularly benefit clubs of various sorts, singing classes, readings, allotments, missionary society branches, and complex arrangements for visiting, were introduced in well-run parishes (for exhaustive analysis of this topic, see *Temporal Pillars*, esp. pp. 145–72).

The achievement of this ideal – which of course was stimulated and broadened by every kind of activity from Lord Shaftesbury's labours to provide more curates to Keble's poetic idealism at East Leach and Hursley – was the task to which the Church was principally dedicated. The evidence on the ground – the mass of Victorian churches in every county – appears to indicate success, but closer analysis suggests disappointment and failure.

The creation of so many parishes required a programme of state activity, organized philanthropy, and practical benevolence on a huge scale. Already while the Napoleonic Wars were being fought, the laws against non-residence were tightened and attempts were made to secure a minimum wage for curates; after the war, the Government was persuaded to give state aid to church building in populous parishes. Pressure was put upon Perceval and on his successor, Liverpool, by a number of men which included Joshua Watson (1771–1855). Watson, a high-church wine merchant who retired from his trade in 1814 and became the centre of a group called the Hackney Phalanx, was the indispensable man of business when it came to organizing the accumulation and distribution of funds for charity, for schools, for churches, and for curates. In the campaign for state help for church building, their argument was simple: that the fifty churches in and about London could not contain a tenth part of the population, which was altogether more than a million. They formed in 1818 the Incorporated Church Building Society with the approbation of Liverpool and the Archbishop of Canterbury; in the same year Parliament voted a million pounds for building churches in populous places. A further half-million was added in 1824. (Here, in fact is the positive 'social policy' of Lord Liverpool!) The money was to be administered by a Commission, of which Watson was a member. They speedily worked out their own rules of operation, like fixing a maximum of £20,000 for a single church, and resolving to work through the bishops. To make the money spin out, pew rents were charged and the parish was invited to contribute to the cost. The original grants were exhausted by 1835. Many churchmen hoped for something of the same kind from Peel, but by the forties the power of Dissent made it impracticable. The Commissioners ultimately built or assisted in building more than five hundred churches. This figure does not exhaust the total number of churches built: many more were the result of private munificence, like Keble's three churches built out of the proceeds of *The Christian Year* (on Watson, see A. B. Webster, *Joshua Watson*).

Schools were also essential to the new parochial ideal; and here the Church fell into one of its gravest and longest-lasting political and sectarian controversies. The desirability of educating the poor was not (indeed) the Church's discovery alone. On the one hand there was pressure from the Benthamites and Dissenters, who secured the setting up of the Royal Lancasterian Institution (subsequently the British and Foreign Schools Society, 1814); on the other, from those Anglicans who set up the National Society for the Education of the Poor in the Principles of the Church of England (1811). The National Society was the creation of the Hackney Phalanx, and of Joshua Watson in particular. Its achievements and its deficiencies were largely, if not entirely, due to him. As an institution for the creation of schools, it was very successful. In three years from its foundation it had raised sufficient contributions for 360 schools in which there were 60,000 pupils. By 1824, 400,000 children were being instructed in 3,054 of the Society's schools. But the National Society was aggressively sectarian, and Watson's original terms under which the Society would make grants required that instruction be given in the Services and the Catechism, that the children attend church, and that no books should be used except those published by the S.P.C.K. The narrowness of the curriculum and ideals of the National Schools was a faithful reflection of the fear of the squires – and of some of the bishops – that the education of the poor would have unsettling social effects.

The intrusion of the State came in 1833 – it gave an annual grant of £20,000 to be divided between the voluntary societies in proportion to the funds they raised. The very success of the National Society made it vulnerable to criticism both from the Dissenters and from those who wished the State to be the provider of education, since it got the lion's share of the grant. In 1839 the Whigs produced a more elaborate scheme which infuriated the Anglicans. The grants to the societies were to be equalized; the State was to set up normal schools for training teachers; and a committee of the Privy Council was to supervise education. Watson declared:

The mind of the State on this great subject is neither more nor less than the transference of the people's training from the Church to themselves. And for this purpose they must degrade the National Society and reform the Universities. . . .

A huge public meeting was called, with the Archbishop of Canterbury in the chair and a platform full of bishops behind him. In the event the Whig scheme was severely mangled. A Committee of the Privy Council did take over the supervision of education, but the normal schools proposal was dropped; an elaborate compromise was made to ensure that inspectors would be bearable to the bishops and to the National Society; and the old system of making grants proportional to the money raised privately was resumed (see the account of the 1839 proceedings in Norman Gash, *Reaction and Reconstruction in English Politics 1832–1852*, pp. 76–9). This was, however, the last complete triumph of the Church of England in this field; the attempt by Sir James Graham in 1843 to make his projected factory education an Anglican preserve met with a different fate. Besides, Dr Kaye was secretary of the new Committee of the Privy Council and was determined to assert the authority of the State. Watson chose the right moment to retire from the National Society – in 1842.

The unvarying faith in a vigorous parochial system as a social cure-all was not, in the end, justified by its results – at any rate if the object was to attract town workers. In the strictly organizational sense, the ideal was not attainable. The Anglican ideal was the *country* parish, and that was something of slow growth. The importation of gaunt Commissioners' churches in the industrial areas was at best a compromise. In an attempt to provide endowments for the clergy, pew rents had to be charged and therefore the number of free seats in the churches was relatively small. The Vicar of St Philip's, Sheffield, reported that in his (Commissioners') church there were 1,200 in rented pews, and 800 free sittings. Moreover, the operatives were reluctant to sit in the free seats because of their 'spirit of independence'. The new town parishes were often one-class parishes, without the nice social gradations of rural England, and Anglican clergymen did not like them. In the providing of schools, the National Society's achievements in the industrial cities were small, since the Society founded its schools where money and interest were forthcoming. The infinitely dedicated Vicar of Leeds, W. F. Hook, was discontented if not hopeless:

I am myself surrounded by a district containing 250,000 souls in which there are thousands uneducated or receiving an education worse than none [he wrote to the Bishop of St David's]; from increase of population, the clergyman meanwhile as soon as one school is built has to commence another and when all is done, he has the satisfaction of feeling that it is only a drop in the ocean.

A deep gloom settled over churchmen when they realized their relative failure in capturing the poor of the cities. The slight

evidence of the Lincolnshire Report, and the larger evidence of
the 1851 Census, suggest very strongly that there was always a
layer impervious to the Church, and current opinion coincides
very strongly with the celebrated observation of Disraeli. When
Archbishop Longley remarked to him that the Church had lost
the towns, Disraeli replied: 'Your Grace is mistaken. The Church
never had the towns.' (The best evidence so far collected on this
problem appears in K. S. Inglis, *Churches and the Working
Classes in Victorian England*; and in Wickham, op. cit., esp.
pp. 70–106.)

The reasons for the Church's failure were difficult to find
then, and are so now. The Church never formulated a social
programme more profound than church building; but there were
exceptional persons who thought it should have one. Thomas
Arnold was the most acute critic of the existing situation, and
he is quoted with approval by Bishop Wickham:

I cannot understand what is the good of a National Church if it be
not to Christianize the nation, and introduce the principles of
Christianity into men's social and civil relations, and expose the
wickedness of that spirit which maintains the game laws, and in
agriculture and trade seems to think that there is no such sin as
covetousness, and that if a man is not dishonest, he has nothing to do
but make all the profit of his capital that he can.

Arnold saw the Evangelicals and the high-churchmen as too
much consumed with their strictly theological views to be able
to do any such thing.

There was, however, one short-lived and halting attempt to
come to terms with the social problem: Christian Socialism. The
name was coined in 1850. The group's beginnings were at the
time of the last Chartist fiasco in April 1848, and it expired as a
movement in 1855. Its leading figures were John Malcolm Ludlow,
a barrister; Charles Kingsley, the Vicar of Eversley in Hampshire, an intensely excitable preacher and novelist; and Frederick
Denison Maurice, a high-church clergyman and Professor of
Theology and History at King's College, London. Socialism was
then 'in the air', partly as a result of Robert Owen's New Har-

mony community, and partly because of French theory and experiment. Ludlow had been brought up in France, and was concerned to Christianize the new movement he observed in Paris in the first months of the 1848 Revolution. Socialism was, he said,

a real and very great power which had acquired an unmistakeable hold, not merely on the fancies but on the consciences of the Parisian workmen, and . . . it must be Christianized or shake Christianity to its foundation, precisely because it appealed to the higher and not to the lower instincts of the men.

Ludlow, Kingsley, and Maurice brought out a penny paper called *Politics and the People* between May and July 1848. It was not revolutionary in its opinions; it disliked universal suffrage, the ballot, physical force, Chartists, and huge meetings. But Kingsley (who wrote as 'Parson Lot') was explosive in his expression – 'My only quarrel with the Charter is, that it does not go far enough.' His observation that

We have used the Bible as if it was a mere special constable's hand-book – an opium-dose for keeping beasts of burden patient while they were being overloaded

was certainly a shock to received notions. The difficulty, of course, was making contact with working men. In 1849, meetings were arranged at which Maurice, Ludlow, and Kingsley did gain the confidence of some of the working men, though the trio were very uneasy at hearing attacks on the Queen and the clergy. It was in reply to one of these that Kingsley stammered out: 'I am a Church of England clergyman – and a Chartist!'

The movement did produce a practical experiment or two. Associations of tailors, builders, pianomakers, and so forth were formed in 1849 and 1850. The workmen were to control them and enjoy the profits of their labour. Ludlow founded another journal, *The Christian Socialist*, which set out a surprisingly coherent attack on the worship of the profit motive and the necessity for a more democratic Church. But it was Kingsley who provided the publicity with his novel *Alton Locke* (1850) and his sermon on 'The Message of the Church to the Labouring Man' (1851), an attempt to show that the gospel message was one of liberty, equality, and fraternity. The Bishop of London suspended him from preaching, but Kingsley succeeded in explaining his sermon away. It raised the Christian Socialists in the estimation of the Chartists, and the *Northern Star* in July 1851 called them leaders of the Co-operative Movement. As an organized body, however, they did not last long, and they came under attack from conservative opinion. Some of those brought into the movement were permanently affected, like Thomas Hughes; Kingsley in later life regarded it as a youthful error. (See the admirable survey by Owen Chadwick, *The Victorian Church*, I, pp. 346–63; S. C. Carpenter, *Church and People 1789–1889*, S.P.C.K., 1959, II, pp. 316–26.)

Lord Shaftesbury (1801–86) – or as he should be called within the time-limits of this study, Lord Ashley – is perhaps most closely associated in the popular mind with a social policy which sprang from religious conviction. But although he mobilized and personified the 'Victorian conscience', acted as 'church minister' when his relative, Palmerston, was at the head of affairs, and spoke of himself as 'an Evangelical of the Evangelicals', he was a man whose activities and opinions were essentially personal. He did not, like Wilberforce, work through a high command or preside over a large parliamentary connexion. He had a set of prejudices rather than a programme, and he conducted his campaigns as a figure raised above the party game – at any rate after 1841, when his instinctive Tory paternalism clashed sharply with Peel's laissez-faire.

He achieved his eminence as a philanthropist when he was in his early thirties by something approaching a political accident. Michael Sadler, the M.P. who had been leading the agitation against existing factory conditions, was defeated in the general election of 1832. Ashley offered his help in the agitation. Entirely unexpectedly, he was asked to lead it. Ashley's opinions on the millowners and the factory operatives were not at that time based on any personal acquaintance with employers or employed, or with northern industrial areas. He shared the vulgar prejudice against millowners that landed proprietors then had, and his emotional and impetuous nature was stirred by the (very partisan) evidence on the condition of the factories presented to the 1832 Select Committee of the House of Commons, which Sadler had stage-managed. The leaders of the Ten Hours Movement, like Oastler and Parson Bull, made Ashley's name known in the factory districts once he had accepted the leadership of the movement, and the vigour and crudity of Ashley's own views on the millowners speedily made him famous there. By his bill of March 1833 the employment of children under nine would have been forbidden; those under eighteen would have worked a maximum of forty-eight hours a week; and employees under twenty-one would have been forbidden to work at night. The Government, however, instituted a Royal Commission to investigate the question and, after it had reported, introduced a bill which became the Factory Act of 1833. Children under nine were not to be employed; those under thirteen were to work eight hours a day, preferably in a divided shift, so that they might receive some education; those between thirteen and eighteen were to work a daily maximum of twelve hours. An inspectorate was to be set up to supervise the working of the Act.

The Act did not work well, and Ashley was critical of its shortcomings. Initial attempts to improve it failed, but in 1840 he secured a Select Committee to look into its working. When Peel became Prime Minister in 1841, Ashley feared that his basic plan of a working day of ten hours would be unacceptable, and so it was. But Sir James Graham produced a bill in 1843 which was a statesmanlike attempt to produce workable factory legislation. It was very much mangled, largely because of Nonconformist objection to its educational clauses (see p. 189), and Ashley opposed it because it brought a ten-hour day no nearer. As passed in 1844, it restricted the working day to six and a half hours for those between eight and thirteen, and twelve hours for women and young persons; the powers of the factory inspectors were strengthened. Ashley's ten-hour day was achieved as a result of the Act of 1847, passed when he was out of the Commons.

The cause of factory reform established Ashley's public reputation. But as a result of working on it his interests became
much broader, and he recognized that the factory operatives
were only a tiny proportion of those who were in need of protection. The Royal Commission he secured in 1840 was intended
to investigate children's employment in general. It produced
only one (illustrated) report, and that was a sensation: the report
on mines. The Act of 1842, prohibiting all women, and boys
under ten, from working down the pits, and appointing inspectors, resulted. Many other groups in society – boy chimney-
sweeps, dressmakers, milliners, and brickfield workers among
them – secured his help. He became – in the age just before social
surveys – the authority on destitution in London, and much of
his later activity arose from that (see G. F. A. Best, *Shaftesbury*,
1964, esp. Ch. 4).

The major attempts by the refurbished Church of England
to face new social problems, then, were to found more parishes
and more schools in the interests of salvation, civilization, and
subordination; a tiny and temporary group suggested Utopian
socialism; and one layman marshalled the forces of Evangelical
philanthropy. The total effort was prodigious.

Old Dissent

After the French Revolution broke out, the sympathies of the
two ornaments of Rational Dissent, Price and Priestley, were
with the Revolution. It was Richard Price's sermon to the
London Revolution Society (a body revived to commemorate
the 1688 Revolution) in November 1789, in which he asserted
that the 1688 Revolution established the right of the governed
to choose, and, if need be, cashier their governors, which provoked Burke's *Reflections on the French Revolution*. It was
Priestley's house which was attacked in the Church and King
Riots in Birmingham in 1790. How far the Dissenters in general
followed the views of these ageing luminaries is a problem not
solved, though the response of the Baptist congregation at
Norwich to the news of the acquittals of the Radicals in the

State Trial of 1794 suggests that they had some support. They
rose at the pastor's direction and sang 'Praise God from whom
all blessings flow' (the story is told by E. P. Thompson: op. cit.,
Pelican ed., pp. 148–9). But the stand of the Rational Dissenters
did not make their sect – they were Presbyterian Unitarians –
any more popular: quite the reverse. Everywhere they were
giving ground to the more orthodox sects. Their academies,
often badly run but now suspected to be training grounds for the
seditious, closed.

The distinctive attitude of Old Dissent had always been a keen
sense of their political exclusion. With the repeal of the Test and
Corporation Acts in 1828, the Dissenters were free to play a
more direct part in English political life without fear of action
being taken against them. But the 1828 Repeal Act was merely
a beginning to them. They were still consumed with grievances.
Moderate opinion, such as the statement put out by the Dissenting Deputies' United Committee in May 1833, was specific: they
objected to having to marry in the parish church, to paying
church rates, to the assessment of Dissenting meeting houses for
the poor rate, to the possibility of being denied burial in the
parish churchyards, and to their exclusion from the universities.
They wished the registration of births and deaths to be a legal
requirement. The Whigs, who still in the thirties considered
themselves the representatives of Dissenting opinion, attempted
to deal with some of these: there was a Dissenters' Marriage Act
and obligatory registration of births, marriages, and deaths, in
1836. The most objectionable remaining burden, however, was
church rates, and no proposed solution – whether providing
revenue from the Land Tax (1834) or making arrangements to
pay it from the Church's existing revenue (1837) – could secure
enough support among Anglican Whig backbenchers.

More grave than the demands of the Dissenting Deputies were
the problems of the provision of eduation for the poor and the
threat to Protestantism which Rome and the Tractarians seemed
to offer in the thirties, forties, and fifties. These helped to drive
the Dissenters into more extreme attitudes, and eventually, at
the general election of 1847, to sever their conventional alliance

with the Whig party. 'Extreme attitudes' for nineteenth-century Dissenters usually meant moving from making particular complaints to talking of the disestablishment of the Church of England and the bringing about of a kind of 'free trade' in religion in which, as it were, all churches commended themselves to the public for support on equal terms. (Both the idea and the metaphor then enjoyed a certain popularity among city Dissenters.) An extreme attitude in education meant opposing state provision for education altogether. Neither of these provisions was practicable, but they were somehow satisfying to those who mouthed them or filled columns of their journals with them.

As has already been seen, the Whigs chose in 1833 to assist the provision of schools by offering grants to the voluntary societies in proportion to the money they themselves could raise. This worked to the disadvantage of the British and Foreign Schools Society, which by the 1830s had largely shed its Benthamite supporters and was dominated by Dissent. Equalization of the grant was proposed in 1839, but Anglican opposition prevented the proposal from getting anywhere. When the education clauses of the 1843 Factory Bill foreshadowed Church of England control of this projected new branch of education – schoolmasters in the factory schools were to be approved by the diocesan bishop, and the school boards were to have an Anglican majority in practice – the Dissenters successfully opposed the bill, even securing the assistance of the Wesleyan Methodists in their campaign. The return of the Whigs in 1846 did not improve the situation at all. Russell's proposals for education involved an increase in state grants to the societies, but the National Society would again secure the lion's share. The figures for the allocation of state funds for new school buildings after 1839 exist: between 1839 and 1850, four-fifths of the money went to the National Society and only one-tenth to the British and Foreign Schools Society. In April 1847 a National Education Conference was called by the Dissenters. Its resolutions were, by any previous standard, wild. In education they became 'voluntaryists' – that is, opposed to government provision altogether. In a mood of deep disenchantment with both parties, they set up a Dissenters'

Electoral Committee to encourage parliamentary opposition; and they demanded disestablishment.

The climax to all this was something against all the political rules – the desertion of the Whigs. In 1846 twenty-six Dissenters were returned to Parliament, and altogether sixty M.P.s were pledged against the extension of state-endowed religion. This extraordinary indulgence in the luxury of protest brought them no conceivable advantage – quite the reverse – and is an indication of how amateurish they were as politicians. But they did not take such a step because of the problems of educating the poor. It was not just the fear of the expansion of the power of the Established Church which aroused their hostility, either, but the increasing fear of a 'Romanizing' Church, and of the Roman Catholic Church itself. Edward Miall, the most active of the Dissenters' publicists, resigned as a Congregationalist pastor in Leicester in 1839 in part because he disliked these tendencies. This vigorous anti-Popery was something new: traditionally, the liberal principles of the Dissenters had included Roman Catholic Emancipation, as in 1828–9. In part the new feeling was also brought about by both parties' handling of the Irish situation. The Tories increased the state grant to Maynooth Roman Catholic seminary in 1845, and Russell for many years tinkered with the idea of the State's paying Roman Catholic priests' salaries in Ireland (see N. Gash, *Reaction and Reconstruction in English Politics 1832–1852*, esp. pp. 60–118).

One other issue gave the Dissenters the opportunity of taking up anti-Establishment attitudes. The Anti-Corn Law League saw its campaign as being not merely against landed gentlemen, but also as being against that other essential component of the landed interest, the Church of England, whose tithes were calculated on the price of corn. Bright wrote in 1842:

The Church clergy are almost to a man guilty of the present distress by upholding the Corn Law – they having themselves an interest in the high price of bread.

The League, therefore, made a great point of enlisting the support of Dissenting ministers in their campaign. Dr Norman McCord

played its loyalty indicated a basic uneasiness. The governing
sses (full of prejudice, no doubt) found it difficult, if not
ossible, to accept Methodist protestations. Sometimes Metho-
n was lumped together with Dissent, as it was by the Mayor
Liverpool in 1792 when he complained of the number of
thodist and other meeting houses' in the vicinity:

equently [he added] the youth of the County are training up
the instruction of a set of men not only ignorant but of whom
k we have of late too much reason to imagine are inimical to our
Constitution.

ey, the Bishop of Rochester, thought the Methodists' main
s were 'sedition and atheism'. It was this basic suspicion
was behind Sidmouth's bill of 1811 which would have
a preacher's licence to anyone not having the support of
utable householders and which speedily provoked official
ist action alongside the Dissenters (see p. 169). Once the
ists had scotched the bill and secured the 'New Toleration
ere was a new element in their declarations of loyalty –
e – and there was even an address to the Prince Regent
Their protestations were rather guilty in another sense
ll, many of the Luddite sympathizers so snubbed by
and Jackson were clearly Methodists or Methodist
zers.

g and Jackson remained official figures in Wesleyan
n for another generation, and consequently their
to reform and civil disturbance, whether that meant,
le, Peterloo or Chartism, became the standard ones.
not merely pious opinions: action was often taken to
malcontents. In 1819 (when Rev. Richard Watson
rd Sidmouth that no man would be tolerated as a
a Methodist Society who joined a political club or
adical meetings) a Manchester local preacher was
signing a declaration against the magistrates for
at Peterloo, and scholars at a Sunday school in the
pelled for wearing Radical badges. Chartism wa
condemned – the Wesleyan preachers of Ba

has shown that the great Manchester meeting which nearly
seven hundred ministers attended in August 1841 was not
exactly a spontaneous manifestation of support, nor was it in
any way a body representing the opinion of seven hundred congregations; it was in fact a stage-managed affair (see *The Anti-
Corn Law League*, Allen & Unwin, 2nd ed., 1968, pp. 103–7).

The present state of knowledge does not make it easy to assess
the Dissenters' appeal to industrial workers. Dr Kitson Clark has
some evidence that the Baptists were active missionaries in
Leeds in the 1830s, and that the Congregationalists also took this
function seriously. But their contribution to municipal life once
the repeal of the Test and Corporation Acts and the passing of
the Municipal Corporations Act laid it open to them was remarkable. Their election to the reformed House of Commons was slow
in coming after the Reform Act, but their admission to the corporations of newly constituted industrial boroughs was rapid.
After the 1835 Act the first mayors of Manchester, Leicester, and
Derby were Unitarians, and out of a council of forty-two elected
in Leicester in 1836, twelve were Unitarian. It was in Birmingham particularly that a Dissenter-inspired 'civic gospel' evolved.
Local government in a new corporation could have been a humdrum matter, but in fact it was leavened with a remarkable
idealism which was generated by a distinguished group of
Dissenting ministers. Most of them flourished in the second half
of the century, but the originator of the civic gospel, George
Dawson, became the minister of Mount Zion Baptist Chapel in
1844, when he was twenty-three. He subsequently opened his
own Church of the Saviour in 1847. He was a very uncharacteristic figure for a nineteenth-century pastor in that he was untouched by the Evangelical Revival and thought like a Rational
Dissenter, rejecting all formal creeds. The social content of his
addresses was, however, relevant enough to Birmingham civic
leaders of the nineteenth century – his congregations often
included them. The 'common end and purpose was to clothe the
naked, feed the hungry, and instruct the ignorant'. Enterprises
like the provision of free libraries were given the importance and
glamour of a crusade, and the middle classes of the city were

induced to give their labour and their wealth in the service of their town. The inspiration for all this did not spring from Birmingham, though; much of it was distinctively Unitarian and originated with James Martineau (see G. Kitson Clark, *The Making of Victorian England*, Methuen, 1963, pp. 161, 165; and Asa Briggs, *Victorian Cities*, pp. 195–8).

Wesleyan Methodism and its Offshoots

When the Reform agitation was at its height in 1831, the Annual Address of the Wesleyan Methodist Conference included the words:

Let not worldly politics engross too much of your time and attention. Avoid all undue eagerness and anxiety on subjects which, however much their importance might be magnified by the men of the world, are only of moment in the estimation of the Christian, as far as they can be rendered subservient to the best interests of mankind.

In them may be seen the authentic sentiments of John Wesley. Politics were dangerously worldly; they took time better spent in spiritual or at any rate chapel activity; they provoked needless splits within the Methodist societies. The common view of the history of the whole Methodist body in the first half of the nineteenth century is that a series of rebellions took place against the reactionary and authoritarian rule of the Conference, and in particular of Bunting; but in fact each of the offshoots, out of belief, prudence, and self-preservation, made official observations much like those of the parent body just quoted. This is not to say that individual Methodists did not have political opinions or did not participate in the politics of their time; their personal inclinations, the circumstances in which they found themselves, and the training and esteem which they obtained inside the Methodist organization, often impelled them to do so. One group, the Primitive Methodists, made their appeal principally to working people, and these impulses were strong. In the West Riding, where Wesleyan Methodism was so very powerful, Wesleyans were often Luddites or Chartists. Only occasionally was

an official line for political action laid down b[...] the politics involved were usually those of h[...] of self-defence. The traditions inherited fr[...] largely transmitted by Bunting – often made[...] Connexion very difficult; the 'special rel[...] Church of England particularly so.

In the Revolutionary period the attitud[...] well known: whether the attitude is called [...] tic depends on the opinions of the writer, b[...] opinion of the 1790s. The Leeds Conferen[...] 'unfeigned loyalty to the King, and sin[...] Constitution'; the Conference Address o[...] Methodists were 'not likely to meddl[...] change'. It was rather like Wesley spea[...] apart from that, the Methodists had[...] with the infidelity that was assoc[...] opinions, or with the unrespectable[...] Tom Paine.

The official Conference attitude [...] and opinion at a more local level d[...] the war period. Dr Thomas Coke a[...] the Duke of Portland, the Home [...] his suspicions that a 'Grand A[...] against the Government. He wa[...] three Methodists suspected of [...] expelled from the Connexion. [...] tendent at Halifax during the [...] 1812, and he brought down[...] declining to conduct the bu[...] attempting to break into a mi[...] closed the gates of Greetland[...] cuit against Luddite symp[...] corpses of their executed co[...] to be delivered over them[...] R. F. Wearmouth, *Method[...] of England*, Epworth Pres[...]

However, the fulsome[...]

dis[...]
cla[...]
im[...]
dis[...]
of [...]
'Me[...]

Cons[...]
unde[...]
I thi[...]
happy[...]

Horsl[...]
object[...]
which [...]
denied[...]
six rep[...]
Methoc[...]
Methodi[...]
Act', th[...]
gratitud[...]
in 1814.[...]
– after [...]
Bunting [...]
sympathi[...]
Buntin[...]
Methodis[...]
attitudes[...]
for examp[...]
They were[...]
get rid of[...]
assured Lo[...]
member of [...]
attended R[...]
expelled for[...]
their action [...]
city were ex[...]
as vigorously[...]

District resolved to exclude any Chartists from their number.

Yet the development of the Chartist Movement is in many ways a testimony to the way in which Methodism in its various forms made up (or had made up) a vital part of the working-class experience, and Chartism may be viewed as a species of secular Methodism, in part run by ex-Methodist preachers. The camp meeting (copied from the Primitives: see pp. 202–3) was adopted as a method of outdoor assembly for a large concourse in 1839, and a meeting on Hood Hill between Barnsley and Sheffield was described (offensively) in detail by the *Sheffield Mercury*: 'the sacred formula [*sic*] of Divine Worship were parodied by giving the proceedings the appellation and method of a religious service' with a sermon and a hymn. Camp meetings continued to be held in the North and Midlands until 1850. There was also a Chartist love feast in Sheffield. The unit of Wesley's organization, the class, was also used in an adapted form by the Chartists; like the original Methodist class, it was used as a fund-raising body as well as for spreading and confirming ideas, and the class leaders assumed a particular prominence. The method seems first to have been adopted in 1839 in Oldham; it spread rapidly and was soon used as far north as South Shields and as far south as Birmingham. During the next year the system is reported in Bristol and Wiltshire. The scheme of Feargus O'Connor to constitute Chartism as a 'religious society' in 1843 was based on classes:

Each class, when constituted, shall choose for itself a leader subject to the confirmation of the Branch Board. The duties of leader will be to arrange for conversational meetings with his class at a place of meeting most convenient; to hold a friendly discussion relative to the principles and objects of the Association, to read the tracts and authorized documents and reports of the general body; to collect the subscriptions of the members and weekly hand them over to the branch secretary. . . .

This method appears in various forms until 1848, when the Attorney-General said that in its latest guise it was illegal.

It was not merely the organization that the Methodists provided, but the personnel. Membership of the Connexion, and a spell as a local preacher, were frequently temporary stages in the path of training and self-improvement which labour leaders followed, and the history of Chartism in its most active period is full of ex-preachers who used their old revivalist techniques in the service of the movement. Thomas Cooper, active at Leicester, had been in turn a Primitive and a Wesleyan. Ben Rushton of Halifax, active in the Yorkshire camp meetings of 1839, had been a local preacher in the New Connexion until about 1821. John Skevington of Loughborough, active in Leicester and in Chartism until his death in 1853, was a former Primitive. Joseph Rayner Stephens, a Wesleyan minister expelled in 1834 not for Radicalism but for his public support for disestablishment of the Church of England, was the most influential figure in Lancashire Chartism. There was a Methodist contribution to the working-class movement, even if it was not what the Conference wanted.

The official political activities of the Connexion were not Whig, Radical, or Tory in the first half of the nineteenth century; they were designed for the greater good of the Connexion or of mankind. The activities leading to the 'New Toleration Act' have been mentioned. The anti-slavery campaign occupied them closely and was supported with particular energy by Thomas Coke, whose knowledge of mission work in the West Indies was extensive, and by Richard Watson, secretary of the Conference and an early biographer of Wesley, whose contribution to the final stages of the campaign seems to be undervalued in the general histories. The work of the Methodists in the West Indies – there were 23,000 slaves who were members of the Connexion in 1833 – gave their observations particular weight. In the furiously fought York election in 1806, when Wilberforce stood in some danger of being defeated, three circulars requesting support for him were issued by Methodist ministers and laymen. Wilberforce was described by them as a man 'whose political sentiments and unwearied exertions to procure an abolition of the slave trade have endeared him to us and to our Society at large'. Conference actually told the Methodists to use their votes in the general election of 1830 to help secure abolition, though Watson's action in intervening in the Leeds election to persuade Methodists to vote for the Whig, T. B. Macaulay, and not the Tory, Michael Sadler, caused some controversy. In the organization of the huge meeting at Exeter Hall and of meetings in the country at large, Watson was very active. There were 224,000 signatures of Methodists on the mammoth petition for immediate abolition in 1833.

Education was the other political issue which made intervention necessary, and severely tested Anglican–Methodist relations. To give Methodism a prime place in the history of the formal school education of the poor would be a mistake, as has already been suggested. The Sunday school movement received some support from them, and Wesleyans preened themselves on the moral improvement they effected, on keeping the children off the streets on the Lord's day, and on the effect Sunday schools (open to virtually all) had in bringing in adherents to the Connexion. In fact, teaching children to write at Sunday school was formally forbidden by Conference in 1814, though the instruction seems to have been ignored in places. It did not become an obligation for every chapel to have a Sunday school until 1837. The building of Wesleyan day schools was not begun until the same year: 22 schools (and 9 infant schools) were provided. It was not until 1844 that the work was taken up with great vigour. There were 434 day schools by 1857. The figures showing government grants in aid between 1839 and 1840 indicate that the Wesleyans received only about one and a half per cent of the total, or about £7,500 (for most of these figures, see Maldwyn Edwards, *After Wesley*, pp. 100–9).

The change of strategy in 1844 is easily explained; it was on grounds strictly sectarian. Until the early forties, Wesleyan Methodism retained something of Wesley's horror of Dissent, and abhorred any thought of disestablishment of the Church of England. (Some of the offshoots, like the Bible Christians of the South-west, and the Wesleyan Association, were not of this opinion.) In education it supported the Anglican position so late as 1839, when the Whigs threatened state control of education and equalization of grants between the voluntary societies. In 1843, however, there was a revolution in attitudes. Graham's bill threatened an extension of Anglican power in a new field of education, and the projected factory schools would have had Anglican headmasters. The Methodists protested in strength, and Ashley, Peel, and Graham himself understood why. The growth of Tractarianism in the Church of England was the reason.

It has been publicly stated [said the Annual Address of Conference in 1843] that one ground of our strenuous opposition to the lately projected measure of public education was its obvious tendency to give to the clergy of the Established Church, an unfair and undue control over the religious teaching in the schools which it would have established. We think it right to confirm this statement, not out of any hostile feeling towards the Established Church as such, for this has never been the feeling of our Body, but with a view to hear our own distinct and solemn testimony upon those grievous errors which are tolerated within her pale.

In 1844, therefore, the Wesleyans took to building their own schools on a large scale. Still, though, they did not wholly go along with the Dissenters in the later 1840s. After Russell's proposals of 1846, most Dissenters strenuously objected to the intervention of the State in education. But the Wesleyans declined to be upset by Russell's action, and once they were assured there would be no aid to Roman Catholic schools, they were recognized by the Educational Committee of the Privy Council in 1847, and got their government grant. As with all the Conference politics of Methodism, the object was survival and increased influence.

[21] PRIMITIVE METHODISM AND THE WORKING CLASSES

Primitive Methodism started in 1811 and became one of the constituents of the (united) Methodist Church in 1932. Throughout its history as an independent entity it was identified with the working class, and particularly so by the rest of Methodism. Thomas Cooper, whose autobiography is a celebrated document in labour history and who was the inspiration for *Alton Locke*, felt it in the few months during which he fell under Primitive influence in 1819: it consisted of 'poor men who knew little of books, but who found happiness in prayer' and 'demurred to my reading any book but the Bible, unless it was a truly religious book'. (He turned to the Wesleyans shortly afterwards.) The long preliminaries to Union in 1932 revealed the same opinions.

It was said that Wesleyans and Primitives were not of the same social grade [Walter Runciman wrote in the *Methodist Recorder* in 1920]. It was no use shirking the fact. He longed to see the manager of the colliery sitting in the same pew with the hewer. In Lincolnshire, he did not want to see the farmers in the Wesleyan Church and the labourers in the Primitive Methodist Church.

On account of this working-class identification, increasing interest in the Primitives has been shown by some labour historians. (E. J. Hobsbawm has revived interest in them in two notable contributions: his article in *History Today* in 1957, 'Methodism and the Threat of Revolution in Britain', and his lecture in *Primitive Rebels*.) Dr Hobsbawm sees the Primitive Connexion as an important element in the prehistory of labour movements, providing by its organization a kind of training ground for labour leaders and a model for the construction of labour organizations, and by its chapel life putting some satisfaction and colour in the lives of the rural and industrial poor. These arguments were well recognized inside Methodism – particularly by Robert Wearmouth, himself an ex-Primitive – though Dr Hobsbawm has discussed them in the more subtle context of early European and American labour history, and under the influence of Marx and Weber.

The period from 1807 until the 1850s may fairly be described as the Primitives' heroic period, when their permanent proletarian image was formed. The place of origin of the sect was the Staffordshire–Cheshire border, the half-rural, half-industrial country dominated by Mow Cop, a hill at the south end of the Pennines. Its founders, all of whom fell foul of Wesleyan Methodism for eccentricities of government and evangelistic technique, were Hugh Bourne (1772–1852), William Clowes (1780–1851), and others less eminent. The first preaching plan dates from 1811 and the name 'Primitive Methodist' from 1812, though the movement has a prehistory dating from the beginning of the century. Bourne and Clowes were men of dissimilar personalities who brought two distinct strands (respectively Camp Meeting Methodists and Clowesites) together. Bourne was born at Bemersley, the son of a small farmer; he was by trade a carpenter with other related interests. Clowes was a native of Burslem whose maternal grandfather was a Wedgwood, but who himself was a working potter in Burslem and, for a time, in Hull. Bourne was easily embarrassed at making public appearances, and his characteristic mode of preaching was with his left hand pressed to his face while he looked through between his fingers. Clowes was thoroughly extravert – his violent drunken episodes in Leek, Hull, Barton-on-Humber, and elsewhere are elaborately chronicled in the standard histories – and became the archetype of all 'Ranter' preachers. Bourne's conversion came about in 1799, the result of reading some familiar matter like Alleine's *Alarm to the Unconverted*, some records of early Methodism, and some Quaker writings – all of which had their effect on his movement. Clowes was converted in January 1805 at a prayer meeting in Burslem.

In Bourne's Methodism there were three essential variations of evangelistic method. After his own conversion, he attempted successfully to do the same the next year for a relative, Daniel Shubotham, a shoemaker. He did it by reading Quaker and Methodist extracts, praying, and making an individual exhortation: he called this technique a 'conversation meeting' and afterwards attached the greatest importance to it. He also tried class meetings in which the leadership was regularly changed – a practice which suited his odd shyness. But his principal innovation was the encouragement of camp meetings. An American Methodist, Lorenzo Dow, had stimulated these huge outdoor meetings lasting several days. Dow had visited the Staffordshire area in 1807, and did so again for the Primitives in 1818. Bourne's followers were attracted to Dow's method not merely because of its novelty, but because it could be staged as a rival to the dissipations of the local Wakes, and because it bore a similarity to some of Wesley's own performances. In planning and executing such functions, Bourne reckoned without the respectability and new orthodoxy of Conference. It met at Liverpool in 1807, and its full decision was that:

Even supposing such meetings to be allowable in America, they are highly improper in England, and like to be productive of considerable mischief, and we disclaim all connection with them.

Clowes was after 1805 a Wesleyan class leader enjoying frequent contacts with Hugh Bourne, though reluctant to provoke his own expulsion by too close an identification with him and his camp meetings. The problem caused him some perturbation, but he eventually fell in with the meetings and appeared at them after 1809; the following year he was omitted from the preaching plan of the Burslem circuit. He took with him those members of his two Wesleyan classes over whom he had gained a particular ascendancy, together with some other admirers; and by their invitation he took to preaching to them in the kitchen of Joseph Smith of Tunstall. He also undertook missionary tours in Lancashire and Derbyshire as well as in Staffordshire, so that the kitchen in Tunstall became the headquarters of a rudimentary Clowesite circuit.

The foundation of the Primitive Methodists was not the signal for all-out expansion, but rather for consolidation. In 1811 there were two hundred members; when the first Conference was held in 1820, there were 7,842. The concern for consolidation did not overcome the natural zeal of the preachers, and by 1820 effective missionary tours had been undertaken in the villages of Derbyshire (Derby became the second circuit in 1816), Nottinghamshire, Lincolnshire, and (in 1819) Hull. Growth thereafter was very rapid: in 1821, there were 16,394 members; in 1831, 37,216; in 1841, 75,967; in 1851, 106,074.

The most obvious reason for this expansion lay in missionary technique. Until 1870 virtually all the energies of the Connexion were devoted to home missions. Their distinctive method was the camp meeting. The first of these, an event regarded with veneration as long as Primitive Methodism lasted, was held on Mow Cop on 31 May 1807, and this prototype is worth a close examination. A huge crowd gathered from early morning to hear a variety of speakers (or participate in a variety of religious experiences) on various parts of the ground. 'Stands', or piles of stones to stand on, were set up, and the crowd broke up into sections. Some heard Clowes recount his Christian experience; some heard a Captain Anderson recite his life story in verse; an Irishman contributed an account of the 1798 Rebellion. The whole event was punctuated by prayers, pious ejaculations, and hymn singing. This technique was deliberately encouraged by Hugh Bourne, and hundreds of these meetings were held.

Such an institution was capable of spiritual (and theatrical) development. The camp meetings were lengthened – one at Barlestone in Leicestershire went on from Sunday until the following Friday. Some were held in the dark and illuminated by lanterns – a chance 'invention' at Hinckley in 1818. In the work of spreading Primitive Methodism they obviously enjoyed great strategic importance. One at Nottingham in 1816 had 12,000 people present; one at Oldham in 1821, 14,000; and one at Waterloo in Cheshire opened up the evangelization of the whole Welsh border region. George Borrow, who had experience of them in East Anglia, described one in Lavengro (1851). The company of preachers 'in sober coloured habiliments of black or brown, cut in a plain and rather uncouth fashion, and partially white with dust' were in a wagon without its horses – a familiar platform for 'Ranters' – facing a crowd which 'consisted entirely of the lower classes, labourers and mechanics, and their wives and children – dusty people, unwashed people, people of no account whatever, and yet they did not look a mob'.

The familiar figure in Primitive Methodist evangelism was the individual preacher, equipped with a bible and a hymn-book. These working men offered to their audiences an appeal at a variety of levels. Their theology was unsubtle – free grace for all, the compelling prophecies of Amos and Ezekiel, and an inclination to curse their enemies, a procedure which, if successful, became part of Primitive folklore. William Clowes, suffering grievously from noisy interruption when addressing a camp meeting on Harris Moor above Whitehaven in 1823, warned the interrupters that they might be 'hurried into eternity' before twenty-four hours were up. Many of them were – in a pit explosion the day after. The presence of preachers in a village lent an opportunity for sport at their expense – they were a ready target for eggs, and if the squire and the parson took exception to them there were more exciting doings, even a temporary imprisonment. The preachers' obscurely heroic way of life was frequently re-told by the preachers themselves and by their adherents, and was in itself attractive in the way that such things always are. Joseph Reynolds wrote of his experiences in Cambridge in August 1821 to the Tunstall circuit which sent him:

When I left Tunstall, I gave myself up to labour and sufferings, and I have gone through both; but, praise the Lord, it has been for His glory and the good of souls. My sufferings are known only to God and myself. I have many times been knocked down while preaching, and have often sore bones. Once I was knocked down and was trampled under the feet of the crowd, and had my clothes torn and all my money taken from me. In consequence of this I have been obliged to suffer much hunger. One day I travelled near thirty miles and had only a penny cake to eat. I preached at night to nearly two thousand persons. But I was so weak when I had done, that I could scarcely stand, then made my supper of cold cabbage, and I slept under a haystack in a field till about four o'clock in the morning. (Kendall, *History of the Primitive Methodist Church*, p. 59)

Hugh Bourne himself repeatedly travelled forty or fifty miles a day with nothing more than two or three boiled eggs to eat. (Some of this abstinence was due to a horror of growing fat.) Thomas Russell, an extremely successful missionary, once had to wash his garments three times in the course of a day to get rid of rotten eggs.

The Ranter preachers who bore these feats of endurance were not all men. Indeed one of the irregularities of the Staffordshire revivalists was the regular employment of women preachers – many hundreds before long. Nine were received into the ministry by Conference in 1834. To read accounts of their careers is a useful corrective to received ideas of Victorian femininity. The labours of Sarah Kirkland, Mary Porteous, Jane Brown, and many others, in missionary activity, were enormous. They were received more civilly than the men, and those spectators with missiles in their hands kept them there.

As in the original Methodist Revival, hymn singing was an essential part of evangelism, and was so recognized from the beginning. In 1809 Bourne adapted a hymn-book put together originally by Lorenzo Dow. He endeavoured to supersede it with his own in 1812, and the *Small Book* established itself as a best seller and something well worth pirating by provincial printers. The appeal of the original hymns was the same appeal as the preachers had. The hymns offered free grace:

> Grace is flowing like a river;
> Millions there have been supplied,
> Still it flows as fresh as ever
> From the Saviour's wounded side:
> None need perish;
> All may live for Christ hath died.

They offered eventual relief from persecution:

> Wicked men I'm not to fear
> Though they persecute me here;
> Though they may my body kill,
> Yet my King's on Zion's Hill.

They offered military metaphors:

> Hark! Listen to the trumpeters
> They sound for volunteers.

Such hymns were often sung to tunes better known in more secular surroundings.

Hugh Bourne was as determined as John Wesley to use cheap printed material to missionary effect. One of the outbuildings of the farm at Bemersley became his bookroom, and, in a way strikingly similar to Wesley's, hymn-books were compiled, collections of simple medical and household advice published, and the *Primitive Methodist Magazine* launched.

The single-mindedness of the Primitives in planning and executing missionary activity was extraordinary. The whole organization was geared to spreading the gospel. As circuits were formed, so they became missionary agencies. Hull was reached in 1819; and by the end of 1822 Clowes was able to announce:

The ground is all broken up between Hull and Carlisle. . . . Our circuit extends from Carlisle in Cumberland to Spurn Point in Holderness, an extent of more than two hundred miles. What is the breadth of the circuit I cannot tell; it branches off in various ways: one to Whitehaven and one to Gretna Green in Scotland.

From Tunstall, the Black Country, Cheshire, Lancashire, Warwickshire and Worcestershire, Shropshire, and Wiltshire were all invaded by 1824. From Nottingham, Lincolnshire, Derbyshire, South Yorkshire, and East Anglia were penetrated by 1825.

Economic factors are sometimes mentioned in explaining the progress or the falling away of numbers in the sect. Dr Hobsbawm writes:

As a working-class sect, they were particularly sensitive to cyclical fluctuations and the movement of unemployment, and indeed normally explained any fluctuation in their numbers primarily in economic terms. (*Primitive Rebels*, p. 137)

This is of course true, in a simple 'times are bad' or 'times are good' sense; but the Primitive Methodists themselves, and their only considerable chronicler, Kendall, are much more analytical and self-critical than that. They explained rises by the power of prayer and by evangelistic technique, and failures by personal backslidings and by mistaken decisions. For example, the attempted suspension of mission work in the interests of consolidation ('the Tunstall Non-Mission Law') was soundly condemned; the crisis of 1825–8, when 'the Connexion was in a tottering state' was economic only in the sense that there was financial recklessness – the major cause was the 'drones and ineffectives' who had been attracted into the Connexion. The more one investigates the purely institutional history of the Methodist divisions in the nineteenth century, the less certain the economic analysis of membership figures is.

Yet the distribution of Primitive Methodism by 1850 indicates reasons other than strictly organizational and religious ones for the spread of the sect. Its success was most marked in the Northeast, in the Black Country and the Trent Valley, in East Anglia, and in the Thames Valley. It never enjoyed great success in cities. A mission consisting of two men was sent from Leeds circuit to London in 1822. Clowes came from Hull and was there for twenty months in 1824–5, but he talked of 'the chariot rolling on slowly and heavily'. He left only 170 members when he set out for Cornwall. There were only 286 in 1837, and London became the head of a district only in 1853. The successful appeal of the Primitives was largely to villages. Dr Hobsbawm has an instructive comparison (his figures are for 1863–4) between the membership figures for Newastle upon Tyne (700) and those for two villages in County Durham, Shotley Bridge with 800 and Thornley with 700. There are even stranger centres of activity. Scotter, an apparently insignificant and entirely rural community ten miles north-east of Gainsborough, was between 1821 and 1823 at the head of a district (and subsequently of a circuit). The 1829 Conference, at which the Deed Poll of the Connexion was approved, was held there. In 1830 a revival swept through villages of the same kind and social structure in north-west Lincolnshire. Vast energy was employed by the early missionaries in the neighbourhood of places like Pickering in the North Riding and Nenthead in Cumberland, where communities were tiny. In

East Anglia, the membership in 1825 was 1,542; in 1842 it was 9,072.

What explains this extraordinary pattern of distribution? The continuing failure in London is easily enough explained. The methods used there were much the same as were used to convert a village – that is, to send one or two men. It was exceedingly difficult for a connexion with its roots in the North Midlands to exercise oversight in London, and the passing of London successively from the Hull to the Leeds to the Norwich circuits seems to suggest that it was something of an incumbrance.

The explanation of why it became so successful a rural sect is more difficult. Wesley was (as we have seen) not particularly successful as an evangelist in rural areas, and no doubt Ranter preachers were sometimes filling in the gaps. Dr Hobsbawm uses something like this reasoning, though in rather a guarded way, in observing that the Primitives often failed to colonize a region where other sects 'fulfilled the same function'. But in two of the regions that he uses as examples, the West Riding and Lincolnshire, both Wesleyan and Primitive Methodism did very well, in fact. Since it is in many parts of the North of England one of the commonest spectacles to see both Primitive and Wesleyan chapels within a matter of hundreds of yards apart, this 'gap-filling' explanation will not do. The explanation of the double strength of Primitive Methodism and Wesleyan Methodism in the same communities may lie partly in the social stratification inside a community – that is, the Wesleyans were appealing to a more 'respectable' element than the Primitives. Partly, no doubt, the novelty of Primitive methods had its effect. Dynamic as it still was, Wesleyan Methodism was suffering from ossification in the Primitives' eyes.

In the rural villages, as distinct from small industrial communities, it is held that the opposition of the squire and parson was a serious obstacle to the sect:

Clericalism and landlordism, or both acting in concert, often unmercifully applied the screw. Local preachers received notice to quit their holdings; those who opened their cottages for preaching were evicted; to show hospitality to the preacher – above all to give him a night's

shelter – was to run the risk of becoming homeless or workless. . . .
Undeterred by the parson's threat of persecution, Mr Watts set out
for the village [in Hampshire]. The clerical autocrat went round to
his parishioners ordering them to keep indoors and have every door
and window shut. And they did as they were told. (*Kendall*, op. cit.,
p. 61)

Dr Hobsbawm and Professor Rudé (*Captain Swing*, Ch. 9) insist
that the act of setting up a chapel and absenting themselves from
church represented an act of considerable independence and
courage on the part of villagers. At Appleby in Lincolnshire the
building of a chapel was absolutely forbidden from 1819 to 1894,
and the services were held in a cottage.

In spite of these observations from widely differing points of
view, it is impossible to be so sure about this resistance. Otherwise Primitive Methodism could have been snuffed out except in
those rural-industrial settlements thrown up during the Industrial
Revolution and which had neither squire nor parson. The
attitude of the gentry was not one of cast-iron opposition. There
is a strong suspicion that they were in fact content that they
should be Anglican but that Primitive Methodism was good for
the servants – an attitude which accords well with the intense
stratification characteristic of the Victorian countryside. There
was one Primitive Methodist squire – Robert Shafto, Esquire, of
Bavington Hall, Northumberland, who gave hospitality to the
preachers, appeared on the preaching plan himself, and regarded
the direction of the Sunday school as his particular province.
But he may be regarded simply as an eccentric. Kindness, a
virtue which historians are at present rather reluctant to admit
ever existed in the Victorian countryside, sometimes helped. Mr
Young of Alford in Lincolnshire permitted the Primitive minister
to deliver the *Magazine* to his servant, talked to the minister,
let him lodgings, contributed to missionary funds, and even
attended chapel (these examples may be found in Kendall,
Origin and History of the Primitive Methodist Church, respectively
Vol. II, pp. 159–62, and Vol. I, p. 451). An amused tolerance of
Primitive independence at Middleton-in-Teesdale was shown by
the Duke of Cleveland. Written requests to the Duke for a piece

of land on which to build a chapel at Bowlees were blocked by an unsympathetic steward. One of the dalesmen bearded the Duke and was granted the land (J. Ritson, *The Romance of Primitive Methodism*, p. 228). Kendall makes the general observation that the clergy and gentry of the North of England were considerably more interested in and indulgent towards the movement than elsewhere. Besides, the landlords were not always convinced that the spread of the new sect was to their disadvantage; on the contrary, it might well have served to moderate the rick-burning and machine-breaking of the 1830s. Robert Key is said to have checked a wave of burning in Suffolk. Any indication that they aided the spread of the Captain Swing Riots is really of an inconclusive and circumstantial kind, like Professor Rudé's observation that in North Walsham, where the Swing Riots began, the Primitive circuit was easily the largest of that Connexion in East Anglia (Hobsbawm and Rudé, op. cit., Ch. 9).

What did the labourers themselves derive from it all? There was something of a poor man's club about the chapel. Once it was constructed, it was a refuge from the outside world with its social divisions. The plainest of all evidence – the names of the chapels – indicates that. 'Zoar' was a particular favourite, and 'his fugitives shall flee unto Zoar' (Isaiah XV, 5) seems to have more than theological significance. Inside the chapel, working people spoke to working people. The Primitive Methodist Connexion was largely run by self-educated lay men and women. A proposal to set up a theological college was defeated in 1844, though it finally came in 1863. Architecturally the chapels remained ordinary plain boxes – Kendall's official history is full of their pictures – and they gave way to Gothic, with all its expense and ecclesiastical associations, only late in the century. Inside these chapels the singing, the preaching, and the pious exclamations of the congregations provided an element of emotion and colour which their world almost entirely lacked. The inn or the beershop, and the rapidly proliferating benefit societies (either parochial, or branches of organizations like the Buffaloes or the Free Foresters) provided their only serious rivals. (The spread of these societies is not well known, but see *Captain Swing*, Ch. 3.)

If the Connexion was homogeneous socially, then it had some effect in forming the political ideas and stimulating the political activities of the working class. The link between Primitive Methodism and labour politics is not, however, simple and direct. Officially, the Primitive Connexion, like the Wesleyan, disapproved of Radical activity. The Primitive Conference of 1821 might have gone the other way, but Hugh Bourne (who owned the chapel where the Conference met) interrupted a speaker with the words: 'That man is a speeching Radical, a man who is employed in speaking against the Government, and he must not sit in this place.' Bourne himself indicated how theology, gratitude, and prudence directed such a step:

I told them that Scripture required us to be subject to the Government under which we lived; that the King was favourable to liberty of conscience and had conferred a favour on us, for, when Prince Regent, in June, 1812, he had signed an act which opened our way to hold camp meetings, and which gave us more liberty of conscience and worship than we had before enjoyed; that up to the present time, we had stood well with the Government; and that if on that occasion the Conference set up against the Government, as the Government had an eye on us, measures might be taken to stop our camp meetings, and the Connexion might receive an injury from which it would never recover. The opposite party attempted reply after reply. But I got into strong and even peremptory language. After a time the speeches against the Government slackened and the more thoughtful began to intervene. . . . Such was the effect that during the meeting, no one lifted up a finger against the Government. (Wearmouth, op. cit., p. 212)

Official statements were made subsequently which sufficiently indicate the tensions of a working-class congregation during the period of the Chartist agitation – like this eloquent document from the Primitive Methodist Norwich Circuit (11 September 1839) which Dr Kent quotes. The meeting before the Quarterly Meeting expressed its dislike for 'Bro. Bowthorpe's new-fashioned way of preaching' and did not consider that his 'conduct was justifiable on the 30th June in walking from Ringland through Drayton to Norwich in the rain then stand up [*sic*] in the open air near our chapel to the ingery [*sic*] of our cause to make a speech for the Chartists'. Bowthorpe and his sister resigned (*Age of Disunity*, p. 136).

Somewhat lower down the organizational pyramid, the Chartists sometimes won this contest for support. Thus the Primitive chapels at Glossop, Thornley, Unsworth, Morley, Huddersfield, Bloxham, Gateshead, Byker Hill, and Newcastle gave facilities for Chartist gatherings.

By the very nature of their communities and their occupations many Primitives were drawn into the organization of working-class activity and to the leadership and membership of working-class organizations. Something has already been said (p. 195) of how Methodist classes and geographical divisions were transferred from religious to political uses; the distinctively Primitive technique transferred was the camp meeting. Thomas Cooper's *Autobiography* goes into details of his leading the poor stockingers out of Leicestershire villages in the summer of 1842 to 'induct them into the knowledge of Chartist principles'. The singing of hymns was a familiar Chartist practice, too, and though the traffic in hymns was usually from Primitives to Chartists, the Primitives were given to adapting hymns from any source so long as they were effective; there is at least one example of the Primitives taking over a Chartist hymn with suitable emendations.

The best-known Primitive Methodist leaders of various labour movements were of a later generation than that now being considered – the list given by Dr Hobsbawm includes one or two who were still alive in the 1950s – but the list of early leaders is sufficient to indicate that Primitive Methodism did have an educative function for leaders, by its mode of conducting business, by the opportunities it afforded for speaking, and by the rigorous morality that it insisted upon. Thomas Cooper, who has already been mentioned, was a leader in his native Gainsborough for only a few months before becoming a Wesleyan; eventually he became a secularist. All three were stages in a course of self-education which was so severe as to drive him to breakdown. John Skevington had been a travelling preacher in 1823–4, but he was 'severed from the Connexion' in 1836, possibly at Hugh Bourne's insistence, partly for his radicalism. He was sent as representative to the National Convention in 1839:

As an advocate of the principles of the People's Charter, I found nothing on inspection to condemn in them, nor in my advocacy of them [he observed], but a firm conviction that though a man may be a Chartist and not a Christian, a man cannot be a Christian and not a Chartist unless through ignorance.

Skevington was imprisoned in the renewed Chartist disturbances of 1842, but enjoyed considerable public standing in Leicester and became a town councillor in 1852. John Markham, the most significant of the Leicester Chartists, a shoemaker turned auctioneer, was a local preacher until his expulsion from the Connexion. Joseph Capper, a Primitive preacher and a blacksmith, shared a platform with Cooper at Hanley and was imprisoned for sedition in 1842. Despite this arrest, Capper, and indeed all these men, were reformist rather than revolutionary in intention – though Skevington, whose hold over a crowd was always remarkable, was once told that he 'only had to speak the word and we will tear up every stone in the Market Place'. (For further details of these leaders see G. D. H. Cole, *Chartist Portraits*, 1959, pp. 141–6 on Cooper; J. F. C. Harrison in *Chartist Studies*, ed. A. Briggs, pp. 130–1 on Skevington and Markham; Kendall, op. cit., Vol. I, pp. 336–40 on Skevington and Capper.)

There is some indication, too, that besides providing one avenue for working-class leaders, the democratic and proletarian atmosphere of the chapel did something to manufacture the spirit of fraternal independence necessary for the successful establishment of trade unions. The most famous and oft-quoted statistic in Primitive Methodist history is an indication of this. When Lord Londonderry evicted the striking miners of the North-east in 1844, two-thirds of the members of the Durham Primitive Methodist Circuit were left homeless.

Emotional experience, education, an apprenticeship in the

methods of conducting public business: these are obvious
enough legacies of Primitive Methodism. Leaving the list there,
however, would be to leave out what so many of the contemporary
commentators regarded as its most vital effect – the moral one.
Thomas Burt, at a late period the Durham Miners' leader and
an ex-Primitive, was insistent upon this necessary ingredient for
training trade unionists and their leaders. Hugh Bourne began
his religious reading with early Quaker literature, and his
Primitive Methodism retained a strongly ascetic character. The
Hull circuit in 1832 suspended a preacher for being late at chapel;
but his other offences included speaking sharply to some children
at breakfast and eating the meat of a pie but refusing the crust.
The Connexion (including Bourne himself) early identified itself
with teetotalism. Altogether the new sect may be said to have
aided the work of rehabilitating the labourer from the position
of extreme degradation which he had reached by the end of the
Napoleonic Wars, and in an epoch when labour organization was
uncommonly difficult. Indeed it did more: it accomplished what
seemed to many sensitive souls in Victorian England an impossible task – a successful mission to the working class. Presumably
this is what Borrow was referring to when he wrote of the
preachers 'carrying the light of the Gospel amidst the dark
parishes of what, but for their instrumentality, would scarcely
be Christian England'.

[22] TOWARDS VICTORIANISM

Methodism, Evangelicalism, and Victorianism are commonly
thought of as forming a progression: a revival beginning with
Wesley, effecting an entry to the Established Church and to the
governing classes by the agency of Wilberforce and Simeon,
revivifying the sects, encouraging the general body of the Church
of England to emulation, and at length imposing a high serious-
ness upon society at large. Further, it has been argued, the

political effect of such a development was the diffusion of conservatism in social and political thinking – a conservatism originating in the mind of John Wesley.

More accurately stated, however, the progression began with the attraction and power of the doctrine of justification by faith to a number of obscure Anglican clergymen in the fourth decade of the eighteenth century. Wesley, with immense gifts of organization, adaptation, and authorship, became the most eminent of these. His abilities and his disregard of ecclesiastical authority had created a connexion on the verge of secession by the time he died. It had, notwithstanding the larger numbers who might attend its services, a small membership – though its organization fitted it for future expansion.

When Charles Simeon and the Clapham Sect raised Anglican Evangelicalism to power and influence in the 1780s, Wesley was in part an inspiration, and in part a warning to them: an inspiration in that they would do for the upper classes what Wesley had done for the lower, but a warning that he had in so many ways gone contrary to the Anglican way of doing things. The Methodists and the Evangelicals were of course kindred in many ways – in their humanitarian and missionary interests, in their political conservatism, in their elaborate concern for detailed organization at every level – but ecclesiastically they were not the same. The Evangelicals were bent on making the old system work.

The greater part of the Church of England was attached to a more tepid and more reasonable doctrine, the machinery of the Church was antiquated and adjusted to an agricultural and hierarchical society, and it was part of the English system of government. To say that Methodism or Evangelicalism changed all that is to attribute excessive power to them both. They had, however, powerful aid – from the French Revolution and from the wars that arose from it, first of all. The great fear was that society would disintegrate. The greatest service religion could provide, therefore, was to encourage social cohesion. Much sprang from this proposition: the Methodist Conference professed its utter loyalty to it, and Wilberforce saw it as the opportunity to commend virtue to the upper classes. The necessity to overhaul the administration of the Church became clear. A new view of the parish as a kind of police unit became the fashion, with a resident squire, a resident clergyman, a school, and a variety of parochial activities, some of which had been pioneered by Evangelicals. In that war period the theory behind the Victorian practical achievements in reorganization, church building, and school building was formulated.

Anti-Jacobinism was one stimulant to the churches; industrialization was another. To most churchmen and Dissenters the spiritual plight of the new towns was fearful. In the new situation Methodism stood at a considerable advantage as a proselytizing institution. Its system of itinerancy, the way in which its machine could take in new missions and chapels, its hymns, its elementary theology barring the possibility of Heaven to nobody, the emergence of Primitive Methodism which providentially renewed the appeal of the movement to the working classes when Wesleyan Methodism might have been hardened by respectability, the attractions of office-holding and of the chapel as a focus of community activity – all these helped the mission. The Church of England responded to industrialization less clearly and certainly. By its governmental and financial reorganization, it abandoned much of the natural power and influence it had previously enjoyed. In the eighteenth century and before, it was an integral part of society; to expect it to adjust to an urban and often one-class society in one generation was too much to expect. The rural parish, more efficiently run, remained an ideal. When the Ecclesiastical Commissioners turned to working out what the circumstances of the new-type nineteenth-century bishops should be, they planned rural palaces and incomes appropriate to noblemen. But what might be termed the natural advantages of the Established Church enabled it to overcome these understandable misjudgements. At the end of the Napoleonic Wars it could command funds from the State to initiate a church building programme; by the 1840s, though, it no longer could. But the voluntary instinct took over, and church and school building became the conventional charitable activity of the time. The resources of the Anglicans, the challenge of battle with Nonconformity, and the principle by which state grants for education for so long matched self-help, enabled the Church to achieve much.

The triumph of the churches in large areas of society is commonly thought of as the triumph of the conservative ideal. Wesley's instinctive conservatism; Wilberforce's anti-Jacobinism and his reforming activity carefully channelled into unexceptionable philanthropy; Anglican concern with subordination; the studied attempts of the Methodist Conference to confine their political activities to humanitarianism and to securing necessary legal rights – the sequence seems clear. But it is not. The ideals of the leadership could not be transmitted so narrowly, nor could the machinery they devised be restricted to do merely what they intended. In the first of industrial revolutions, social change could only take place by the use of the machinery that was there, and much of the machinery was religious. The process of rising in society was one which the sects – and particularly Methodism – facilitated. It provided the experience of oratory and business, the wherewithal for self-education, and the opportunities for gaining community esteem, which were necessary qualifications for working class leadership. Eventually the political activism could clash with Conference ideals and expulsion might result – but the experience had been gained. Similarly with working-class organization. The classes, the quarterly meetings, and the camp meetings of Chartism were a sufficient indication of the Methodist contribution to it. The labours of the Evangelicals also produced unintentional effects. The techniques of extra-parliamentary agitation they developed were adaptable to other ends; and their stock-in-trade, philanthropy, was the first instinct which modified the rigours of laissez-faire. The impulse of the Revival was diffused into many directions; to chart them neatly is impossible.

Further Reading

As well as those quoted in previous lists, the following are important:

Asa Briggs, *Victorian Cities*. Pelican, 1968.
  Chartist Studies. Macmillan, 1959.
G. F. A. Best, *Shaftesbury*. Batsford, 1964.
Owen Chadwick, *The Victorian Church*, Part I. Black, 1966.
R. Currie, *Methodism Divided. A Study in the Sociology of Ecumenicalism*. Faber, 1968.
Maldwyn Edwards, *After Wesley. The Social and Political Influence of Methodism in the Middle Period, 1791–1851*. Epworth, 1937.
N. Gash, *Reaction and Reconstruction in English Politics 1832–52*. Oxford University Press, 1965.
E. J. Hobsbawm, 'Methodism and the Threat of Revolution in Britain'. *History Today*, February 1957.
  Primitive Rebels. Manchester University Press, 1959.
E. J. Hobsbawm and George Rudé, *Captain Swing*. Lawrence and Wishart, 1968.
K. S. Inglis, *Churches and the Working Classes in Victorian England*. Routledge, 1963.
H. B. Kendall, *The Origin and History of the Primitive Methodist Church*. 2 Vols. Dalton (P. M. Publishing House), 1903.
  The History of the Primitive Methodist Church. Dalton, 1919.
  The first of these titles is the official history, and is one of the most remarkable records of nineteenth-century provincial and working-class life, copiously illustrated, in existence.
J. Kent, *The Age of Disunity*. Epworth Press, 1966.
G. Kitson Clark, *The Making of Victorian England*. Methuen, 1962.
J. Ritson, *The Romance of Primitive Methodism*. Dalton, 1909.
R. A. Soloway, *Prelates and People: Ecclesiastical Social Thought in England 1783–1852*. Routledge, 1969.
E. R. Taylor, *Methodism and Politics 1791–1851*. Cambridge University Press, 1935.
A. B. Webster, *Joshua Watson. The Story of a Layman: 1771–1855*. S.P.C.K., 1954.
E. R. Wickham, *Church and People in an Industrial City*. Lutterworth Press, 1957.
G. M. Young, *Victorian England. Portrait of an Age*. Second edition, Oxford University Press, 1953.

Political and Religous Framework, 1795–1850

(excluding Evangelical activity to 1833: see Part III)

1795. Methodist Plan of Pacification – in effect, the departure of Methodism into Dissent. Preachers were permitted to administer Communion if a majority of the stewards and leaders belonging to the chapel (and Conference) agreed

1797. The Methodist New Connexion (Kilhamites) – it objected to the continuing domination of Methodism by the preachers

1807. Beginnings of Primitive Methodism
(1807: Camp Meeting at Mow Cop; 1808: Methodist Conference condemned the technique; 1820: First Primitive Methodist Conference; 1829: Deed Poll of the Primitive Methodist Connexion approved)

1808. Royal Lancasterian Society founded

1811. National Society for the Education of the Poor in the Principles of the Church of England founded
The two 'voluntary societies' most famous in instituting schools for the poor: the first, as the *British* Society, became dominated by Dissenters; the second, the *National* Society, was determinedly Anglican under Joshua Watson's management

1812. 'New Toleration Act' repealed the Conventicle and Five Mile Acts and gave Methodist preachers the legal privileges of clergymen

1814. Jabez Bunting became Secretary of the Methodist Conference. He continued as Secretary until 1820, when he was President for the first time. He remained a dominating figure, in various official positions, until his death in 1855

1818. Incorporated Church Building Society established
Parliament voted £1m. for church building in populous places

1819. Peterloo

1827. Methodist Controversy over the installation of an organ at Brunswick Chapel, Leeds. There were two causes for alarm – the 'tyranny' and the 'churchiness' of the centre. It caused the secession of the Protestant Methodists (1829)

1828. Repeal of the Test and Corporation Acts

1829. Catholic Relief Act permitted Catholics to enter Parliament and to occupy all but the very highest public offices

1831. Congregational Union set up

1832. Reform Act
Baptist Union

1833. Irish Church Temporalities Act
Government grants to the Voluntary (Schools') Societies began
Keble's Assize Sermon at Oxford – conventionally, the beginning of the Oxford Movement

1835. Ecclesiastical Duties and Revenues Commission established – for the reform of the Church of England

1835. Municipal Corporations Act

1836. Established Church Act set up the Ecclesiastical Commissioners, who carried through over many years measures equalizing bishops' sees and revenues (1836 on), against pluralism (1838 on), and suppressing excess revenues of cathedrals (1840 on)
Tithe Commutation Act
Registration Act
Dissenters' Marriage Act

1838. The People's Charter

1839. First Chartist Petition presented

1842. Mines Act

1843. Controversy over the Educational Clauses of Graham's Factory Bill. Methodists and Dissenters both objected to the prospect of Anglican control over factory education

1844. Factory Act

1846. Repeal of the Corn Laws

1846–8. Methodist 'Fly Sheets' Controversy. The 'Fly Sheets' were pamphlets protesting principally at Bunting's domination of Wesleyan Methodism. Their author was probably James Everett, who was expelled in 1849 and who, with Robert Eckett, formed the Wesleyan Reformers (1850)

1846. Russell's proposals for increased state aid to education

1847. Dissenters' Electoral Committee. Dissenters renounced their traditional support for the Whigs in the general election

1848. Third Chartist Petition
Beginnings of Christian Socialism

Index

displayed its loyalty indicated a basic uneasiness. The governing classes (full of prejudice, no doubt) found it difficult, if not impossible, to accept Methodist protestations. Sometimes Methodism was lumped together with Dissent, as it was by the Mayor of Liverpool in 1792 when he complained of the number of 'Methodist and other meeting houses' in the vicinity:

Consequently [he added] the youth of the County are training up under the instruction of a set of men not only ignorant but of whom I think we have of late too much reason to imagine are inimical to our happy Constitution.

Horsley, the Bishop of Rochester, thought the Methodists' main objects were 'sedition and atheism'. It was this basic suspicion which was behind Sidmouth's bill of 1811 which would have denied a preacher's licence to anyone not having the support of six reputable householders and which speedily provoked official Methodist action alongside the Dissenters (see p. 169). Once the Methodists had scotched the bill and secured the 'New Toleration Act', there was a new element in their declarations of loyalty – gratitude – and there was even an address to the Prince Regent in 1814. Their protestations were rather guilty in another sense – after all, many of the Luddite sympathizers so snubbed by Bunting and Jackson were clearly Methodists or Methodist sympathizers.

Bunting and Jackson remained official figures in Wesleyan Methodism for another generation, and consequently their attitudes to reform and civil disturbance, whether that meant, for example, Peterloo or Chartism, became the standard ones. They were not merely pious opinions: action was often taken to get rid of malcontents. In 1819 (when Rev. Richard Watson assured Lord Sidmouth that no man would be tolerated as a member of a Methodist Society who joined a political club or attended Radical meetings) a Manchester local preacher was expelled for signing a declaration against the magistrates for their action at Peterloo, and scholars at a Sunday school in the city were expelled for wearing Radical badges. Chartism was as vigorously condemned – the Wesleyan preachers of Ba an official line for political action laid down by Conference, and the politics involved were usually those of humanitarianism or of self-defence. The traditions inherited from Wesley – and largely transmitted by Bunting – often made the position of the Connexion very difficult; the 'special relationship' with the Church of England particularly so.

In the Revolutionary period the attitude of Conference was well known: whether the attitude is called patriotic or sycophantic depends on the opinions of the writer, but it was the ordinary opinion of the 1790s. The Leeds Conference of 1793 expressed its 'unfeigned loyalty to the King, and sincere attachment to the Constitution'; the Conference Address of 1798 declared that the Methodists were 'not likely to meddle with those given to change'. It was rather like Wesley speaking from the grave; but apart from that, the Methodists had no wish to be connected with the infidelity that was associated with revolutionary opinions, or with the unrespectable working-class disciples of Tom Paine.

The official Conference attitude was often reflected in action and opinion at a more local level during the more tense times of the war period. Dr Thomas Coke addressed a series of letters to the Duke of Portland, the Home Secretary, in 1801, expressing his suspicions that a 'Grand Association' was being formed against the Government. He was happy to tell the Duke that three Methodists suspected of rebellious notions had been expelled from the Connexion. Jabez Bunting was the superintendent at Halifax during the Luddite disturbances in 1811 and 1812, and he brought down the wrath of the Luddites for declining to conduct the burial service for a man shot while attempting to break into a mill at Cleckheaton. Thomas Jackson closed the gates of Greetland chapel in the Sowerby Bridge circuit against Luddite sympathizers who planned to bring the corpses of their executed comrades into the chapel for addresses to be delivered over them (for these and other examples, see R. F. Wearmouth, *Methodism and the Working Class Movements of England*, Epworth Press, 1937, Ch. II).

However, the fulsomeness with which official Methodism

has shown that the great Manchester meeting which nearly seven hundred ministers attended in August 1841 was not exactly a spontaneous manifestation of support, nor was it in any way a body representing the opinion of seven hundred congregations; it was in fact a stage-managed affair (see *The Anti-Corn Law League*, Allen & Unwin, 2nd ed., 1968, pp. 103–7).

The present state of knowledge does not make it easy to assess the Dissenters' appeal to industrial workers. Dr Kitson Clark has some evidence that the Baptists were active missionaries in Leeds in the 1830s, and that the Congregationalists also took this function seriously. But their contribution to municipal life once the repeal of the Test and Corporation Acts and the passing of the Municipal Corporations Act laid it open to them was remarkable. Their election to the reformed House of Commons was slow in coming after the Reform Act, but their admission to the corporations of newly constituted industrial boroughs was rapid. After the 1835 Act the first mayors of Manchester, Leicester, and Derby were Unitarians, and out of a council of forty-two elected in Leicester in 1836, twelve were Unitarian. It was in Birmingham particularly that a Dissenter-inspired 'civic gospel' evolved. Local government in a new corporation could have been a humdrum matter, but in fact it was leavened with a remarkable idealism which was generated by a distinguished group of Dissenting ministers. Most of them flourished in the second half of the century, but the originator of the civic gospel, George Dawson, became the minister of Mount Zion Baptist Chapel in 1844, when he was twenty-three. He subsequently opened his own Church of the Saviour in 1847. He was a very uncharacteristic figure for a nineteenth-century pastor in that he was untouched by the Evangelical Revival and thought like a Rational Dissenter, rejecting all formal creeds. The social content of his addresses was, however, relevant enough to Birmingham civic leaders of the nineteenth century – his congregations often included them. The 'common end and purpose was to clothe the naked, feed the hungry, and instruct the ignorant'. Enterprises like the provision of free libraries were given the importance and glamour of a crusade, and the middle classes of the city were

induced to give their labour and their wealth in the service of
their town. The inspiration for all this did not spring from
Birmingham, though; much of it was distinctively Unitarian
and originated with James Martineau (see G. Kitson Clark, *The
Making of Victorian England*, Methuen, 1963, pp. 161, 165; and
Asa Briggs, *Victorian Cities*, pp. 195–8).

Wesleyan Methodism and its Offshoots

When the Reform agitation was at its height in 1831, the Annual
Address of the Wesleyan Methodist Conference included the
words:

Let not worldly politics engross too much of your time and attention.
Avoid all undue eagerness and anxiety on subjects which, however
much their importance might be magnified by the men of the world,
are only of moment in the estimation of the Christian, as far as they
can be rendered subservient to the best interests of mankind.

In them may be seen the authentic sentiments of John Wesley.
Politics were dangerously worldly; they took time better spent
in spiritual or at any rate chapel activity; they provoked needless splits within the Methodist societies. The common view of
the history of the whole Methodist body in the first half of the
nineteenth century is that a series of rebellions took place against
the reactionary and authoritarian rule of the Conference, and in
particular of Bunting; but in fact each of the offshoots, out of
belief, prudence, and self-preservation, made official observations
much like those of the parent body just quoted. This is not to
say that individual Methodists did not have political opinions or
did not participate in the politics of their time; their personal
inclinations, the circumstances in which they found themselves,
and the training and esteem which they obtained inside the
Methodist organization, often impelled them to do so. One
group, the Primitive Methodists, made their appeal principally
to working people, and these impulses were strong. In the West
Riding, where Wesleyan Methodism was so very powerful, Wesleyans were often Luddites or Chartists. Only occasionally was

BR 758
.A66
1973

274.2 Armstrong, Anthony.
A

The Church of
England

DATE			
SEP 24 1974			
OCT 7			
NOV 3 1978			
NOV 22 1978			
MAR. 25 1983			
APR 25 1983			
NOV. 15 1985			